ROGUES TO RICHES

Books by Murray Teigh Bloom

MONEY OF THEIR OWN

THE MAN WHO STOLE PORTUGAL

THE TROUBLE WITH LAWYERS

ROGUES TO RICHES

Murray Teigh Bloom

ROGUES
TO RICHES

The Trouble with Wall Street

G. P. Putnam's Sons New York

For Phil and Jerry

Acknowledgments

Most of my information sources and interviewees are already named in the book. In addition, there are several who were helpful, even though they aren't named. For fascinating data and stories on some international financial practices I am deeply grateful to my dear old friends, the late William Blake of London and his wife, Christina Stead, and to Jacques Coe of New York.

Peter L. Bernstein, the brilliant investment adviser, took me through several primary grades of my financial education when I was an officer and a director of a minor mutual fund. Robert L. Heilbroner, the splendidly lucid economist—who was a fellow fund director—provided several excellent suggestions. Helpful in various ways were Charles M. Macko, a sagacious New York financial analyst, and Gerald M. Loeb of San Francisco.

I am also indebted to George Bookman and Chuck Storer of the New York Stock Exchange staff and to Bob Deindorfer who used to work there. Allan D. Sutton of David J. Greene & Co. kindly provided some needed statistical work-ups.

Sherley Raices, my typist and a stock market buff, managed to complete the manuscript in time without losing her faith in the system. The book was written at the MacDowell Colony in Peterboro, New Hampshire, and once again I am obligated to them for the boon of my stay.

Contents

Part III | *The Winners*

Introduction

It is easier to write about money than to obtain it; those who gain it jest much at those who know only how to write about it.

—Voltaire

The information game on Wall Street is based on the natural assumption that no one knows all the time, or even very often. If anyone did, he'd have all the marbles and the game would have been over long ago—except for those who discovered early that he knew and did what he did, if they could find out. At best, you might know sometimes, and even then the knowledge would be only partial. And because the information is so fuzzed over and uncertainly timed, one of the basic rules for speculators is: Don't try to buy at the bottom or sell at the top. Settle for less.

Centuries before Dow Jones, Duc François de La Rochefoucauld, who coined some of the pithiest maxims of all time, saw the hopelessness of this problem: "To know things really well we must know them in all their ramifications; these being infinite, our knowledge is always superficial and inexact."

Wall Street for most Americans is a playground for their wild daydreams of backward-in-time certainties. What if they bought Xerox when it was still Haloid and paid $2 a share

and ran it up into millions? Or Polaroid? Or Syntex? If only.
But what if you *really* knew?

Several months ago I made a pest of myself with some friends
by asking them to place themselves in a curious scenario I
outlined: They wake up tomorrow morning and discover they
are suddenly, inexplicably, frighteningly back in 1938. "You're
twenty-two years old and have $500 in your pocket. You know
everything that's going to happen from 1938 to 1971—or at
least as you ordinarily remember from that period—and there's
no going back." Since all these time-travel gambits have an
elaborate rule codification, we have to stick to The Condition:
You can't grossly change history. You can't go over to Germany
and kill Hitler or make a pest of yourself at the Navy Department with warnings that they'd better listen good when that
radar sergeant out in Hawaii tells them some strange planes
are on their way That Sunday. But apart from these strictures,
your knowledge is yours to use as far as you want.

Just as a general warning and guideline, I'd throw in a
lovely line from Richard Burton, the other one, the nineteenth-
century adventurer: "It is a very curious and not altogether unpleasant sensation, that of not being believed when you are
speaking the truth."

Naturally, most of those asked dipped into their own experience for their reconstruction of what they *would* have done.
An old friend, an engineer who is sales manager for a specialized electronics firm in Los Angeles, thought a couple of
minutes and came up with this path to fortune:

"I'd have gone down to Brazil and bought up quartz crystals.
They're going to start getting scarce by 1939. You could have
picked them up at $1 a pound, and in the middle of the war,
they were selling for $20–$30 a pound. So now let's say I
have $10,000–$12,000 by the end of 1942. I'd buy bonds on
major New York City buildings like the Commodore Hotel
or the Waldorf-Astoria. You could have picked them up for
10–15 cents on the dollar then. Or maybe I'd have bought an
interest in a small metalworking shop or stock in marginal
tungsten or cobalt or molybdenum mines. You could have

increased your stake fifty to one hundred times in any one of those operations."

A divorced woman: "I wouldn't have married my first husband. I'd not make a lot of the other personal mistakes I did."

The rules of the game were a little murky on that. What if she couldn't make *any* major changes in her foreordained life pattern? "I'd commit suicide. To have to live those years over again. Ugh!"

My friend, Bob, a millionaire, said sensibly: "I'd do nothing different." And thereby ensuring that he become a millionaire, as he did.

Many of them started rummaging in their memories for good stocks to buy in 1938. I pointed out that in general, $500 wasn't going to take them too far; that the money was primarily to make sure they didn't become breadline bums. Still, one thought she'd buy AT&T and hold it for a long rise. Very long—it wouldn't come until the late 1950's. Her husband would have "taken over good houses" in the prosperous suburb where they lived because those houses tripled and quadrupled in value in the next fifteen years. By this time I got tired of trying to explain how little you could do with just $500 if you had to wait so long for it to appreciate.

(If there was one stock you were going to pick in 1938 for the fastest possible appreciation, it would probably be Missouri Pacific Railroad preferred stock which was selling for 20 cents a share because the road was practically busted. If you wait until the railroad is back on its feet and highly profitable by the middle of World War II, the stock rises to more than $10 a share, or a rise of more than fifty times.)

One of the sharpest approaches came from Gus Tyler, an old friend who is assistant president of the International Ladies Garment Workers Union and a man of great political savvy and involvement.

"I don't know one stock from another, but if I'm back in 1938 and I know what's going to happen politically for the next thirty-two years, I'd do all right financially. Not just the election bets I'd win. I'd really become *the* political prophet of the ages. Louis Bean would seem like a character who just made a couple of lucky guesses. Within a few years the papers would have me on the front pages with my prophecies along with the Gallup and Roper polls a couple of days before each election. You *know* Roosevelt is going to be elected in 1940 and again in 1944; that Truman will make it in 1948; Stevenson won't make it in '52 or '56. You know all this and more, you got yourself enormous power and prestige. Somehow money would come along."

Judith Crist, the film critic, quickly sized up the opportunity: "I'd start a weekly newsletter. You could mimeograph it, even, but if you called every shot, you'd have them clamoring for subscriptions at $100, $200, or $500 a year. You'd make Kiplinger or Whaley-Eaton look sick. You'd probably have the FBI all over your neck, but that wouldn't hurt."

Others have played my little game. One of the best-known players was Ralph A. Rotnem, a veteran stock analyst, now retired to a Massachusetts village with a perfect name right out of a three-generational novel: Prides Crossing.

Back in 1957, when he was director of research—*i.e.*, boss analyst—of Harris, Upham & Co., Rotnem devised his Scheherazade tale of the four brothers. The format obviously goes way back: the king who was always sending his sons out in the world to see who would fare best; the king who was always setting tasks for the four suitors for his daughter's hand. And there is one folktale from the Kashmir Valley of India about a maharaja who made no bones about it. He was sending his three sons for a real test; no dragons' tails, no fair maidens rescued with splendid derring-do, no sacred relic of the Lord Buddha. He laid it on the line: *His successor would be the son who acquired the greatest fortune.* The two eldest brothers went and traded with their small stakes and gained considerable wealth, but the youngest, a feckless fellow, went and loafed along the seacoast, encamping here and there as it pleased him. One day he met a gosain, a holy man, who was so impressed with the lad's piety and goodness he decided to give him a helping tip when he heard what the maharaja's game was.

"Send your servants," he told the prince, "into the city to buy as much corn as possible and then throw some of it into the sea every day until it is gone. Then wait and you shall reap an abundant harvest."

The prince acted accordingly. Every day for six months he threw some corn into the sea until it was all gone. He waited for something to happen. A week went by. Nothing. "The gosain has deceived me," he cried. "I am a ruined man. What will my brothers and father say when they hear I've thrown all my money into the sea? How they will laugh at me! I'll never be able to show my face again. Tomorrow I leave this cursed place."

But when the prince and his retinue were about to leave, something happened. The corn that the prince had thrown into the sea had been eaten by a big fish, and as the news of the prince's liberality spread far and wide, shoals upon shoals of fish came together to the place. The king of the fishes also came with them. At last the supply suddenly stopped.

"Why is this?" the king fish asked. "We have been receiving corn for the last six months, and now for several days we have had nothing. Has the prince been rewarded for his kindness to us?" "No," replied the other fish. "Well, then," said the king fish, "go immediately and recompense the prince. Each one of you take a ruby from the sea and give it to him."

It goes on and on, as these folktales will, but in the end, of course, the youngest son had far and away the largest collection of priceless rubies and great wealth and his father, the maharaja, ordered that the youngest son should succeed him. Which was very sensible, since not only did he have the largest fortune but he seemed to have a great in with holy men and the king of the fishes.

(There is no modern lesson to be learned from the youngest prince's adventures. No sense telling anyone to become a corn or commodity speculator or to be kind to the poor fishes or suckers, as they might be called today. Only disaster lies that way.)

But the idea of brothers' being sent out with a modest stake to make their way is a perfect vehicle. In Ralph Rotnem's version, each of four brothers is given $1,000 by their wise old father on New Year's Day, 1915. "Go, my sons," he tells them, "and do what you will. No communication, no contact for the next forty years. Then on Christmas Day, 1956, you will gather here at your old homestead and you'll see who did best."

The first son, poor fellow, was very, very conservative. He put his $1,000 in high-grade corporate bonds and held them for the forty years while he probably plodded away at some miserable clerical job and led a blameless family life. In 1956 his bonds had increased in value only to $1,220. But in the meantime, the dollar had shrunk in value, so in 1956 his $1,220 would buy only about $700 worth of goods.

The second brother was a trifle less conservative, a little more imaginative. He invested his $1,000 in the stocks making up the Dow-Jones Industrial Average. By 1956 his stake had grown to $9,100, and considering the toll of inflation, his purchasing power was a little more than three times larger than he would have had with his original $1,000 in 1915.

The third brother "was a harder worker. He decided that there were such things as business cycles, that there were bull and bear trends in the stock market and he would try to benefit from them." He was also extraordinarily prescient and sold at the peak of every bull market, kept his money in cash in bear markets, and reinvested his original capital and his profits at the bottom of every bear market. By the end of 1956 he found that his $1,000 had grown through the nine bull markets of the forty-one years to $1,910,000. Allowing for a decline in dollar value, he had a purchasing power of $707,000.

The fourth brother, the fortune-favored fourth brother, the blessed Benjamin, knew that some industries "make greater progress than others. He must invest in the particular industry that was benefitting most from the economic conditions of the day." He always stayed invested. In 1915 he was in autos, into steels in 1916, back to autos in 1917, to department stores in 1919, and so on. Even in the Evil Days of 1929–33, he made money because he put everything in gold stocks that rose 44 percent while everything else went to hell. He continued calling his shots perfectly through the thirties, the forties, and now in 1956 he comes to the old homestead for the reckoning. He's a modest fellow, and he drives up in a quiet little Buick, instead of arriving with a retinue of armored cars, each bearing $1 billion in cash for his less fortunate brothers. He could afford to give away $3 billion because he has racked up the score of all times: He has amassed $26 billion by always being right in the market. It has probably had an awfully deleterious effect on his character and his marriage, but he's clearly won the old man's game.

You don't abandon gorgeous characters like that. Rotnem kept getting pleas from the readers of the Harris Upham "Market Review" to do reprises. In 1968, Rotnem carried them forward another twelve years. Now nearly seventy years old—we presume they were healthy quadruplets—each has continued in his preordained path. The conservative bondholder is living on Social Security and a miserable pension. His $1,000 bond investment is now worth only $651. The second son, the Dow-Jones Industrial Average fellow . . . but the rest is foreordained. The fourth son is no longer just the Mysterious Richest Man in the World. Long ago he could buy or sell the Rockefellers, the Du Ponts, the Rothschilds, the Mellons—put together. He could wipe out Howard Hughes and Jean Paul Getty in a whimsical day. He *is* the world of capitalism, the man with all the chips, the Final Winner. He has $4 trillion. And the Buick.

The market experts, the gosains, the wise holy men, the patriarchs urging us to go forth and make our splendid fortunes, come in many guises in our time. They publish market letters and get anywhere from $25 to $500 a year for their invaluable advice. They write and publish books about the stock market and investing. Or they write market letters sent free to the customers of their brokerage firms. There are hundreds of these. Or they simply give advice because they have passed a test given by the New York Stock Exchange and they can now call themselves registered representatives instead of the old-

fashioned customers' men, or brokers, or even—ugh!—salesmen.

The stock market has also attracted another kind of salesman: the seller of dreams, or novelist. For example, Sholom
Aleichem, the great Yiddish writer who described the life of
the *shtetl*, the simple Jewish villages of the Polish-Jewish pale
where the Jews were permitted to live in the nineteenth century. (*Fiddler on the Roof* is based on his folktales.)

Before he could live on his writings alone, Sholom Aleichem
was a full-time broker on the Kiev Stock Exchange. He traded
stocks as well as commodities such as grain and sugar. He lost
his money and his wife's considerable inheritance—as well as
his mother-in-law's estate—in the terrible trading year 1890.
He continued dabbling in the market until 1903—and continued to lose. He did get an enduring character out of it,
though: Menachem Mendel, a small-time trader who dealt in
tips and scalping fractions of a point. A born but amusing loser.

One of the few writers to do really well in speculation was
François Marie Arouet, Voltaire. He was a realist and sensed
that if he was to be a writer, he would need the freedom of
money. Lots of money. He couldn't see himself living meanly
in a garret waiting for patrons to come through with crumbs.
He once explained his drive in terms that sound oddly modern:

> I was not born rich, far from it. I am asked by what art I have
> managed to live like a farmer-general [read: millionaire]. . . .
> I saw so many poor and despised men of letters that I decided
> long ago not to add to their number. In France a man must
> be anvil or hammer; I was born anvil. A small patrimony
> becomes smaller every day, because eventually all prices go
> up, and because the governments often lay their hands on
> both income and capital. . . . There is always one way or
> another by which a private individual can profit without
> incurring any obligation to anyone; and nothing is so agree-
> able to make one's own fortune: the first step is painful, the
> others are easy. . . . After living with kings, I have made
> myself king of my own domain. . . .

Voltaire attained financial security in one year. How? With his first book royalties Voltaire invested in Paris municipal bonds. But the city defaulted. The Paris authorities, writes his latest biographer, Theodore Besterman:

> . . . then decided to reimburse the holders of their bonds, the drawings to be held by lot. Owners of bonds could buy lottery tickets to a value of one in a thousand; that is, the holder of bonds having a face value of 1000 francs was entitled to buy one ticket at a cost of a franc. The prizes were financed in part by the income from the sale of tickets, in part by a monthly contribution of 500,000 francs from the national government . . . the drawings were monthly, and consequently each month those who bought tickets made a profit of something over a half million francs, which was distributed among themselves by luck of the draw. If, however, any one person could obtain all the tickets available in a given month, he would automatically make the whole profit.

Voltaire saw the possibilities of a marvelous can't-lose deal. He got together with the great mathematician Charles Marie de La Condamine, and they organized syndicates to get all the lottery tickets right away. The syndicate made a profit of 6,000,-000–7,000,000 francs. Voltaire made 500,000 francs, which would be the equivalent of $1,000,000 today. He made another killing soon after, with an issue of Lorraine bonds. With his wealth he lived like minor royalty for the rest of his life—and wrote what he wanted to, without worrying if it would please this patron or that; whether a state pension or grant might be cut off. In short, he splendidly solved the writer's universal dilemma: getting enough of a stake to assure independence.

In so doing, he also qualified for the label of genius from another French writer, Jean de La Bruyère, who had once been treasurer of the city of Caen. He died when Voltaire was two years old. La Bruyère wrote:

It takes a kind of genius to make a fortune, especially a large fortune. It is neither goodness, nor wit, nor talent, nor strength, nor delicacy. I don't know precisely what it is: I am waiting for someone to tell me.

No one ever did tell him, and he depended largely on a pension from the Bourbons. But modern writers, instead of waiting for someone to *tell* them how to make a large fortune, have tried to find out for themselves. The place most of them have looked into is the stock market. Their quest is understandable. As Edmund Wilson once put it, there is "nothing more demoralizing than a small but adequate income."

Besides the writers who went into the stock market, there are also those who merely leaped on it and wrote about it. At any given moment there are some 130 books in print on investments, speculation and playing the market. Regardless of whether they are merely primers, gee-whiz how-to books or even modified exposés, all the 130 books are told essentially from the *outside*. The occasional insider who wrote—or had it written for him—wrote with inordinate discretion. It began bothering me: How come the insiders don't write and really Tell All?

I once discussed this problem with Vartanig Vartan, a financial writer for the New York *Times*. He agreed that it wasn't being told from the inside. He thought libel was a major problem. He was getting around that problem by writing *novels* about Wall Street on the side.

Alan Abelson, a very knowledgeable columnist for *Barron's*, thought the answer lay in the New York Stock Exchange rules. "The public doesn't know it, but the exchange exercises a censorship over the writings of members and their employees that makes the Catholic Church's censorship seem amateurish."

David Denison, the assistant director of advertising for the New York Stock Exchange, more or less confirmed this. "Yes, we have to approve books on finance or Wall Street or investment written by partners, registered reps, analysts, even an unregistered employee of a member firm. Even if he did a novel about Wall Street."

As the exchange's "Guidelines for Member Firms' Communications with the Public," dated March, 1970, puts it:

> Books on investing authored by member firm personnel are also subject to Exchange standards and the Advertising Department will review manuscripts. . . . It is important to submit such material well in advance since more time is required for review and corrections can be troublesome and costly if the publication process is in the latter stages.

In a sense, this book is an attempt to understand the drives, the strategems, the character of certain kinds of money-makers in our society. From the *inside*—as much as possible. The people in the following pages spend most of their time making money—or trying to—by speculating, by looking for The Method, by persuading others they've found it.

While the book is, in part, a how-to on moneymaking, it is also a guide for the prudent man in the marketplace.

There was a worldly Jesuit named Baltasar Gracián who in the seventeenth century wrote "The Oracle: A Manual of the Art of Discretion." It is a shrewd, cynical, moralizing, earthy handbook for the guidance of life by the wise. In one of his apothegms, No. 232, he wrote:

> Be a bit of a business man. . . . Very learned people are easy to deceive because, although they are versed in abstruse matters, they lack the more necessary knowledge of everyday affairs. . . . The wise man should, then, try to have something of the trader about him, enough to prevent him from being swindled and even ridiculed: he should be a practical person for, if practical matters are not the highest, they are the most materially valuable things in life. What is the good of knowledge if it serves no useful purpose. And in these days, true knowledge consists in knowing how to live.

To enable such a man to be more practical in the modern world of finance and speculation, I have devoted a large part of the book to the frank, inside talk of several successful operators in that marketplace—to Phil and Jerry, their allies and enemies. The world they live in and operate in is often far removed from the textbook world of finance and speculation, but it is the one that exists today. This one.

PART I | *The Insiders*

1. The Weighers

Very few people are as smart as they portray themselves. Most of our successes are luck, not planning, knowing, judging wisely.

—H. W. HEINSHEIMER

Finding out who was first with an invention, an expression, a custom, is the unique occupation of recorders of the curious and graduate students who cast around desperately for thesis subjects. For them and other interested readers here are a few financial firsts:

The first boiler-room operator in U.S. history was Archie Andrews, a tall, thin, ascetic New Englander who invented the boiler room and its telephonic ganglia to suckers in the hinterlands. This was around 1910. Andrews was the first to realize that the telephone, then first coming into common use, had infinite advantages over mere tout letters. He operated boiler rooms on and off, profitably, until the coming of the SEC in 1934. He retired gracefully to Greenwich, Connecticut.

Possibly the first operator of a *paid* market letter was Carsten Boe, a Danish immigrant with a heavy accent who built up a subscription list around 1895.

Probably the first market letter operator who *sued* to collect what was due him for pushing a stock in his letter was A. N.

Ridgeley, who published "Ridgeley's Financial Forecasts" from 1902 onward. In 1908 he sued a market plunger, James R. Keene, who had reneged on a deal after Ridgeley had valiantly and effectively pushed Southern Pacific stock in his letter.

And the first weigher of the effectiveness of market letter tips, of the accuracy of tipster buy-and-sell recommendations, was an estimable and wealthy gentleman named Alfred Cowles. When Cowles' name was mentioned to people in Wall Street, they were always surprised he was still alive. "It must have been forty years ago he came up with that classic report," one man reacted. "He still around?"

Fortunately, he is, and in April, 1970, I arranged to talk to him in his winter home in Palm Beach. He's now seventy-nine, about 6 feet tall, and his thin gray hair is combed straight back. His skin is slightly splotchy and freckled, the neck crepey. He wore a white shirt with an open collar.

"I'm getting along," he said. "And for a man with a plastic aorta in my heart and a game leg, I'm doing all right." He's also somewhat deaf and has cataracts.

He and his second wife bought their Palm Beach home in 1962. Up to then, they had wintered there in rented homes. Their ten-room house is one of five French Empire one-story homes built around an enclosed square, artfully surrounded by the rich, glossy leaves of trained *Ficus nitiea* hedges. The luxurious, high-ceilinged rooms had been done by society decorator Billy Baldwin in his early black-and-white period. "One of the first houses he did," Cowles recalls, "before he became really big in decorating."

We sat out in the back, looking over Lake Worth, and Cowles talked about himself.

"I came out of Yale—I was in the same class with Cole Porter, by the way—and I went to work as a reporter on my uncle's newspaper in Spokane for a couple of years."

He explained that his branch of the Cowles family is only distantly related to the Cowles of *Look* magazine. One of Alfred Cowles' grandfathers had been a founder of the Chicago *Tribune,* along with Joseph Medill.

"I liked the work on the paper until I got hit with TB. It was pretty common in those days and the only cure was lots of rest in a good climate. So they shipped me off to Colorado Springs for therapy, which consisted mostly of resting in bed and hoping for the best. I had it on and off for ten years, a real stretch.

"When it seemed arrested for good, I started working with my father, who was an investment counselor. This was around 1926, and he handled many of our family accounts through his firm, Cowles & Co. There was a lot of money being handled, and I became interested in the whole process of passing on financial tips. I was subscribing to many different services, and it seemed a little wasteful to me. Why not find which one was the best and just take that one? So I started keeping track records in 1928 of the twenty-four most widely circulated financial services—right up to July 1, 1932. Meanwhile, I had helped found the Econometric Society—I was the first secretary and treasurer and, I suppose, its main angel—and at the time of our first annual meeting, I gave my report on what I had found on the accuracy of the prognostications of these twenty-four services." (Econometrics is the application of statistical and mathematical techniques in solving problems.)

The timing of his report was a kind of doleful underscoring of the nation's plight. He read his paper, "Can Stock Market Forecasters Forecast?" before a joint meeting of the Econometric Society and the American Statistical Association in Cincinnati on December 31, 1932, the lowest point of the U.S. economy in the present century. The summary of his paper, still often quoted, is worth repeating:

Twenty-four publications engaged in forecasting the stock market during the 4½ years from January 1, 1928, to June 1, 1932, failed as a group by 4% per annum to achieve a result as the average of purely random performance. A review of the various statistical tests, applied to the records for this period, of these 24 forecasters, indicates that the successful records *are little, if any, better than what might be expected to result from pure chance* [author's italics]. There is some evidence, on the other hand, to indicate that the least successful records are worse than what could reasonably be attributed to chance.

In short, if you had selected stocks purely at random, throwing darts at a page of the NYSE daily listings, you probably would have done at least 4 percent better than the expert forecasters.

He also checked on the performances of experts hired by the twenty-five leading fire insurance companies, who had a great deal of advance premium money to invest for the companies. These experts, he found, "achieved an average record 1.20% annually worse than that of the general run of stocks. The best of these records . . . fails to exhibit definitely the existence of any skill in investment."

Then, not to neglect the system players, the experts following the Dow theory on stock movement, he checked the performance of its leading exponent, William Peter Hamilton, of the *Wall Street Journal,* who published forecasts of the stock market over a twenty-six-year period, from 1904 to 1929. He did slightly better than average but poorer than if he had simply let his money stay "in continuous outright investment in representative common stocks for the period. On ninety occasions he announced changes in the outlook for the market. Forty-five of these predictions were successful and forty-five unsuccessful."

In short, Alfred Cowles had checked all the available public prognostications and found them occasionally no worse than average and often, far worse.

"Of course," he recalls, "I got a lot of complaints. Who appointed me to keep track? Also, I had belittled the profession of investment adviser. I used to tell them that it isn't a profession, and of course that got them even madder."

In 1944, Cowles decided to update his studies on forecasting, and his report appeared in an issue of *Econometrica* magazine. His summary:

The records of eleven leading financial periodicals and services since 1927, over periods varying from 10 to 15½ years, fail to disclose evidence of ability to predict successfully the future course of the stock market.

Of the 6,904 forecasts recorded during the 15½ year period, more than four times as many were bullish as bearish, although more than half the period was occupied by bear markets.

Still, there was one positive finding. He had studied one forecasting service back to 1903 and found that its results were 3.3 percent better than the Dow-Jones index stocks. It was nothing to get excited about, he pointed out, but it indicated that you *could* have made a great deal of money in following what he called the "inertia" principle. *That is, if you bought at turning points in the market, after prices for a month averaged higher, and selling only after they averaged lower for a month. If you followed this simple rule, you would have done very well in the forty-year period.*

"Looking back, my approach seems terribly obvious. Why hadn't anyone done it before? I suppose you needed time and money, which I had. We didn't name names of the services I checked out and perhaps that was a mistake, but still, it was being done as a very sober academic and professional report and we didn't want to get down to the level of nasty finger-pointing."

He saw another aspect that should have been obvious, even before he began. "Market advice for a fee is a paradox. Anybody who really *knew* just wouldn't share his knowledge. Why should he? In five years he could be the richest man in the world. Why pass the word on? After the first year with every stock hit right, his only problem would be how to hide his buys and sells so that he didn't develop a coterie of followers out to do exactly what he did. That would defeat his purpose, of course.

"There's another element here that makes the professional analysts and advisers uncomfortable. The element of luck *is* terribly important in the market. They like to deny it because it reduces itself to the client deciding whether or not he's dealing with a *lucky* man, instead of one with all sorts of impressive initials after his name.

"Even if I did my negative surveys every five years, or others continued them after I'm gone, it wouldn't matter. People are still going to subscribe to these services. They want to believe that *somebody really knows*. A world in which nobody really knows can be frightening. I don't come to belief easily. I'm an agnostic—married to a Christian Scientist. She's tried to convert me, of course, and I *want* to believe, but I can't."

Since the early thirties, Alfred Cowles has been the investment counselor for some seventy members of the Cowles family trust. He preferred not to talk about the size of the family's trust holdings, but another source indicated that it ran "well into nine figures."

As a registered investment adviser, Cowles has been getting $\frac{2}{10}$ of 1 percent of the market value of the family holdings, which include his own sizable investments. He is a millionaire many times over.

"How do we invest? Basically, we're advised by Brown Brothers-Harriman. I don't always follow their advice, but on the whole they've done a good job. Averell Harriman was a classmate of mine at Yale. They have some thirty analysts on the staff, and they're good men but I don't think they have any really *special* knowledge. We've done well in the family trust because we've stuck pretty much to high-grade, diversified stocks and not jumped in and out."

Where should people go for investment advice?

He smiled dimly. "I was afraid you'd ask. I haven't the faintest idea. It would be easier if the analysts and advisers were required to maintain a year-to-year box score. That would give the public *some* kind of guide, at least."

He was still proud that he had initiated the concept of "weighing" the investment letters and advisers but prouder still of having helped found the Econometric Society and the Cowles Commission for Research in Economics, one of the most important agencies of its kind in the world.

"I started the commission with a $40,000 contribution and watched it grow. Now the commission has about $750,000 and gets about $250,000 a year income, some of which it gets from other foundations. It's done a lot of good work and helped some of our top economists at important stages in their careers. Professor James Tobin was our research director until 1969. He's also president of the American Economics Association and Sterling professor of economics at Yale, where the Cowles Foundation is now headquartered."

In his handsome white-and-gray marble hallway, Alfred Cowles had a last observation: "There does seem to be one safe investment. Houses. We bought this house eight years ago and it's doubled in value since. No investment advisers, no tipsters, nothing."

A month later in New York I talked to Professor James Tobin and a colleague of his at Yale, Henry C. Wallich. Tobin, a tall, handsome man with gray-black hair and expressive eyes, was enthusiastic over the work of the Cowles Foundation and many of the important economic monographs it had helped underwrite.

Henry C. Wallich, who is the Seymour H. Knox professor of economics at Yale, was familiar with Cowles' pioneering work and was enormously interested in the overall problem of establishing track records for analysts and market letters. He had once been in the business as analyst for a New York Stock Exchange firm.

Born in Berlin in 1914, he studied ancient languages there before going on to Oriel College at Oxford, where he took a degree in economics. He was in the import-export business and banking in South America for two years before coming to New York and becoming a security analyst. His speech is still Oxford, strained through a German background. He wears bifocals; his hair is combed straight back; and he has the sedate, careful look of a bank trust officer. In person, he doesn't look half as pugnacious as in his picture over his *Newsweek* column.

"I still supervise some of my old accounts, mostly old ladies

I've known a long time, but I don't take any fee. Cowles' old comment, 'If you really knew you wouldn't talk but just quietly become the richest man in the world,' is patently true. So the assumption must be that the professional analysts don't really know. There's another factor with analysts that has nothing to do with *knowing*. One analyst with personality and force of character can influence a surprising number of other analysts. But that has nothing to do with *knowing*.

"Yes, there are a few superior analysts who do see farther than the rest, and they do turn in a consistently superior performance. But even they can't escape permanently the iron laws of the market. The market learns their methods and uses them until things start averaging out again. You see the workings of this best in mutual funds. Every good study shows that, on average, the funds do not do better and usually do worse than just random selection of stocks.

"There's one good development that has to go a lot further, though. I think we're beginning to see the demand by investors for periodic evaluation of investment performance, something almost unheard of before. The only trouble is that when you get a permanent means of evaluating investment management, the managers become impelled to switch stocks more often to improve performance and that can and does lead to instability in the marketplace.

"Still, it would be better to have some means of permanent track record than not. If you're buying investment advice, you have the right to know how good the man has been."

Another academic type who is on record in favor of score cards is James H. Lorie, professor of business administration at the University of Chicago. In 1968 he announced:

The measurement of performance and the evaluation of those responsible for performance is going to be with us from now on. . . . The people responsible for manipulating these huge assets are going to have to be accountable. . . . Report cards are going to have to be issued.

These are fine sentiments, and they are held by others, but nothing seems to be done about them.

Joe Mindell, a widely respected New York analyst, who had studied philosophy and science at Columbia before switching to the stock market, recently talked about the problem.

"For years I tried to keep track records on the technical analysts, to see how closely they came in their prophecies on the market. I finally gave up after ten years. The charts and patterns always looked lovely and impressive, but what's the good of a pattern that works—except when it doesn't work? A friend of mine, a doctor, inherited a million bucks and he looked around for a competent investment adviser. Now, he was no fool. He wanted to know what kind of track records they had; how well had they managed other people's money. He got a marvelous runaround. Why don't you get in touch with him? He'll tell you what happened."

He was a surgeon at Mount Sinai Hospital in New York. As he recalled the incident, he went to several reputable, independent advisers: "I told them I wanted to see how they had done on some typical accounts of theirs. Naturally, I didn't want *them* to pick out their two or three particular winners. I wanted a *random* selection from their current accounts. I suggested that my accountant would select the accounts in some purely random fashion; or if they didn't want that, I was willing to take a mutually acceptable accountant to do the random selection. I was being very flexible. I was even ready to accept their own accountant's choice if he'd certify that he had selected the accounts by some acceptably random process. Now, you must admit I was being reasonable. But even though I was ready to bring a sizable account with me, they wouldn't hear of my approach. I even argued with them; all I was asking is the kind of analysis of accounts that they and their analysts regularly were giving to stocks in which they recommended investment. But every one of them turned me down. Flat. As far as I know, none of them would agree to it, even today. Oh, I made some other arrangements for my money."

Sandy Hohauser, who is considerably younger than the surgeon and not nearly as polite, wouldn't be put off that easily. He had only $250,000 to invest but he was going to do it right.

He's thirty-six, tall, and wears his long brown hair in a Prince Valiant bob. He speaks very quickly, and often his words come tumbling out over each other like a teletype outracing its keys. He got his degree in architecture at Yale in 1955, after having attended McBurney Prep School in New York. He and his wife both inherited money and live in a nine-room brownstone duplex on East Sixty-fifth Street in Manhattan, with their three children.

His home is far more attractive than his grubby, cramped, and disheveled offices at 1 Union Square. "Not much of a showcase for an architect," he admits with a mirthless smile. "But then, I don't have a lot of clients coming down here because I don't have a lot of clients." He does have a minor reputation in his field because of a recent book he did on architectural models. He has two assistants at his office—not for architectural work, though. They are Cooper Union students who work part time for him, at $3 an hour, keeping his stock and statistical charts up-to-date.

"In late 1965 when my wife and I came into our money, I decided to do this systematically. I'm *very* systematic. Well, I had to find out about the investment business. So I took this night course in investment they give at NYU. Mostly women: a lot of elderly widows who were left money and a few twenty-year-old gals who know they're coming into money. But it wasn't for me.

"Obviously, the way to do it was to find the broker with the best track record and stick with him. Okay, how? I had an idea: I'd ask the fifty thousand registered reps to submit their own trading records, Xerox copies of their accounts, and I'd pick out the best one, the one with the solidest track record. But after I thought about it a little, that didn't seem too feasible.

"I heard about these sharp little hedge funds, where the partners were making all kinds of money because the fund manager was getting 20 percent of the profits—giving him a hell of an incentive—by going long *and* short on stocks. So I looked into them. I called some of the largest NYSE firms and told them I wanted to put substantial funds into a hedge fund. They made appointments for me with ten hedge funds. All of them wanted to look me over first, maybe to make sure it wasn't Mafia money." He giggled at the idea of being mistaken for a mobster.

"A great way to be taken to a nice free lunch. Eight of nine hedge fund people decided I was partner-worthy. But then I told them I was a natural cynic and wanted to see, at a minimum, their record for the past year. Fine. They gave me records for the past year.

"The only trouble is, I felt the records had been doctored heavily. So then I asked if I could see the fund's books. 'But that's not the way we work,' they said. 'We're really great, and you'll be happy with us, Sandy.' They still call me every few months, but I never did get to see their track records."

He kept looking, a long-haired dogged Diogenes wandering around Wall Street. "At the end of the 1966 bear market I wandered into a broker's office and I gravitated to this registered rep's desk. I had been watching the tape idly but also kept a sharp eye on the salesmen at their desks. This one seemed active and knowledgeable, and he became my broker."

Just like that? No checking, *nothing?*

"Of course, I *checked*. I had him show me his buy and sell slips. Great. Of the one hundred ten slips, one hundred were profitable and only ten losers. He seemed great on short-term trading, one- and two-day deals. He sounded like the man for me. He gathered about two dozen other loyal clients for this hedge fund and raised about $400,000. We all assumed that he was going to apply his magic touch in day trading. But he didn't. What he did was pick up a lot of lettered stock—stuff that he had to hold for at least a year—at a discount, just as many go-go funds were doing that year.

"At some point I started getting a little worried, and I began taping all my phone calls to him. I'm pretty careful, you know. Then he called a meeting of all the fund partners—for 6 P.M., the day before Decoration Day. Pretty crafty. He naturally assumed most of us would be away for the long weekend. But I came. He told us flatly unless we put up more money, we'd be sold out. Turned out he'd been operating on margin, and the margin calls were coming in fast. I told him to go fuck himself. Well, that investment is probably worthless by now, but I'm suing him. I think the SEC is investigating."

He now turned to the "Wall Street Transcript," which runs in full the in-house recommendations of various analysts working for brokers.

"I studied two thousand comment analyses during the 1966–67 period and found that there was a 60–40 bent to be bullish. I could only conclude that if 60 percent tell you the market looks good, it means they don't know. If only 50 percent are bullish, run for the hills. My general feeling is that in-house analysts are 80 percent inaccurate. And I surveyed hundreds of them."

Despairing of finding an honest registered rep or an accurate market analyst, he decided to check on the market letters and their recommendations. Since it would entail elaborate and costly checking, he thought it would be a good idea to have others in on it, too.

"So I started a new service, 'Rating the Services: A Review and Rating of Market Letter Services.'" He showed me the solicitation letter in which he wrote:

> INFORMATION—That's the Name of the Game
> Which Stock Market Letter Services
> Outperformed the Others?
>
> We are in the process of conducting an *extensive study of investment advisory services* aimed at the sophisticated investory, stock broker and investment adviser who is intelligent enough to let others do the research and then act upon the results. . . .
>
> Information and judgment are the two tools upon which the consistently successful investor must rely. Today's alert investor has at his disposal numerous advisory services. . . . What do the past performances of these advisory services reveal?

Each quarterly issue of Rating the Services will contain approximately thirty pages and 30,000 words. It will list, dissect and compare the performance of various investment market letters. These services account for 95% of the total yearly subscriptions to services.

How did he find out the number of subscriptions each service had, since this is generally tightly guarded information? "I did a lot of checking, talked to a lot of market letter operators. I gathered that the last time the industry had a count, it was estimated that there were 250,000–300,000 long-term subs; that in any one month there might be 500,000 long- and short-term subscriptions in effect."

He mailed 18,000 letters and got 200 subscriptions in March and April, 1968. Since he is methodical, he did a breakdown of his subscribers. "About 19 percent were from New York State; 14 percent California; and 13 percent Illinois. Interesting: 25 percent of all of them asked to have the letter sent to a post office box." He also did a rundown on the names of the subscribers. Based on the sound of the names, he found that the percentage breakdown of names appeared to be:

45 percent...... WASP names
17 percent...... Germanic names
13 percent...... Jewish names
10 percent...... Irish names
2 percent...... Italian names

The only trouble was that most of the 200 subscribers didn't enclose their $45 check as they were supposed to. This made him start rethinking some of his basic premises.

"I always keep a careful track of my time expenditure. I realized to do the service properly I'd have to take on two assistants—and I'd still have to work eighty hours a week on it. Even then, if I did as good a job as I projected, I'd quickly have a breakdown. So reluctantly in May, 1968, I sent out another letter announcing that the service had been aborted because of technical difficulties. Of course, I refunded the checks I had received.

"I still thought it was a good idea and maybe I could sell it to some other market letter service. I went to a couple of dozen. Most of them thought it was out of their line. And a few thought it interesting, but it would represent a conflict of interest. After all, what if their service turned out to have a poor track record? I asked some of them: 'What would happen if I published my letter and your rating turned out to be very poor, say, forty-ninth or fiftieth?' I was flabbergasted: They didn't think it would *affect their sales at all.* They said their clients just wanted their hands held. I find that hard to believe. How could people be so unscientific? Maybe they were just trying to put me off."

Meanwhile, a lot of registered reps trying to get Hohauser's investment business kept calling him. "I'm pretty crafty with them," he told me. "When they call with a recommendation, I immediately write down their comments and then check to see how the stock turned out. Then after I accumulate maybe six or seven such items from a broker, I send him his box score. So far, I've run scores on 30–40 brokers. They know I keep records. No, they're not much good."

Despairing of competent outside counsel, Sandy decided to find his own system of beating the market.

"I did 1,000 hours of research, using the 300 market indices I keep up-to-date. Finally, I developed a system for operating through no-load mutual funds. It's about time; I've been non-profit long enough."

He wouldn't describe his "m.o.," his *modus operandi.* "My fund selection method is fifty pages long," he said. "And I figure it's worth at least $100,000, so why should I *give* it away?"

In November, 1970, he was optimistic about his system. "I think we really got it now. We had a dry run for the past few months on my method. It involves stock volume and price momentum. Technical stuff. All dry runs so far, but they show I'd have made at least 100 percent profit for 1970, even. When will I actually put money in? Let's see how the market shapes up. One other thing: I recently surveyed fifty pros in the market—millionaires and big traders. You know, not one of them subscribes to a market letter."

In June, 1971, I checked with Sandy again to see how he had been doing in the market. "Great, just great," he bubbled. "My mutual-fund trading system is working fine. So is a short-term trading system. I think I'm ahead $100,000, and most of it is going into the brownstone on which I have an option to buy. On the short-term trades I've been averaging 8 percent profit, except for the bad trades which resulted from bad information or just emotional responses. I'm now embarked on a new project: superlong-term trading to find another Avon, another Xerox. Call me in 1974."

The men most interested in establishing track records of the financial experts should surely not be Sandy Hohauser, who after all had only $250,000 to invest; or the Mount Sinai surgeon with a mere million; or even Alfred Cowles, who never had more than a few hundred millions to worry about. No, the men who should be clamoring for, firmly insisting on, an appropriate and continuing "weighing" system of the experts are the heads of our largest banks, who at the start of 1970 had more than $102 billion in trust accounts which they managed. All commercial banks in the United States at the end of 1968 had about $283 billion they were investing for individuals, trusts, foundations and pension funds.

How well have they done in protecting and increasing these assets for their clients? No one knows—and the banks aren't telling. "We've been overly concerned with privacy," admitted Edward L. Palmer, chairman of the executive committee of the First National City Bank. In April, 1971, First National admitted that it had $11.7 billion in trust accounts, with nearly $7 billion held in blue-chip common stocks such as IBM, Xerox, Avon, General Motors and Eastman Kodak.

The problem got a rare public airing in September, 1968, when James R. Sharkey, Jr., a twenty-nine-year-old Harvard

Business School grad, did a study on bank trust departments. He was interested because he works for R. Shriver Associates of Denville, New Jersey, a computer-applications consultant firm out to sell banks on its services. Jim Sharkey was then—and still is—director of Shriver's Trust and Investment Systems.

Early in 1971 Jim Sharkey talked about the three-year-old study—reluctantly. "It made an awful stink. We innocently thought that the study would get us some business by showing how inadequately a lot of trust companies were managing these trust funds. Instead it turned out that we were the world's worst enemy of the trust companies—by pointing out these weaknesses. So now we no longer hand out copies of the study and try to avoid any publicity on it. Still, I'm glad I did it because there were deficiencies I just had to speak out about. Also we did get a lot of favorable comment—but not from the banks. From people who felt they had been victimized by the trust companies."

What Jim Sharkey did was study the way six top banks handled their trust accounts, including a most detailed investigation of how one of the nation's top twenty-five trust companies did it for individual accounts. He concluded that a big part of the nearly $175 billion that our trust companies were handling for individuals was not getting adequate attention.

The trouble is, Sharkey wrote, that generally a minor bank employee making between $8,000 and $12,000 was making the key decisions on how to invest the funds held by 300–400 smaller trust accounts that might aggregate anywhere from $70,000,000 to $80,000,000. There were other attendant problems:

• Management had little control over his work nor any adequate method of measuring his performance as an investment expert.

• Most of the banks studied had no way of following up to see if the trust man was buying what the bank's research department was recommending.

• While corporate pension and profit-sharing accounts get

a great deal of attention because they know they're being double-checked by knowledgeable corporate moneymen, the individual customers "are largely inarticulate or locked into a trust set up by persons now dead. They have great difficulty getting through to the bank and getting results."

In an interview in 1968 Jim Sharkey gave Robert Metz of the New York *Times* some specific instances of incredibly poor judgment on the part of the bank trust departments he had studied:

A young man inherited a fair-sized trust. "He didn't hear a word for over two years. When he investigated he found 40 percent of the money was invested in municipal bonds." Since he was in the low-income, 20 percent tax bracket, the tax-free municipal bonds made no sense for him. In fact he was getting a net of 4 percent on them when he could have made 5 percent just by putting his money in a savings bank.

Other horror tales poured out. One New York *Times* reader told how he had given $214,000 to a bank to manage because he suspected 1969 was going to be a rough year. "In three months," he reported, "the account was down to $184,000. They sold my good stuff—which held the line, by the way—and bought stuff which promptly went lower."

Other cases: A Philadelphia man told of a trust fund his wife inherited in 1961 worth $108,000. "As of the summer of 1969 the trust has 'grown' to $96,000. Because of the general attrition of the dollar since 1961, the purchasing power of the trust is about $78,000 in terms of the 1961 dollars."

A man who had worked as a trust officer in three leading banks said: "This is one area in which we are wide open. In my opinion a bank is simply not a place where an individual can find good professional money management."

There was a lot of flack from banks about the revelations, which they termed "slightly irresponsible" or based on "isolated instances." There was also a rebuttal of a kind from a federal official, Edwin H. Hanczaryk, senior economist in the Comptroller of the Currency's banking and economic research department.

He had done a study on "Bank Trusts: Investments and Performance" which concluded that "the performance of national bank trust departments has been competitive with that of other institutional investors. Yields from . . . trusts and estates participating in bank common trust funds during the 1963–68 period compared favorably with the results provided by other institutions."

The running arguments on the effectiveness of banks as investment managers gave A. Joseph Debe a good idea. Debe was then the forty-three-year-old vice-president of the Chase Manhattan Bank and in charge of liaison in the bank's investment research division. He invented the Big Money Game and managed to sell it to his superiors at Chase.

Recently he recalled the origins of the plan. "I've been a securities analyst since 1952. I worked for Argus and with Standard & Poor's, and I was always haunted with the notion that there should be some standard method of weighing the value of all the advice given out by analysts. Maybe instead of initials after our names there should be lifetime 'batting averages.' I looked around at Chase. We had thirty full-time analysts. On and off there were some thirty-six leading brokerage firms we used to funnel our stock buying and selling business through. And we'd give them a hell of a lot in commissions. Between them, these firms probably had 500–600 analysts at work. Okay, I said, let's see how good these firms are when they're measured carefully on recommendations from month to month, from year to year.

"The basic idea wasn't new. You have business schools where students hold contests on who can do best on a paper portfolio of stocks. But as a big bank we could offer even better prizes."

What Chase proposed to the thirty-six major stock brokerage firms was that each would manage an imaginary $100,000,000 account. The firms would notify the bank of every buy and sell order on these imaginary portfolios—and their reasons for each order. The bank might or might not act on the advice, but in any case it would reward all the players. Meanwhile the bank would keep score, measuring the growth or decline in value of each of the imaginary $100,000,000 portfolios.

The Big Money Game wasn't being played just for kicks. Each of the thirty-six participants would be given actual orders to buy and sell enough securities to generate at least $3,000 a month in commissions. Then after six months the eighteen firms with the best performance to date would be raised to $6,000 a month in commissions, whether or not the bank had been following their advice. After a year the bank would reward the top three firms with $15,000 a month in commissions, the next six $10,000, and so on down the line until the last eighteen firms would still be getting $3,000 a month for participating.

"There's a fantastic amount of duplication in Wall Street," Debe went on. "Reports, advice, estimates and so on. And an incredibly minute amount of checking or keeping of track records. By investing some $2,500,000 in commissions—money we'd have spent in any case—Chase will be finding out for the first time who are really the best advisers in the street."

Understandably, Joe Debe and Chase wouldn't give out the rankings of the firms involved. After all for $2,500,000 they were entitled to the benefits of the Big Money Game findings. But in May, 1971, the *Wall Street Journal* did manage to ferret out the three firms leading in the game: Baker, Weeks & Co.; Neuberger & Berman; and Spencer Trask & Company. Meanwhile the Chase bank decided to continue the game indefinitely.

"No reason not to," Joe Debe explained. "We're building up a great data bank on six hundred top analysts. Nothing like it ever existed before, and the bank is convinced that it's gotten its money's worth many times over."

In February, 1971, Joe Debe left Chase to become president of a closed-end mutual fund, the Surveyor Fund, listed on the New York Stock Exchange. "It was great fun at the Chase running the Big Money Game, but I left because I'd rather be the head of a rat than the tail of a lion."

And of course he has a very good idea of who the really good analysts are in Wall Street—information that no one ever developed so accurately before.

On the second floor of a converted Georgian house in London is London's own Sandy Hohauser. He is Sir Thomas Crawley-Boevey, eighth baronet. Tim to his friends. He is long-haired and wears the official uniform: desert boots, corduroy trousers and turtleneck sweater. He is forty-two and financial editor of *Which?*, which is to England what *Consumer's Union* reports are to America. In early 1968 he must have tuned in on Sandy Hohauser's wavelength and came up with the same idea: a rating service for the stock market tipster services.

He explained how he got the idea: "You must understand that I have no background in the City at all. I'm a complete outsider in financial matters. I don't invest. Yet people ask me for tips. I just tell them that if I *knew* I wouldn't be working here as assistant head of research for the Consumers' Association."

"Money Which?" is a regular special section in the Consumers' Association's noted periodical, *Which?*, which rates vacuum cleaners, soaps, cars, hand lotions, and so on. "Money Which?" also goes to 360,000 subscribers at about $3 a year and gives advice and the best buys in items such as insurance, banks, interest rates and endowments.

"Stock tips are handed out regularly in our newspapers and various periodicals, and it struck me that somebody ought to do a rating of them. Just how good are these tips? And since I had the vehicle for such a report, it wasn't too difficult. What made it a little easier to do here rather than in New York, for instance, is the custom of share tipsters' making a New Year's list of half a dozen or so shares which they believe will do well during the coming year. So we followed the New Year's tips of the *Financial Times,* a daily, and three Sunday papers, the *Observer,* the *Sunday Times,* and the *Sunday Telegraph.* We also checked out the most widely known investment magazine, *Investors' Chronicle,* and a subscription-only tip sheet, *Inves-*

tors' Chronicle Newsletter. We also checked out their 1966 New Year's tips.

"We had some difficulties right away, when we began checking. For one thing, it isn't always possible in real life to buy shares at a price the tipsters recommend. Oddly, the price happens to go up just before the tip is published. Somebody must know something, I assume. What we found was this:

• "No tipster was able to produce consistently successful results. All of them had poor selections. The *Sunday Telegraph* was top or near the top for both years, but the evidence wasn't strong enough for us to conclude that it would do as well next year.

• "If you are an ordinary, unskilled investor, I don't think the tipsters' predictions will be very helpful. You are unlikely to be following *all* their tips, and if you make an unskilled selection of them, why, the risks are about the same as making your own choices."

There were no plans to repeat the tipster rundown. "It takes an awful lot of work," Sir Thomas explained. "Also, we made a couple of minor mistakes and one of the services cried foul; that we hadn't properly evaluated their tips. This was *Investors' Chronicle*. We made the corrections, but they still didn't come out that high. The subject is of great importance to our readers, though. Of the 360,000 subscribers, about 125,000 of them, about 34 percent, own listed stocks and 39 percent own unit shares, what you call mutual funds."

Clearly, the man to see was Patrick Hutber, the city—*i.e.,* financial—editor of the *Sunday Telegraph*. After all, he had come out first in the survey, two years running. He had once listed "Seven Rules for the Greedy Investor":

• There is no substitute for inside information. There is an unfortunate corollary to this axiom—by the time the news reaches The City [London's Wall Street] it is usually too late.
• Never (or hardly ever) take your broker's advice. . . . They are excellent chaps, charming to their wives and

kind to their children. . . . But their basic job is to buy and sell shares: if they knew which were the best, why would they sell them to you? . . . Make your own mistakes.

• If the company is run by a Leader of Industry, avoid it like the plague. He is too busy leading industry and making speeches . . . one Cockney whippersnapper is usually worth three sacked Cabinet Ministers.

• Never invest in a company that spends heavily on research. . . . Americans have a number of jet-age corporations exclusively devoted to scientific wizardry, which never pay a dividend at all. American investors love them. But you are in investment for a profit. Research programmes acquire their own momentum, and it is your money which all those disinterested scientists are questing for truth. If you can get the Government to pay for the research, of course, it's different.

• Don't "Buy good shares and forget about them." If you must be forgetful buy bad ones. It is the good shares that have catastrophic falls. . . . A good share is one that everybody else is buying and therefore very dear.

• "Back good management every time" is a dangerous belief. Luck counts just as much, particularly the luck to be in the right industry at the right time. . . . There is no justice in investment matters.

Hutber is croaky-voiced, sandy-haired, and slightly hunched over. He sits in a black-leather tufted chair and toys with one of those swinging steel ball games.

"I couldn't do my job in the States. Here, I do get—hell, I solicit—inside information. Your SEC would put me away for life. Things here are, in some ways, the way Wall Street was before the SEC came along. Looking for tips for the paper, I only talk to high-class people. No one tells me a lie twice. What do they get out of it? Well, I'm prepared to do a small service, if they'll do me a bigger one.

"It took me some years to overcome my prejudice against tipping of stocks. Still, even today, weeks can go by without a stock recommendation, but on average, I do provide one tip a week. Mostly, I seek the inside story, the real shenanigans of corporations. And there are a lot. After all, we don't have an SEC, and our solicitors don't seem to have the occasional good luck your American attorneys have suing on behalf of a wronged stockholder. I'd say it's almost impossible for a wronged shareholder to win a civil case in Britain. We have a Board of Trade—like your Department of Commerce—but it has a very limited survey function, I'm afraid."

Financial reporters face many temptations today in London, he went on. "Financial PR is becoming bigger and bigger here, brought over, no doubt, by the besmogged winds from Wall Street. Of course, their object is solely to raise the share price. PR is like prostitution: a great career for a girl, no good for a man. Look, I say to my staff, you lose one hundred thousand cells in your brain each day. You don't have to lose *everything* for the sake of some sordid little profit on a deal thrust on you by a PR man. If you play it straight, you'll have all kinds of opportunities after seven years here. We have some informal rules on the staff. They mustn't buy or sell on short-term deals. They mustn't buy or sell a share if the company is going to be the subject of a story. About once a month, the PR lads come along with a tempting little offer. Or it might be an enterprising broker who is anxious for one of my staff to push a stock. He'll say, 'Old boy, I'll give you a loan account,' which means he'd carry him for one thousand shares for a month. A kind of option offer without cost. Of course, if the stock goes down, the jobber, the broker, is stuck. We've had some touting scandals here. Some years ago, an evening paper's reporters were getting £5 [then $25] for pushing a share. But nothing big, so far. I'm sure we're due for a major scandal on some of these financial tipster sheets that sell privately, like your own market letters. Lots of temptation there, I'm afraid."

Investors, he went on, are babies: "They're children looking for the rich milk of mother's breast . . . they love mommy so much, but if the supply is cut off, they're enraged. So everybody is out seeking a share tip. Me, I haven't been buying shares the past four years."

Congratulated for coming out on top in the "Money Which?" survey, he laughed. "That New Year's list. A lark, after a few drinks. Sure, we selected stocks for the New Year, but no one took it too seriously. Maybe that's the secret of share selection: *Don't take it too seriously.*"

Meanwhile, in another part of London, as the nineteenth-century novels used to put it, there is Basil Taylor who is an innovation: the academic intrusion into the marketplace. The type has become common in the States, but in England graduate studies in finance, particularly share market finance, are comparatively rare.

Basil Taylor is forty-four, brown-haired, and struggling with an academic salary of £3,200 (about $7,500). He has a wife, two red-haired sons, and lives in suburban Wanstead. He also has a book called *Investment Analysis,* which sells slowly but steadily. His title is reader in portfolio investment at the Graduate Business Centre of the City University, Gresham College—yes, *that* Gresham—not far from the Bank of England. [A reader is roughly the equivalent of an associate professor in the States.] After Oxford, he became an investment analyst for an insurance company and then at the British Petroleum Pension Fund. He enjoys academic life, even though the salary is poor.

"Every year we run what my friends call Basil's Benefit. More formally, it is an Advanced Seminar on Portfolio Investment for which I get 38 guineas a head [about $93]. Mostly we get partners or members of the senior research staff. No private investors. [The pink-and-blue announcement of the seminar footnotes darkly, "The Conference Administration takes no responsibility for any views expressed at this Seminar, *nor for an effect whatever they may have on the prices of any securities.*" The Conference Administration is Giles Taylor, Ltd., who turns out to be Basil's eleven-year-old son.]

"We have almost as many analyst reports on stocks as you do in the States. And just as few really read them here, just as in Wall Street. I used to want to offer a £100 prize. I'd announce it only in the middle of a long analysis of a stock. I

know no one would win because no one would see the offer.
I have people stopping me in the street and congratulating me
for recommending buying a share when, of course, I'd actually
said sell it."

He talked about the London securities market operating
without an SEC-like cop. "Everything considered," Taylor
said, "it works quite well. A few minor scandals from time to
time perhaps, but nothing serious. The need to keep *respecta-
able* is far more important here for our brokers, our jobbers,
than it is in Wall Street. They all went to the same public
schools and Oxbridge, or the Guards regiment. There's a great
club feeling at the Stock Exchange. If a broker scalped a share,
word would get around fast and his firm would be cold-shoul-
dered."

In 1968 he upset many of his fellow analysts by suggesting a
"painstaking system of continuous measurement" of all investment advice:

> If the result of management is not a more profitable situation
> at the end of a given period than would have been obtained
> from a portfolio selected at random, *then there has been no
> product at all* and the purchases and sales undertaken have
> been no more than a financial ring-a-roses. . . . Investment
> management is a fruitless exercise if the so-called techniques
> and expertise do not recoup more than their administration
> cost, compared with performance of a portfolio selected at
> random. . . .

Basil Taylor smiled in recall at the stir the article caused.
"Seemed perfectly obvious but I did get a lot of black looks,
more behind my back, perhaps, than to my face. It made a lot
of analysts uncomfortable. Here I was suggesting that they had
to be right more often than not, or else they weren't worth a
shilling's pay, let alone several thousand pounds a year. The
only criterion worth a damn is *effectiveness* and the only way
we can know is to measure it continuously. And we shouldn't
have to rely on 'Money Which?' either. Of course, we don't have
any such systematized 'weighing system,' as you call it. Our

Society of Investment Analysts was only formed here in 1955, and already its members command, by far, the highest remuneration of all professions in Britain. This lovely condition can't go on indefinitely—without them showing that they're earning their pay."

Another skeptic—and advocate of a continuous "weighing" system—is Abraham William Cohen, who as editor of *Investors Intelligence* reads at least sixty market letters and writes a consensus of their recommendations every two weeks.

He is sixty, short, stocky, and sports a goatee-mustache combination that makes him look like a benign Walter Ulbricht, the ex-East German Communist boss. Cohen got out of Harvard Law School during the Depression year 1932 and found it difficult to establish a practice. He went into his father's dress trimmings business after the war and ran a vanity press operation, William Frederick Press, on the side. One of the books that came into his hands was from a Long Island man, named Ernest J. Staby, who had a variant on point-and-figure charting: using *X*'s for price gains in the stock; *O*'s for losses. Staby's system, called Chartcraft, turned out to be a winner, a rare event in vanity publishing. He sold his rights in it to Abe Cohen. Eventually, Cohen gave up vanity publishing and moved full time into Chartcraft publishing. Chartcraft issued point-and-figure charts on all NYSE and Amex stocks and acquired 5,000 subscriptions. Then in 1962, he and his partner, Lee Gray, picked up *Investors Intelligence,* which had been established in 1959.

"The guy I picked it up from had bought out his partner for $250,000, which was fantastic and way overpriced. We picked it up—it was floundering then—for a nominal sum and an agreement we'd take over $100,000 in debts the letter had accumulated. We now have about 3,500 subs at $60 a year and it's mildly profitable. We make much more out of Chartcraft."

Some of editor Cohen's caveats about the sixty or so market letters he reads and digests regularly:

• It's hard to keep score. Some of them are so muddled it's almost impossible to tell if they're bullish or bearish.

• Most of the time they're wrong. Very few of them ever admit they're wrong because they have enormous egos. The professional letter writer doesn't know any more about the market than the odd-lotter (one who buys fewer than 100 shares at a time and is secretly despised by the professional trader, who likes to think it's smart to do the opposite of what the odd-lotter is doing).

• There's a lot of conscious and unconscious plagiarism in market letters.

• Most market letter subscribers have been in the market and lost money and decided they need help. When they occasionally do get good advice, they almost never follow it.

• Many of these services start out nicely, but then they get greedy and start taking payments for pushing a stock.

Abe Cohen says he's "the only man in our social circle who's never been in the market." "I've no time to follow it," he adds with unintended humor. Other comments:

"Wall Street is a terrible place, filled with greedy people."

"One of the market letter operator's favorite tricks is to pick a thinly held issue and push it hard. It's bound to go up that week when his subscribers buy it, and naturally, it makes him look good—for that week. A week later, it will have fallen back, of course."

"During a bull market I'll get at least one call a week: 'Give me a stock I can make a few hundred bucks on for a day trade.' Just like that."

He got onto some of the characters in the business and their tricks. He mentioned Peter Jeffrey, whom we will encounter later, and pointed out that when the SEC closed his "Dynamics Letter" it enunciated a new principle that hobbled some of the market letters.

"In the old days, the letter operator could put all his subscription money into promotion and ads, figuring that he's building his subscription list, and in time, his full-term renewals would be found money since most of them lose on their short-term offers. But in the 'Dynamics' case, the SEC said you have to have the money on hand to refund *all* your subscribers pro rata, if necessary. Which means, of course, that you can't throw all the subscription money into the promotion hopper. The SEC checks that out every now and then, and if they want to get somebody, even if there isn't any other reason, they can always close him down if he doesn't have the refund money around. In a way, the SEC really pays a disproportionate amount of time checking the paid letters and very little time at all on the free brokers' letters."

One of the very few attempts ever made to weigh the value of the advice in these free broker letters was undertaken by two students at the Columbia University Business School in 1946. In their summary in the *Financial Analysts Journal,* Edward F. Underwood, a financial analyst working for Bache in the Philippines, and Myron C. Nelkin wrote that the status of this "free expert advice" is "somewhat paradoxical":

> Obviously they cannot be taken too seriously by Wall Street houses or by their clients, since one can hardly expect to give and receive valuable advice for nothing. On the other hand a great deal of high-price time and brainwork is devoted constantly to the appraisals of the market's future—presumably in the belief that the results are worth the trouble. Are they?

They set out to find, between September, 1929, and June, 1946, how some 616 broker-letter opinions had fared on two items: To what extent had brokerage opinion been able to:

1. predict important downturns or upturns in the market *shortly before* they occur?
2. recognize that a turning point had occurred—shortly *after* the event?

Their basic findings: 221 opinions were correct, and 274 incorrect—"an appreciably poorer result than from tossing a coin." And the brokers were only 49 percent right in identifying a turn *after* it had taken place. In their conclusion, the authors became philosophical. They didn't think it likely that "the age-old practice of stock market forecasting will be disturbed in any wise by our findings." It hasn't been.

Still, someone *is* looking on to make sure the brokers' market letters don't get too far out of line. David Denison, the assistant director of advertising for the New York Stock Exchange, is also its censor. In 1970, he and his staff read and checked more than twenty thousand pages of brokers' letters. But the only actions taken against member firms were a censure and a fine. In one case, it was a matter of "bad taste" and the other market letter writer failed to disclose that he was lifting his information from another letter: plagiarism.

"Ordinarily," Denison, a tall, long-faced man with Franklin half-glasses, said, "the main violations are (1) failure to disclose the current price of the recommended stock and (2) failure of the firm to reveal that it is a big source of the stock it is recommending; that it is making a market in the stock. In addition, we check on possible scalping in a stock: recommending a stock to its customers while it unloads its own holdings in that stock. We check by issuing random questionnaires asking for the firm's holdings in a given stock on a specific date. In 1970, I think we sent out maybe thirty to forty such questionnaires. So far, we've uncovered no scalping."

He didn't think there was much skulduggery in the free broker market letters. "Really, for a scoundrel or rascal, the broker letter is a pretty dubious platform for his operations. He could do a whole lot better elsewhere."

2. | Phil and Jerry

*Every man has reminiscences which he would not tell to
anyone, but only to his friends. He has other matters on
his mind which he would not reveal even to his friends,
but only to himself and that, **in** secret. But there are
other things which a man is even afraid to tell himself, and every decent man has a number of such things
stored away in his mind. The more decent he is, the
greater the number of such things in his mind.*

—Feodor Dostoevski

A *Wall Street Journal* story on February 27, 1968,
was headlined: FIVE ARE INDICTED ON CONSPIRACY CHARGES IN
ALLEGED TERMINAL-HUDSON STOCK RIGGING. The stock was listed
on the American Stock Exchange. The five had allegedly con-
spired to rig the stock of this New York distributor of electronic components. One of the names, Jerry Allen, seemed
vaguely familiar. He was described in the story as:

> Jerry Allen, 40, a principal in a New York investment ad-
> visory service, that publishes a market letter called the Stoller-
> Allen Survey. Mr. Allen . . . was indicted here last month
> by a grand jury in a similar case involving 1963 trading in
> stock of Pentron Electronics Corporation of Chicago. He
> pleaded innocent.
>   Mr. Allen said he had never met any of the other four de-
> fendants. "I believe I'll be vindicated," he asserted, and said
> his defense will bring out "What I believe to be the mal-
> feasance, indeed the perfidy of certain Government agents and
> attorneys."

In going through the clips on the Pentron story I came across another name that was to haunt me later. Along with Jerry Allen, there was:

> Frank Kaftel, identified only as a Canadian; Dr. Marcus Kaftel, a New York physician and a brother of Mr. Kaftel. . . . The court papers also said payments [for manipulating the Pentron stock] were made out to Frank Kaftel, in Paris, "through his brother, Dr. Marcus Kaftel at his office in New York City, in return for Frank Kaftel's providing European buying to support the market for Pentron stock."

I still couldn't place the name Jerry Allen, but I went down to the U.S. Court House to look at the case file. There was a copy of the indictment and several letters from Jerry Allen and his attorneys requesting permission to make trips to Zurich, Switzerland, where he was a financial consultant to a private bank. For this he was receiving $5,000 a month. The judge granted him permission to leave the court's jurisdiction, provided he posted a $50,000 personal recognizance bond.

Now I remembered. I had once run across a Jerry Allen, a minor press agent, while doing a magazine piece back in the mid-fifties. I vaguely recalled a short, chubby, blond-haired fellow.

I wrote Jerry Allen, recalling our brief meeting, and asked if he would see me. Why?

> I'd love to let you talk, off the record if you wish, about the business of pushing a stock; or why people buy stocks; or why people believe or disbelieve what they're told about a stock. . . . From what I've heard you have more genuine expertise than the next dozen people.

Two days later Jerry Allen phoned. Why didn't I come down and have lunch with him and his partner, Phil Stoller?

Early in 1970 we had our first meeting at the Yale Club. We sat at a polished wooden table in the long dining room, and it was obviously a time for sizing up.

Jerry is short, earnest, openmouthed, with a chubby body. Thick blond hair, darkening. Very likable, blurting out things about himself no one in his right mind would ever say. "Sure I'm a whore, like everybody else. . . . Sure I took the $700 [as charged in the Pentron case] to ghostwrite a market letter on Pentron. But they got me for the wrong reason. Things were rough then. Much better now."

How much better? "*Much* better," Jerry said. "Phil and I are very well fixed, financially independent. And I wouldn't do the stupid things I did today for the $700."

It was a much interrupted luncheon. Every ten minutes Jerry walked out to look at the ticker. He'd come back with his face two inches lower. It was a bad day at Gray Rock downtown.

Jerry: "The $5,000 from the bank in Zurich? I get that for giving them tips on U.S. stocks. Hell, we made them and their clients about $3,000,000 on a little leasing deal a few months ago."

Phil Stoller is much taller and thinner than his partner. Hair graying. Long sideburns, dark-blue-striped suit, glasses. A good-looking New Yorker. Lives in Woodmere, Long Island. "The whole bit: two cars, maid, kids, a wife. I went to NYU, School of Retailing. . . . Listen, how do we know you're not from the U.S. attorney's office?"

Jerry: "For crissake, Phil, stop being paranoid. I know him." It's been a liquid lunch for Phil: three double scotches.

They get on to Swiss banks. Jerry: "There's something. At least twenty-five Big Board houses have Swiss offices. Why? They can't advertise there; they can't take Swiss customers, so why do they do it? Sure, most of them are tiny one-man operations, but what the hell. They do it for all these stock deals. . . . All these numbered-account stories are a lot of crap mostly. With a number, there's still a lot of people in Switzerland who will know about your account. Best way to do it is with a Liechtenstein corporation."

Phil is still worried. "You're sure you're not from Larry

Newman [the assistant U.S. attorney who's handling Jerry's case], huh?" I assure him again I'm not; that I haven't had any connections with the U.S. government since I turned in my stripes in early '46.

We got the ground rules settled, finally. They'd talk about deals they handled, names and all, if the statute of limitations had run out on those cases. On more recent ones, they'd be a little more guarded.

We arranged to meet the following week at the midtown executive apartment of a wealthy friend of mine who was away. The day before, Phil called: "Could we bring along a guy who works for us? His name is Joe Arden and he's doing some special research." It sounded odd, but I said, "Sure, bring him along." They turned up on time the next day and introduced me to Joe Arden, a short, stocky gray-haired sixty-three-year-old Brooklyn man who had worked in the post office several years and was on the boys' personal payroll. From a valise Joe took out a roulette wheel and a green felt with the usual number layouts. While Joe was setting it up and Jerry was preparing drinks, Phil took me into the other room to explain Joe's presence.

"I once worked for Bache & Company as a registered rep back in the early fifties. I met Joe Arden, who then was a post office supervisor. Joe had some money and came to me as a client. I had his account from then to the early sixties. There are clients for whom you just can't make the right move. No matter who's making on your list, there's always one who's the odd man out. Nothing works with him. He's always in the wrong situation or the right ones at the wrong time. He had $12,000 to start, and somehow we managed to lose $10,000 of it for him. Then he had a second heart attack and I was out of the brokerage business, but he was still a friend and he was on my conscience because I had managed to lose nearly all his money for him. He was on a small pension, so I said, 'Joe, come to work for Jerry and me. We'll find something for you.' At first he was in charge of the letter mailings when we did the

Stoller-Allen reports. When we dropped that, we got him to playing roulette, craps, and blackjack for us trying to find systems. So we're still trying to beat the table, which is a lot harder than beating the market. And I think we know how now."

"But you told me you *beat* the market."

Phil: "Yeah, but that isn't beating the market. It's easier to beat something where they can't beat you back. In roulette, you can lose all. If you play the market properly, you don't lose too often. A slower way, but surer. Picking a stock is a lot surer than roulette. The fuckin' zero can come up ten times in a row. Not likely, but it has. When you're playing a stock and the right people are in it, and the promotion is right and the background is right, usually you don't lose. Even in a bad market. But in roulette, even with the system we've worked out, you can go bust in a night. Gambling is much more exciting because you have so little stacked in your favor. So many imponderables."

As Joe began playing the wheel, Jerry decided to fill me in on his background. His father was a pharmacist in South Ozone Park, Queens. "I don't know what you want to make of it," Phil broke in. "But my father was a pharmacist also. And Jerry and I both have high IQ's. Apart from that, we're pretty different."

Jerry graduated from Guilford College, a small Quaker school in North Carolina. While there he met his wife, Janis, a pretty, Nordic blonde. They got married while still in school. Her father was a free-lance writer who deserted his wife and daughter. She was at Guilford College on a four-year scholarship.

At Guilford, Jerry was editor of the college weekly and won the coveted Alumni Achievement Scholarship Award in his final year.

"In my senior year I almost got thrown out for making trouble. There was no smoking allowed at the college. Quakers. But a lot of Quaker farmers in the county were making a lot of dough raising tobacco, and I attacked the hypocrisy. After college, I went to Yale and got a master's in English. I came to New York to write, but I had a wife and child and I could see free-lancing wasn't for me. I got a job as a copy boy with the New York *Daily News* and then fell into a press agent job with Twentieth Century-Fox."

He was fascinated with the movie world—and abhorred it. Jerry opened his own publicity office in 1954: J. R. Allen and Associates, handling industrial clients. Then in 1955 he met Bryan Newkirk, a legendary Canadian mining-stock promoter, and gradually Jerry became his full-time ghost and press agent. In 1958 Jerry left Newkirk—by now he had become completely fascinated with Wall Street—and began his first market letter, "Inside Wall Street."

Jerry: "It took only a few hundred bucks. I had read a lot of other market letters, and they were pretty deadly. I was going to make mine lively, and I'd recommend short sales, which damn few other letters do. It grew, and I kept pushing it with direct mail solicitations and ads in the New York *Times* and *Barron's*. At the peak of 'Inside Wall Street' I had 2,000 subs at $65 a year each."

I did some quick mental calculations, which Jerry picked up immediately. "Yeah, I know, you figure I was grossing maybe $130,000 a year and it was just offset, so I must have been rolling in dough. I wasn't.

"Trouble is, you lose money just on subs alone. First, you're up against the damn Xerox. I had one Stock Exchange member firm in Texas. They took a sub at $65 a year and every Tuesday he'd Xerox about one hundred copies and send it out to his customers, free. You have to spend a lot on advertising and direct mail. Then you get a lot of trial subs and they cost you dough. Nameplates and follow-ups. The sucker takes the trial sub. Then another in his wife's name or his cousin's. No, you can't make money on subs alone.

"When I started the letter, I decided I'd do a good honest job and get subscribers just on the basis of my solid recommendations. I'd give them quality stocks to buy and sit on, for maybe a year. But they couldn't care less. They needed fast action. I recommended Penn Central at 13, but that's not what they wanted. They could have sold out in the 60's on that one. They begged for quick zingers where they could be in and out at a fat profit of 100 percent. I'd go around preaching to investment clubs: Buy good stocks and hold them. The way to make money in Wall Street was to buy straw hats in winter— and hold them. They stopped listening, and one day I decided to stop being a virgin."

Temptation came through the vice-president of a leading advisory firm who knew Jerry slightly. "He asked me if I knew of the possibilities in Studebaker. He wanted me to meet someone. So I met this guy. He had 100,000 shares of Studebaker. The market was lousy. And he wanted to move some of his stock. What he wanted was something I'd heard about but never done: a sendout. You know, you send out 100,000 free copies of your letter, in which you push Studebaker. The corporation, of course, wasn't in on this. In return, he'd take 2,000 subs. I bit. I sent out the full 100,000 free copies and later found out that I was a jerk. Most market letter operators pulling this one wouldn't give full measure. They'd mail out only 5,000 or 10,000 copies and save themselves a lot of money. Who was to know?

"Well, once you're no longer virgin, the offers start coming your way faster. Once when —— was young [he mentioned a prominent conglomerate], they wanted a little push. The offer was a little different this time. They had twenty people who were ready to open personalized service accounts with me. They'd each give me $500, and in return, maybe I'd phone them with a hot stock when I had one. It was done very nicely. D——, the head of the conglomerate, wanted the write-up to stick to the facts. I might go a little overboard on the adjectives and adverbs, but I was to stick to the facts, which were pretty rosy then. They used my write-up smart. They got it into the hands of hundreds of customers' men, registered reps, who love to have a good, well-written market letter they can show their customers. That recommend moved a lot of stock that month, and I had a nice consulting income of $10,000."

Other opportunities came along, but Jerry didn't always accept them. "There was a stock, a Midwest outfit, which was up to $71, and I started knocking it as a sure short sale. I felt the stock was a classic swindle at 71. A day after my letter was out, I got a call from the management in St. Louis: 'Hey, Jerry, why don't you and maybe fifty friends come out here on an all-expense party? We'll have a real wingding.' I didn't bite that time, but it hit me right away that they were just as ready to offer the cash such a party might run to—if I stopped knocking them. All kinds of blackmail opportunities when you're running a well-read market letter."

Any market letter, Jerry went on, can make $100,000 a year in payoffs during a bull market. "Don't forget, at the same time you're also recommending solid stocks. But for the zingers I just looked upon the payments as space rates. And 99 percent of all promoters pay off—if they don't, they're dead on Wall Street. Most of the time the arrangement was simple: They'd give you an option on 10,000 shares of a stock which was then, say, at 10. When you got it up to 12, say, you got $20,000. Or you might take an ad pushing your letter and describing in the ad the wonderful opportunity in XYZ stock. They pay for the ad, of course, and you also get new subscribers. Through that period I was reimbursed by some unexpected subscriptions from some of the finest member firms of the New York Stock Exchange, as well as some of the sleaziest promoters. There've been two men on the cover of *Time* who paid me for my services at one time or another."

You needed all the extras, Jerry continued, because the damn letters are very expensive to run.

"My advertising bills would run $50,000–$75,000 a year. On mailings each letter costs you about 15 cents each. And the phone bills were heavy; and to do research on the legit stocks you pushed, you had to do a lot of research and travel. I'd travel 50 percent of the time. And I'd have to pay free-lance analysts to do studies for me. I'd pay a couple of thousand, say, for a good study of the Big Three auto makers if the stocks were hot then. From 1957 on, there was almost a geometric progression in market letter and security analysts, so a lot of services started plagiarizing one another."

The bad times in the market are disastrous for market letters. "Your subs dry up. The attrition rate is enormous. Ninety percent don't renew after the first year. If you hung them up on one stock, they're out trying other letters. If you try to give them honest, direct advice, particularly on short selling, they won't listen. My most accurate and potentially most profitable recommends were on short sales."

He started getting a little cautious and as a result started missing some great deals. "A promoter came to me on a Canadian mining deal, a dog. He said, 'I won't pay you, but if you buy Control Data at 50, it's going to run up.' I didn't take the deal, and it did run up to 150. After a while I had to get more selective on what deals I took. The better talent agents don't lay all their female clients. Only the better-looking ones. Don't forget, at the height of the bull market I was getting two, three calls a day from brokers, over-the-counter dealers and even Big Board members to push this or that. When I later applied to the Board of Governors of the New York Stock Exchange for allied membership, I was turned down. And a big shot on the board then was a prominent Wall Street character who wanted me to push a stock."

Jerry was proud of the literary quality of his letter. "There were three of us who could write well: Brad Thurlow, Walter Gutman and myself. The rest wrote with sticks."

He had some sample issues for me, "just to give you a flavor of the style." There was his "Inside Wall Street" for June 12, 1959 (Vol. II, No. 38):

> Stocks, like starlets, . . . are made, not born. Both require the doting attention of a "daddy" or sponsor, utilizing myriad publicity techniques in an effort to gain customer acceptance. With the acceptance of most blue chips, which fluctuate

against the background of earnings, business conditions, general market trends, most securities "move" (at least for the short term) as a result of Wall Street sponsorship.

And sometimes he had a little fun with his readers: In that same issue, he discussed a new company, Treasure Hunters, Inc., that had just filed its prospectus with the SEC. Commented editor Allen:

> How refreshing! What a cool poetic departure from freight car loadings, from blast furnace statistics, from futuristic terrestrial safaris. How amusing a thought to contemplate stubby stock analysts probing the depths, studying corroding sea chests! What succulent fare awaits the shark. Punsters are having a field day. . . . Watered stock. . . . Bailing Out Stock. . . .
>
> How can one seriously belittle the corporate future of Treasure Hunters Inc. Imagination should be rewarded. To turn away from the Space Age, to forsake transistors in favor of sunken Spanish galleons . . . to instill a sense of manhood, of humor, in an otherwise impersonal business, is commendable. We're going to buy one share of stock as an investment in man's ingenuity. And a decade hence, standing on the moonswept Isles of Greece, we'll sail our certificate westward, encased in a bottle of Bollinger.

The issue had bread-and-butter stuff, too, based on solid market expertise. In it he pushed Gulf & Western at 11, and it ultimately went over 100. He urged his readers to sell their AT&T stock near its $75 top. His proudest achievement was urging the sale of Brunswick at $70 a share. When the bowling alley craze hit the gutter, the stock eventually fell to $6.

He was fond of some phrases he had coined. He was the first to call them "Twiggy stocks: the science-scented, thin issue with few apparent assets that is transformed by virtue of 'thick' money sponsorship into a bloated 'hot number.'" He wrote, "New issue soufflés are concocted by eggheads capitalizing on the public's demand for puffy stocks." Or "Buy Now,

Pray Later" for a rash of overvalued new issues. Or "The Stock Market is a game devised by geniuses to be played by idiots."

Phil: "I coined one we once used: 'The SEC is going after the wrong people. The ones who should be licensed are the customers.' "

What had they been up to after Jerry's market letter operations?

Phil: "I'm a two-bit stock promoter who got very lucky. And I'm grateful. I've been broke three times and now I'm loaded. Here's the way we got there:

"After NYU I fell into selling piece goods—knit goods—for an outfit called William Heller & Company. This was 1954 and I was making myself $10,000 to $12,000 a year and had my own car, lived with my folks on the island, and went to Florida three, four times a year. The good life. One day I had a blind date and she turned out to be the girl I married. She was working for a Big Board firm, Cohen, Simonson, but they had just sold one of their offices to a major brokerage, and she wanted me to meet her boss, an old-timer named Ben Lewis, a real market pro. He was so good I went to the lunch making maybe $250 a week and walked out as a trainee at $37.50 a week. Why? He painted such a vivid picture of what the brokerage business was like and how you could make $100,000 a year and all you had to do was dial the phone and use your contacts and if you picked the right stocks, you'd get rich or you'd get rich even if the customers got poor. It sounded like an exciting biz, and it was better than hauling a 20-pound bag of piece goods up and down lower Fifth Avenue for nine months of the year. So I took the deal.

"When I went into the firm, they had a ninety-day training program and you spent a few weeks in each of several departments. And then one day I landed in the supervised accounts department and right there I moved on to high school. Every firm has these supervised accounts, pretty much on a discretionary basis. They get a fee for this, in addition to the commissions on the stocks they buy and sell for the account.

"Well, the way it worked was this. And of course it's the same thing with all large firms. Every Friday after the meeting of the advisory committee of the firm, I'd wheel the cart out. It was like a supermarket thing, and it had the long cards of each of the supervised accounts. Hundreds of them. I'd give a card to one of the heads of the department who'd look at the card and say: 'Ah, yes. This account is long 500 shares of Bethlehem Steel. Okay, we switch him to U.S. Steel.' I made the notes for this. I'm listening hard; I'm learning the ways the pros do it. The next card I give him: 'Ah, yes. This account is long 300 shares of Standard Oil of New Jersey. Let's switch him to Standard of Indiana.' I'm a little slow sometimes; after all, I'm the new boy and there's something I'll catch on to. Must be something smart and subtle. The third card comes up: 'Ah, yes. This account had 400 shares of U.S. Steel. Switch him to 400 shares of Bethlehem.' Then the next card, which had 500 shares of Standard of Indiana, and it gets switched—even I could figure that out by now—to Standard of New Jersey.

"Well, that was a real learning day for this student. Why was Bethlehem good for one account and not the other? Why was Standard of Indiana good, and so on? The answer was obvious to me. *Their* rationale, of course, was that the switching was always for the betterment of the account's holdings, but any jerk could see the one common denominator was that by all this switching a lot of commission was also being generated for the firm. Coincidence, huh?"

There were other traumatic learning incidents for Phil during his apprenticeship. "When I came to work there, my stepfather, who has some dough, said, 'Phil, my boy, I'll get you off to a good start with your new firm.' So he came down to my desk and wanted to spend money on some *good* bonds. The bond man came in: 'Mr. Stoller, the best we have are these West Virginia Turnpike bonds. Don't worry about them. They'll never break 95.' Well, you know what happened. That was the turnpike that never went anywhere and the damn things fell to the mid-50's and they haven't paid interest in fifteen years or so. Well, my stepfather didn't blame me, but he wasn't going to take that kind of crap. So he sued the firm and they settled out of court and he got back $3,500."

Things got a little unpleasant around the office after that—by this time Phil had passed the registered rep's test.

"In those days you took the test in the office of your firm, and everybody except an illiterate cluck passed. That's changed now. The test is considerably harder and you can't take it in the friendly environment of your own office. After I passed, I went to work in one of their branch offices." Then an opportunity came up in his family's business and he decided to leave the street. The business was manufacturing boutique items, gadgets, jeweled findings for lipsticks and related items.

"One day a guy comes in and I learn another useful lesson: Beware of crazy inventors. This one had an unbreakable heel, and it was at a time when women were wearing those spike heels. He had a patent pending on an aluminum heel. It looked great, so I went out and sold for $150,000 some hefty interests to a couple of shoe manufacturers and opened an aluminum-heel foundry. Things were rolling great when I get a call from an acquaintance in the business. 'Come on down, Phil,' he says, friendly-like. 'I got something to show you.' I go down, and there are boxes and boxes in this long loft of cast aluminum heels. They're not ours. His company had knocked off our heels and we could have spent the next ten years in a patent battle. So that was the end of the heel business. We were busted.

"Here I am with a wife and a child and a half and an apartment in Forest Hills and owing everybody a lot of money. There's only one thing to do.

"Get back in the brokerage business because it's the only place where you can make a lot of money with no money and a minimum of talent. The only place where they give you a desk and a phone and say, in effect, here, go steal. I went to work as assistant manager of a branch of Van Alstyne, Noel, a Big Board member firm. I got another lesson in the way the street works, there. One day we get a flash over the wire: 15,000 shares of Altamil are available net to our customers at 8½. That means that the firm wouldn't be making any commissions of the sale of these Altamil shares. But it also means that it's a special deal for all the registered reps. In effect, for every 100 shares of Altamil a rep could sell his customers, he'd get $50 commission, which was at least three times the normal commission on secondaries, on large blocks of stock sold after the initial issue of the stock. Me, I was a young eager beaver, and I got on the phone and hustled off 3,000 shares to my customers and made myself $1,500 that afternoon. Great, no? Then at 3:45 P.M., after the market closed, the government announced cancellation of a big contract it had with Altamil. Van Alstyne swore they didn't know about the cancellation. Go prove they did. My customers gave me a bad time because the damn stock dropped bad the next day. But I was learning, all right."

"You've been reading," Phil said, "about what a helluva nuisance the small customer is to the average brokerage firm. They lose money on them, and so on. So how come the firms tolerate having such customers? They're not charities. There must be a reason, and there is.

"You're at a big wire house—one with lots of branch offices around the country connected with teletype—and a wire comes in from the main office: We're participating in a secondary of TWA at $91 a share. That was the big blowoff of Howard Hughes' stock, of course, some years ago. The wire adds that there's a discount of $3–$5 a share. What happens? Why, the same broker who wouldn't go near TWA at $91 will get on that phone and work all day and night for a piece of that action. Instead of making maybe $15 for himself as he might on an ordinary sale of the stock, he can now make $100 for himself.

"The customer, the poor customer, is under the illusion he's buying a bargain because there's no regular commission on it. I think it's terribly immoral and the SEC is simply aiding and abetting it. So the reason the firms hang onto those widows and orphans and retired pharmacists in Wichita is not that they're good fellows anxious to make American capitalism thrive the

way the exchange says it should, but because the small customers
are their outlets for new issues and secondaries where the money
really is. End of sermon."

After the Altamil incident, Phil left Van Alstyne, Noel for
another Big Board member firm. They had a new branch for
Phil to manage.

"They wanted me to open this new branch in the Governor
Clinton Hotel, a tiny office, maybe 20 by 20 with twelve brokers jammed into the 400 square feet, as well as two order clerks
and the usual equipment. It would have made a great testing
ground for a new underarm deodorant. Well, they gave me a
contract twenty pages long guaranteeing all the things I'd be
getting as manager of the branch. In a month we're doing
$50,000 worth of commission and things look great. A week
later, the vice-president calls me downtown to the main office.
Our talk goes like this:

" 'Phil, we have a problem.'

" 'What's the problem?' (He expects me to say 'our' problem,
but I'm real cautious by now.)

" 'Well, Phil, a short time ago I did a public issue underwriting on something called Amalgamated Coil. It came out at
$3 and moved up a buck. The trouble is it's now selling for
$3\frac{5}{8}$ to $3\frac{3}{4}$ and we own all the stock.'

" 'How come?'

" 'Well, I decided to support the market. We couldn't let the
stock go down, so we swallowed the shares that came back on
the market from our customers who were ready to take a small
profit. So now we have 36,000 shares and we'—that 'we' again
—'have to get rid of it.' "

Phil laughs. "You got to understand at this time in my young
life I am strictly a blue-chip boy. I put my clients in General
Motors and Du Pont, solid stuff. I'm very cautious. So I say,
okay, let's look at this Amalgamated Coil financial picture. He
shows it to me, and in two minutes I could tell this crap wasn't
only not worth $3; it wasn't worth a dime. Just another little
company with no earnings, no sales, nothing. They were making
coils for TV, radio, and so on.

"Well, I'm a model manager and the boss says: 'Get rid of it. No matter how; get rid of it.' I say okay, but not to any of my people. 'I don't care,' he says, 'find somebody who can sell it to somebody's people.' This is a new world to me, but I'm adventurous. I make cautious inquiries, and a friend of mine says, 'Phil, I want you to meet a certain chubby little guy who'll do anything for a buck.' So one morning he brings around this young gentleman"—pointing elaborately to Jerry—"and introduces him as an 'investment adviser.' "

Phil breaks off, laughing at a private joke. "I was *so* square. I said to young Mr. Allen that my boss had a big block of Amalgamated Coil which he wants to get rid of, and I've been told that if I talked to you, there's a way to get rid of it."

Jerry asked him, "How many shares?"

Phil told him, "36,000."

Jerry asked, "How much?"

"How much *what?*" Phil asked, genuinely puzzled.

"How much money; how much cash per share?" Jerry asked.

"I wasn't very bright," says Phil, "but I wasn't *stupid*. This guy wanted an under-the-table payment to do something that I still didn't understand. I had no idea what it would be worth. So I went back to my boss and asked and he said, 'Okay, if the character can get rid of the whole lot, I'll give him 30 cents a share.' I went back to young Mr. Allen and he agreed. He phoned a few people, and lo and behold, in ten days all the shares disappeared in the market at between 3⅝ and 4. Then one day soon after, my boss and I met Jerry in the vault at the Marine Midland Bank on Park Avenue and he paid him $12,000 in cash. I suddenly realized that my life had been misdirected. I was clearly missing the important things in life. And that was the beginning of the end or the end of the beginning, but a new way of life had opened for me. [In a bull market miracles take place daily: The buyers of the Coil stock came out ahead because the firm was taken over by a larger outfit that paid each of the Coil stockholders $6 a share for their stock.]

"Later, this character and I got friendlier because he seemed interesting to me and he had a very good advisory service.

Finally, we got together. What happened is that I went to Reuben Rose & Co., a member of the exchange. I was a partner and Jerry came in as our director of research and editor of the house market letter. We had a little trouble with the stock exchange then. They were holding up Jerry's registration as a registered rep. Lee Arning, the exchange vice-president, told me that for my own good I shouldn't have anything to do with Jerry. I threatened to take the issue to the papers—after all, Jerry hadn't had any SEC trouble or anything up to then—and after six months they finally and grudgingly gave Jerry approval. Things worked out fairly well for a while."

Jerry had a copy of his first market letter at Reuben Rose. This was April 12, 1962, he explained, and the market was way down. The issue is headed "Chris-Crafts and Caviar," and the key line was "This is the time to buy, not to sigh." Some of it went:

> Why should a dip in the Dow-Jones Industrial Average take precedence, in the mind of many investors to a basic fact . . . namely: the craving of mankind to upgrade their standard of living. Our optimism is nurtured by the observation that the world is experiencing "a revolution of rising expectations." The majority of people are no longer content to pay homage to economic predestination. The all-too-prevalent feeling, "That's not for the likes of me," has succumbed to idealistic possession of Chris-Crafts and Caviar. Those with bicycles want cars; those with blisters, bicycles. . . . Everyone wants a piece of the pie.

The Reuben Rose arrangement was blasted by a smart con man.

Phil offers a little background: "At Reuben Rose I was sales manager and partner because I had brought $25,000 with me. Reuben got a seat when he was twenty-two—bought for him, of course. Reuben was also a specialist on the floor of the New York Stock Exchange. He had Post 30, the dog post. There they handled a lot of inactive odd-lot crap: mostly obscure preferred rail stocks. And he had lots of spare time. Maybe, he had 190 stocks there.

"Well, shortly after I came in with Jerry, the firm hired a fellow named George Herman to run our OTC—over-the-counter operations. One of his first fast-moving stocks was in an OTC firm called Jerome Richards & Company. It was the first OTC firm to go public. They issued 50,000 shares at $4. Our man, George Herman, was handling a lot of the Richards stock, and it went up to $10. Jerry and I got a little curious—we just couldn't see this little OTC firm being worth $500,000, no matter what. The more we looked into it, the more suspicious we got. We talked it over with my partners in Reuben Rose, but they didn't want to get rid of a guy who was doing so well for them. I went to Lee Arning at the exchange to tell him what I knew and suspected, and still nothing happened. Jerry and I were getting more and more worried and we decided to get out. We knew there was going to be a big stink on this eventually, and we didn't want it to smell us up. There had to be a tidal wave, and we wanted to be safe, high up somewhere, when it hit. But before we left Reuben Rose, I went to the National Association of Security Dealers, the NASD, which polices the over-the-counter brokers. There was a compliance officer there named Robert J. Sayegh, a nice, bright boy who had gone to NYU and gotten a degree in business administration, now at Mayflower Securities. I told him everything."

Sayegh, who's thirty-eight, was for nineteen years a compliance officer at the NASD, the cop. He thought Phil and Jerry were "two very talented, very persuasive characters—and two of the sharpest connivers on the street. Personally, they're nice guys; I like them, but professionally—boy! The George Herman operation was an incredible swindle, and it's to their credit that they spotted it so early, long before we or the exchange did. When Phil came to see me and told me that he had gone to the exchange and given them his suspicion that the Herman thing was crooked, I really didn't believe him. I checked with Arning, and, by God, Phil had been there six months before and even insisted on making a recorded deposition. When we got on the case, Phil was completely cooperative and very help-ful. He had done us a good turn, I must admit."

Phil sketched in the clever swindle George Herman had pulled on more than one hundred shrewd over-the-counter brokers all over the country.

"The crazy thing about this operation was that the stock of Jerome Richards—he got the names from two guys connected with him, a Jerome something and a Richard something—went from 4 to 20 in a *bear market*. Now that takes doing. The pub-lic didn't get hurt at all; it was strictly intended to victimize shrewd broker-dealers all around the country.

"What Herman would do was this: First he gave the stock of the new corporation, all 36,000 shares, to people he could trust. Then he started reporting buys and sells of the stock in the pink sheets—the daily records of all OTC stocks to be found in every brokerage office—at 5, then 6. Now he started moving it around. He'd call a friendly broker in, say, North Carolina, and say: 'Pete, I want you to take 5,000 shares of Jerome Richards at 6 and tomorrow you're going to sell it to George over in Atlanta for 6½. It's all set and George knows about it. You're going to make $2,500 on it. Okay, now you owe me $2,500 worth of commissions, right?' "

Phil explained that these over-the-counter dealers usually bought and sold New York Stock Exchange and American Stock Exchange listed stocks through large New York brokerage firms that were members. They got part of the commission for bring-ing the business to the larger firms. So the business of placing their major stock buys and sells with a New York member firm in return for other favors was routine. It's called reciprocal business.

"So, in time, the OTC dealer in North Carolina will come through to George Herman and Reuben Rose with $2,500 worth of commissioned business. Even Steven. The dealer in Atlanta, Georgia, gets the same deal when he passes the 500 shares on the next day to a dealer in Kansas City. And so on and on. Every-thing's on the up and up. George Herman is building confidence in himself and the Jerome Richards stock. Meanwhile, he's got the price up to 18, 19, and finally 20.

"Now George Herman decides its time to blow off the load of stock. Throughout, he had 107 dealers involved, and the 17 holding the stock near the end got stuck. No one wanted their Jerome Richards stock and no one was paying them anymore. So they lost more than $500,000 on the deal. Eventually George Herman was indicted, found guilty, but he skipped. Ran to the Philippines, I heard. He came back, got a suspended sentence, and I hear he's selling used cars somewhere. The NASD suspended his registration, of course, and even Reuben Rose got a brief suspension. Everyone congratulated us on getting out early, and Jerry and I figured we had moved up to graduate school."

Jerry broke in. "You're making us sound a little too good. Don't forget, we got to run through going bust three times, and we're not even broke once yet."

"That's coming," Phil said. "We're about to lose our first fortune, but just to keep the chronological record straight, we went on to another member firm, Lieberbaum and Company, in late 1963. The old man had made a lot of money, first as a bagel manufacturer and then in Polaroid. He had been a big producer—a registered rep with a wealthy following—at Dreyfus & Company, and left them, and with sons started this firm. He had a good reputation, but he had just had a disaster with a thing called Electronics Capital where he lost a bundle of his own money and clients', too. So now they needed new blood and we were it.

"Again, Jerry was our director of research and editor of our market letter, and I was the sales manager. The deal was $20,000 a year in salary for each of us, plus commission. Actually, I went in as a partner."

Jerry took over. "We had Rodin's 'Thinker' on our cover, and one of the issues I put out took a little knock at the new title some analysts were giving themselves, CFA, or Chartered Financial Analyst. I wrote:

The market is an attitude, not an art. A skill, not a science. No one should quibble with efforts to upgrade the standards of the Street. . . . But is there a subtle danger in having a security analyst prescribe fiscal nostrums, operating under a pseudo-professional mantle? The title "Chartered Financial Analyst" adds authenticity to the treatment of subject matter that somehow defies precise dissection or prognosis.

"As you can see," Phil added with a toothy smile, "we were again making friends wherever we went. But there are still a lot of people we have to alienate. Wait.

"At Lieberbaum one day, we were there six months or so, one of the other partners calls us in and says, 'Boys, we got a problem.' I look at Jerry and wince. I could tell what it was real quick, by now. Everybody had something to sell which was worth a lot less than they wanted and usually wasn't worth anything. And I was the guy to find the guy to sell it. They had underwritten some crappy company down South. Suppose, they said, you *do*—a nice little word, quiet, unloaded—*do*, 50,000 shares. We knew the outfit. A bust-out stock, one that has no value and must go to zero. The firm was days away from bankruptcy. It was too much, even for us, and we politely declined. There'd been other frictions, and maybe it was time to get up and move. We weren't going anyplace."

But while they were at Lieberbaum, they did get interested in another kind of market operation. "This was *pure* gambling," Phil recalls. "Commodities, of course. Our lives became cocoa and potatoes, and it was the fastest ride we'd ever had up to then. We ran up $8,000 to $250,000 in nine months." A brief grounding in the commodity business:

"First, there's the CEA, the Commodities Exchange Authority, the equivalent of the SEC. They regulate the kind and amount of commodity contracts that can be bought and sold by the public but not by the producers—a marvelous little inequality that's worth millions. If you're a speculator, me, you're only allowed to own 150 contracts of potatoes, which is 150 carloads. But if you're A&P, a potato grower, a maker of french fries, you can buy and sell as many contracts as you want because, presumably, you may have to do this to insure your future supplies of potatoes a year from now. And in addition, certain commodities are not regulated. These are primarily silver, platinum, and cocoa, mostly foreign commodities. [The value of *all* commodities traded in 1970 was about $150 billion, compared with the $103 billion of securities traded on the New York Stock Exchange.]

"The big attraction is that you can get into the game with very little margin: 7–10 percent in cash is all you need. A great trap. The average potato contract is turned over seventeen times a year. That carload of potatoes somewhere up in Maine is bought and sold seventeen times a year by people like me who have no intention of accepting the carload. The firms dealing in commodities do great. The customers' man working for a commodities firm averages four times the commission of the stockbroker's registered rep. Under 3 cents a pound for potatoes, you can buy a contract of 50,000 pounds—that same carload again—for $250. The round-turn commission on potatoes is $30 a contract or 10 percent of the money actually put out. Every time your broker makes a round trip for you, he gets 10 percent of your money. A healthy vigorish. Lucrative as hell and practically free of back-office headaches. There is no such thing as transfers, stock certificates, dividends, nothing—just a piece of paper from the firm to you. The cost of processing a potato contract carrying a $30 commission was a floor brokerage fee of $2 to the broker and maybe 50 cents for total handling charges. The firm can easily net $24 to $27 on a $30 commission. The same is pretty much true of the other commodities. A great business. What it comes to is that the commodities market is simply a medium for the users and producers to get rich at the expense of the public that gets inveigled into speculating on commodities. The public has to lose because it's not designed so that you should be able to make money on it."

We got back to cocoa. Just how did they go bust the first time?

"I built our little pyramid from $8,000 to $250,000 in nine months. I owned 212 contracts. Each called for 30,000 pounds of cocoa. We went into cocoa at 12–13 cents a pound. And only belatedly did we realize the nature of the game which was played by experts against us and every other greedy speculator. When cocoa rose to 30 cents, the users of cocoa—Hershey, Nestlé and Cadbury—figured enough is enough. The price was getting too high. When they want to break the market to get the price down, all they have to do is sell and sell and sell as the price falls. They sold cocoa they didn't own to people who couldn't accept it. So they sold and busted all the speculators. In two weeks our $250,000 profit turned into a $70,000 loss. Hell, it was just six trading days. Sixty thousand dollars a day went down the drain."

One of the things Phil figured out after he had lost the dough in cocoa was that the real winners were his brokers. "We gave them $50,000 in commissions on our trades. Real dough. So we picked ourselves up and got another small stake and decided we ought to be in on the commission end of commodities. Potatoes, this time. I figured I had a gimmick there. We teamed up with a guy, Harry, who was in the potato business. We started a retail business in potato commodities, and I got the idea that maybe we ought to have a mutual fund to trade in potatoes. I had figured out a trading pattern that seemed to work for ten years back. You bought at a certain time each year and you never lost. We called the fund SPUD Trading. Cute, huh?

"But at the Mercantile Exchange they didn't like the idea. I got called down. I was told they didn't like what I was doing and I wasn't welcome as a partner in Harry's firm. I asked why, in all innocence. They just said they didn't want any mutual funds dealing in potato futures. It quickly dawned on me that they just didn't want any large cohesive group with a nice bankroll that could prevent producers and users from manipulating the market. The potato business is the guy with 1,000 contracts fighting the guy with 2 contracts. Guess who has to lose. But if we become the operation with the 1,000 contracts—spread out over several clients, of course—that gives us a lot of dangerous clout. So, *out*."

Phil expanded on the pitfalls of commodity trading, and potatoes in particular.

"You go down to the atypical exchange and watch the one hundred or so brokers around the ring. They're all driving Caddies. So are their partners back in the firms they represent. How come the customers aren't? The brokers do great because none of them are trying to figure out if the turnip market is going up or down. They don't have to. They've got each other. Let me explain how it works on the floor of the Mercantile Exchange."

Commodities, he explained, are not rigged like rigging a stock, because there are as many people who want to buy as want to sell. And, practically speaking, there's an unlimited supply of a commodity. It's the floor regulations that make great daily larceny possible.

"Let's suppose on this day the turnip market is thin, there are few offers to buy. Now, Broker A gets a big buy order from the firm he represents, say, 100 carloads of turnips. He has a friendly broker across the ring with whom he works in tandem. He winks at his cohort or uses some other signal. Maybe it's a wink with ten fingers showing. This means he has an order to buy 100 carloads of turnips. Okay. He gives his friend across the ring the signal. He waits thirty seconds. The fellow across the ring, meanwhile, buys 100 carloads for his account at the current price. Then as soon as his buy order is complete, his friend who's holding this 100-carload buy order will shout, '100 to buy.' And who gets the order? Why, his friend across the ring who's just picked up that 100 from someone else. Except that now the 100 carloads is priced two points higher. A point on turnip futures means $5 on 50 lots, $10 on 100 lots, or possibly $500 for a little bit of signaling, and that's why these guys are driving Caddies. They divide up the profit of their little deal." *

Phil's firm was making good money on commodity commission business.

* In late July, 1971, the New York Mercantile Exchange agreed to desist from certain practices identified by the Commodity Exchange Authority as violations of federal commodity law. The agreement grew out of an investigation of trading in Maine potato futures on the exchange.

"Things were going great. Just one problem. Our partner, Harry, wasn't happy just raking in those $25 commissions [it was raised to $30 recently] on each round trip. He was a habitual gambler and he was betting the wrong way on potatoes, and he lost all our dough. We had a lawsuit and I won, and we got back all our dough, but after paying the lawyers, we were, in effect, broke again. We had just finished paying off our cocoa debts. The firm was dissolved. Harry kept his seat. So there we were in the mid-sixties with no money, no business hope or aspirations.

"I can't give you names on this one. Here are Jerry and I, kind of broke, very low in spirits, and suddenly we get a call from a character we knew slightly. He had a deal for us."

The deal was that he and his group had a stock then selling for $6 on the American Exchange. The firm was about to buy an oil company on the West Coast. His idea was that Phil and Jerry should promote the stock.

Phil: "Actually, we'd been out of the securities business for two years by then, and we couldn't promote our way out of a paper bag, but what the hell, we could *try*. But we were a little cautious. We did some checking, and sure enough, the West Coast oil deal was in the works and that should give some spark to this $6 stock. So we made the deal. We spread the word around about the stock as well as we could. We were pretty gimpy touts by then, but we simply told all the friendly brokers we knew about the pending absorption of the West Coast oil company by this Amex-listed company. We called no more than a dozen people, but the market was right and the damn stock went in a straight line from $6 to 14⅞ in nine weeks. We were given a big block of stock with options, which we paid for. But we were pretty cautious; before we went into the deal, we checked and rechecked. Was the block they were selling *available to sell?* Had it been registered with the SEC? Yes. It wasn't letter stock—stuff you bought at a discount and had to hold onto for a year or so before you could sell it. Everything seemed on the up and up.

"The stock moves up nicely to 11. Great. All of a sudden, brokers start calling: Where the hell is the stock you've been selling! A certain Canadian firm was supposed to be selling the stock for unnamed parties. We didn't want to know who they were. All along we assumed the deal was legit, that the oil merger would go through, in which case the stock could be worth $15–$20. The brokers screamed at us and we screamed at our Canadian contact. Then one day after he could have heard us up there without the phone, he said, 'Maybe you boys'd better come up. We have a little problem here.'

"We fly up on a very cold day. We sit around his office, and he tells us *we* made a little mistake. *We* didn't have all the stock originally mentioned."

"They sold 112,000 shares which they didn't have," Phil said. "They told me not to worry because soon the stock will go down when the public learns that the oil merger isn't going through. They had to revive me."

"You don't last in this business by copping out during disasters," said Phil. "So we sat down and thought. I said, 'Look, if the stock *is* going down, at least let's get on record that we're going short.' It meant that his broker firm would put up the money to borrow the stock so that they could go short. Then when the stock started collapsing, they could buy back the stock at much lower prices. We got back to New York and I had calmed down a little.

"The next day I get caught in a snowstorm coming in from the island, and I can't make the market opening. By the time I got to the office the damn stock was up to 14⅞ and moving fast. It was trading 10,000 shares every other minute, practically. I think it did 140,000 shares that day.

"Now this is serious as hell. We *got* to get the damn stock down. Jerry and I get on the phone to call all the brokers we had gotten in on the deal. Get out, we said, the dam is about to go. Our luck: The more fervently we told them this, the less they believed us. Obviously, we were lying to them. They figured the oil deal was really going through and we wanted

them to dump their holdings so we could buy it up. So what
do they do? They buy more stock.

"Then our first break. There's a rumor the SEC is looking
into the deal. Thank God for the SEC. The stock starts dropping down to 10¼, and now we come up against another
crowd of stubborn believers—the chartists."

There are two kinds of analysts in our business, Jerry explained. "There are the fundamentalists, who are like us in a
way. They analyze a stock on the basis of its profit projections,
new deals coming up, new devices, and such. The other kind
are the technicians. They say, 'We don't give a shit about
profits and inventions. All we want to know is how's the stock
doing on the charts: How many shares are being bought and
sold; how much is it moving up?' They got a private language:
head and shoulder, upside breakout, spike bottom and other
nonsense. All their bar charts and graphs, they think, tell them
what the smart insiders are doing, with all their buys and sells
showing up on these charts."

"Chartists," Phil said with enormous scorn. "The trouble
with these charts is that they won't tell you when an iceberg is
ahead, or something important. There's a good reason for the
street saying: The technicians don't live in Palm Beach, only
the promoters. These characters don't know what a company
is doing; they even boast of it.

"And because they're such damn sheep, they're useful sometimes. Back in the '62–'63 period General Plywood was getting
a play. There was a big lawsuit pending which would bring
them millions if they won. We bought our group a lot of the
stock at 8. When it got to 11, we had almost 400,000 shares.
Then the technicians took a look at it, and they solemnly pro-
claimed that after having examined their charts and the en-
trails of a few dogs, the major breakout for General Plywood
would be 13⅞–14. They're never hesitant with a few modest
maybes or possibles. No, they come right out firmly. God bless
'em. Well, if they had a major breakout scheduled for our
stock, why, we had to oblige them, of course. So we ran the
stock up a few points with more major buying, to the 14½

mark, and every technician in the land was yelling 'Breakthrough! Breakthrough! Buy General Plywood!' And a lot of
people listened and ran the stock up to 25½. We got our crowd
out at 22–23. Nah, General Plywood lost the lawsuit."

Phil was inordinately pleased with the maneuver. "We were
a little like the astrologer who says, 'You're going to fall on
your ass tonight,' and then runs over to your house and puts
a banana peel near your bottom step. Chartists!"

And now those despised chartists were forming another road-
block in Phil and Jerry's efforts to get their stock down so that
their group could buy in their shorts at a profit.

The chartists looking at the stock, which had fallen to 10¼
on the rumors of some SEC investigation, said nonsense. This
was a stock to buy and its first upward objective was 23. Phil
and Jerry went back to the phones and called a few chartists
working for some of the more influential market letters.

"We pleaded. We begged. We said, 'For God's sakes, this is
an inflated stock that's going to drop. The oil merger is off.
The SEC is going to bust it wide open.' No one would listen.
They knew us. We were double-dealers and the rest. They
knew the stock was going to 23."

Jerry has relived the situation a few times in nightmares.
"We're telling the truth and nobody believes us. Friends dis-
trust us. People we've made money for in the past are shaking
their heads and wondering how two nice guys could try such
a crummy trick. If we were ever going to cut our throats, that
was the week to do it. The stock keeps moving up again, and
we're $500,000 in the hole."

Once again they were saved by what Phil calls "a splendid
set of bureaucrats called the SEC. They stepped in and saved
our sanity and lives. In their usual fumbling, stupid way they
come in and announce an action against the company and its
stock. Obligingly, the stock drops to 6½ in a week and our
friends up North buy it back to cover their shorts. We should
have given the SEC a tremendous payoff because without them
we'd have been in one helluva jam. So a fiasco that became a
debacle which became a catastrophe finally worked its way out

—with the help of the SEC marines. End of story. Oh, yes, we made $117,000 on the deal. And we declared it in our taxes that year."

Phil was thinking about why they had been effective in getting the stock to double. "When you call brokers, it pays to have a real fervor. After all, Jerry and I *believed* that stock would go up. Of course, the merger never went through and the insiders knew it wouldn't. *We* didn't. It wasn't easy to convince all our friends to get out at 13–13½. Most finally did, reluctantly. In this business you have to trust a guy until he fucks you."

After paying off their debts, Phil and Jerry were happily solvent again. Now the same group came to them with another stock deal. This time it was Chief Consolidated Mining, selling then for $3. The group managed to buy 400,000 at that price.

"We accepted the deal again with them. The 400,000 shares were turned over to a group outside the country at 4⅛ so that there was a $400,000 profit involved. The stock moved up to 9¾. The same people we'd had in the other deal we got into this one. We had them buy at $4 and get out at 8–9½. Chief rose; it was primarily a mining operation; silver was having a sharp rise then. Unfortunately, the mine flooded, timbers collapsed, and in time the stock did, too. Well, we made a bundle on this operation before then."

The same operation was used four or five times in quick succession. It's simple, says Phil: "Find a stock that sounds good and promote it. Get paid for promoting it and sell it off. Your only worry is about getting your people out in time. Well, there came a time when Jerry and I had a lot of money. We decided it was time to start a new kind of market letter which would expose the whole business of promoted stocks. We called it the 'Stoller-Allen Survey.' We ran a full-page ad in the *Times* headed BUY NOW, PRAY LATER, and another in *Barron's* pushing what we called our 'Twiggy Index,' skinny stocks that had been oversponsored and overpriced. We had about 2,000 trial subscriptions and maybe 600 regular ones at $65 a year, but we couldn't really make it. We made a lot of enemies and drew some libel suits from some of the companies we were knocking. When you knock stocks, you can't be popular. It was strictly a legit operation. No payoffs involved at all."

Phil was adamant. "Absolutely no payoffs. But"—he smiled—"we did have clients overseas who would go short when they knew we were about to knock some popular high-riser. After all, at the bottom of the market letter, in small type, it did say that we may or may not have an interest in stocks we discussed. Most people reading those lines—and ruining their eyes in the process—would assume that we might be long. We were short, of course."

They had made a lot of money by then, but just then the SEC came in and got Jerry indicted. (This was the story I had read in the *Wall Street Journal*.)

"When I was indicted in January, 1968, for something that took place in 1962–63, a lot of brokers I knew were very commiserating. 'There but for the grace of God, go I' was the thought most of them expressed. In Wall Street when you say SEC, they vomit. All of them had the same problems. And a lot of my friends had had their hands in the cookie jar, the way I did. I was philosophical about it because I know I'm not a virgin. I never protested the indictment but only the coercion the government used to get me to trap others. But I wouldn't implicate anyone else. True, I pleaded not guilty, but there were other reasons for that I'll go into later.

"We were then living in a small town in New Jersey, Nutley, and there was some problem there. Being indicted is tantamount to a conviction in some people's minds. Well, there had been a little bit of jealousy. When my neighbors were driving Fords, I was driving a Cadillac. In the business we're in, the pressure of an indictment is more social than business because in my business an SEC indictment is a normal risk of business. Basically, an indictment separates your real friends from your false friends. When the publicity hits, you cringe a little, I suppose, but it wasn't a case of embezzlement or anything like that. I'd be ashamed of that. But being indicted as a stock manipulator is almost a badge of honor in our society. Maybe a sour badge, but still. . . ."

Jerry moved his family to Manhattan and a large, expensive apartment. Many more men get indicted in Manhattan than in Nutley, and the city provides its own protective smog for the accused.

In 1968 Phil and Jerry, both loaded, closed down the "Stoller-Allen Survey," paid off the unfulfilled subscriptions, and as Phil puts it, the fun started.

"We were going to play the game straight," Phil began. "If a stock was too high, we'd short it; if it was cheap, we'd buy it. If the stock was really good, we'd do a promotion and get paid for it. Our nucleus was still only twelve or thirteen people with lots of buying power. But if they're the right twelve or thirteen, you can start an avalanche. They'll talk to twelve o⌐ thirteen others, and so on . . . the chain-letter effect. We were comfortable, and we decided we wouldn't take any more pay-offs to push dogs.

"Soon after this new wave of righteousness hit, we got a visit from a couple of Las Vegas hoods. They had a stock that was then selling for 14 on the Amex, and they'd heard we were the right characters to get it up to 50 or 100. We looked at it, an outfit in the restaurant supply and laundry supply business. Of course, it was our friend, Parvin-Dohrmann. Jerry and I looked over the figures and talked about the two hoods, and we decided it wasn't for us. The people didn't seem very nice, and as I say, we didn't need such types anymore. We had it by now. We turned them down and they went elsewhere."

Phil and Jerry were in Switzerland for a couple of months on business. "Three months later I take a look, casually, at Parvin-Dohrmann and I can't believe it: The damn thing is 49⅞. I turn to Jerry: 'I don't know who they got to do the deal, but he's great.' Now we had to get in on it and we decided it was a perfect short. Our friends here and abroad were alerted to the possibilities and most of them began shorting it at 50–52. Now it moves up to the mid-70's and we got back on the phones and had our clients and friends double their shorts. A month later it's 103. All kinds of news hitting the tickers on Parvin-Dohrmann. They've acquired the Fremont Hotel in Las Vegas, then the Aladdin. It moves up more. We go over the figures and their reports, and it still seems like a swindle to us. We went short again at 113. We had a session with a friend of ours at *Barron's,* Alan Abelson, who does what the street calls a knock column, 'Up and Down Wall Street.' Alan goes over the reports and figures, and in his completely negative piece you could see this wasn't worth $113 a share. After his column came out, the stock plummeted 10 points. But they had to show up Abelson, so a big buying push came on in the next few days, and the stock moves up 15 points in the next two days. At 127½ we got our clients short again. Now we were sweating all the way. We knew what it was worth—damn little—but no one else did. Or wanted to know. Our last short went off at 141 in April, 1969. We were very nervous because we had a loss on paper more than all the dough we had.

"Then the Amex halted trading in it the end of April, and we got it made. It reopens trading in May and starts dropping down to the high 60's. They halt trading again in mid-October, and when it reopens finally again, in February, 1970, it falls to 35. By then the whole thing was a mess. The SEC stepped in with accusations of stock rigging, the old management moves out, the stock changes its name to Recrion Corporation, and there's a million civil suits. A great mess. We closed out our shorts, of course, and did pretty well. We could have made millions for our crowd, but the brokers squeezed us, closed out our shorts prematurely, and we didn't make as much as we could have."

One day before they got so heavily involved in shorting Parvin-Dohrmann, they got a call from a broker they knew.

"This is a guy named Morty Tover and he ran an outfit called Hancock Securities, now out of business. He was sponsoring a stock called Jayark. It had once sold for a buck a share and now was $50. He was sure it was going to $200. What it was, was a self-contained projector for educational and teaching setups. According to Morty, it was the greatest thing since Polaroid. We told Morty we'd investigate. They were assembling the item in the old Keystone Camera plant in Boston. Jerry and I flew up and went through it, then came back and studied the figures. What we saw was three years of broken promises. The sales in that period had zoomed up—yeah, from $100,000 a year to $102,000 a year. As far as we could figure, the outfit was insolvent. We got together with Morty and said, in effect, 'Morty, you're in the wrong church and wrong pew and wrong stock. This is absolutely worthless, a piece of shit, and we're going to short it for a client.' "

What convinced Phil and Jerry even more was the news they got from good sources that Bell & Howell and SONY were coming out with very similar outfits. And since they had better merchandising setups, their products could easily displace and overtake the Jayark unit.

When the boys get down on a stock, they do it all-out. Not only did their friends and clients short it at 50, but they went to Bob Sayegh at the National Association of Securities Dealers —the one they had gone to on the Jerome Richards case.

"We told him the whole story of what we found out. And the fact that we were shorting the stock. The NASD wrote us a nasty letter that we weren't altruistically motivated; we weren't acting in the public interest but for our own selfish purposes, and, accordingly, they'd do nothing."

Now they went to their traditional enemy, the SEC.

"There's a nice Brooklyn boy in their New York office named Marvin Pickholz. We went up and insisted on having a stenographer present to get it all down. We laid out our findings: Here was stock with three years of lies in the annual report and absolutely false projection of future profits, and the thing was a fraud. Pickholz made a recommendation to the SEC to suspend the stock from trading, but nothing happened."

They called their friend, Abelson, at *Barron's* and suggested he look into Jayark; that it would make a fascinating item. Abelson did just that, and his column on August 12, 1968, shows how beautifully a sharp financial reporter can explode a fat bubble:

> All these years what the world has needed, it turns out, is not a good five-cent cigar but a "simple audio visual device to help a complex society communicate." We're indebted for this revelation to a public relations concern called Robert S. Taplinger Associates. What's more, the world's in luck. For a company called Jayark Corp. has developed just such a device.

Abelson talked to distributors in the field. They were unimpressed. To the Jayark president, Reuben Kaufman. He was filled with splendid projections: The company, he said, had a huge backlog of orders and would earn $2 a share that year on sales of $7,000,000. Abelson called Keystone in Boston, where the camera device was being assembled, and found that it had made fewer than 100 prototype models; that commercial production wouldn't start for a few weeks; and that anyone who thought 1,000 units would be produced in September was "dreaming." Finally, Abelson pointed out that the current market valuation of the company was $42,000,000, an utterly incredible figure, considering its meager production. It was a beautiful job of bubble bursting. The stock started falling.

The SEC eventually found that all of Phil's and Abelson's comments were true; and more. Not only had the Kaufmans been selling a lot of stock without registering it with the SEC, but also they had issued:

> . . . untrue and misleading statements in press releases, information memoranda and reports to shareholders, including Annual Reports of the Jayark Corporation, which they distributed and caused to be distributed to the news media, investors, prospective investors and to registered representatives employed by brokers and dealers.

The Kaufmans, without admitting any of the many allegations, consented to a permanent injunction on the practices charged against them.

A few months later, on August 19, 1970, Phil proudly produced an item in the New York *Times* "Bankruptcy Proceedings" column. Jayark had applied for a Chapter 11 arrangement.

"A quiet joy when I saw it," Phil says. He was a little mollified that the SEC had taken action against Jayark. But he was still suspicious. Why did they keep it so quiet? "All they were worried about was that Jerry and I and our clients shouldn't profit from a short on Jayark."

They did profit, of course. "One of our best," Phil admitted.

Alan Abelson, the columnist at *Barron's,* is forty-five, about 5 feet 8, jowly, and has a prominent cleft chin. His wife runs the local bookstore in their suburban town. Until 1966 he had been managing editor of *Barron's* and then decided to do his present column, "Up and Down Wall Street."

"We felt we needed a countervailing force to the eternal optimism you hear expressed on the street."

He began as reporter on the old New York *Journal-American* but moved over to financial reporting on the paper to get a $5 raise. He worked for Leslie Gould, an enterprising editor given to financial exposés.

"Gould was a rarity in those days. He never took a dime from anyone when a lot of financial editors and reporters were on the take. One afternoon rival had a financial editor whom everybody in the street called '$500 a column ——.' Today, there's less of that."

He went on to *Barron's* and rose to managing editor. In 1966 he began his present column, which is generally considered the most influential "knock" column in the financial community. "They call me irascible—and a whole lot worse, of course. I suppose you need a certain amount of bile for a column like mine."

"When Jerry and Phil came to me with the Jayark story, I checked it out carefully and it was even worse than they told

me. After my column on Jayark appeared, I got a call from an
an SEC character. Well, I'm a good citizen, and I said, 'Okay,
come over to my office and I'll talk about it.' He said, 'Uh, no,
come here—because I can't carry the recording equipment over
to your office.' I told him to fuck himself. Obviously, their only
real concern was that Phil and Jerry had been in touch with
me."

Abelson has a lingering sympathy for the SEC and its min-
ions. "It's an impossible job. To do a real, thorough job the
SEC would have to have twenty-four-hour trained monitoring
of every phone and a spy in every broker's office. This is a
business based essentially on conversation and verbal orders.

"The SEC is always a few years behind on indictments.
Mostly because they know little about the inside operation of
the business, the way it *really* works. Most of their employees,
particularly on the middle levels, are in a revolving door. They
begin to get some useful knowledge and they're hired away by
the industry they were policing. All the SEC work now, all
their proposed reforms, should have been done years ago. Still,
you've got to give the SEC one big major credit: They kept
Bernie Cornfeld out of U.S. mutual funds and that alone may
have saved the funds from a devastating debacle."

In the early days, he went on, when he was occasionally
called upon to address groups of security analysts, he'd get very
nervous:

"After all, these were *experts*—trained men with initials
after their names and whatnot—and what right did I—with
a lousy master's in English—have to be telling them what I
thought? It didn't take long to lose my nervousness, though—
as soon as I realized that for a lot of them, their IQ's were
perfectly matched with their ages."

He gets his biggest kicks from the reaction of promoters
after he's knocked one of their stocks in his column. "They'll
deliberately try to push the stock up even further—just to show
me up. Now that's a real tribute. Of course, all it means is
that a lousy stock will simply have to drop that much further.

"This is a business that consists of a bunch of little entrepreneurs and their business is to sell. The pushcarts have been moved a few blocks downtown. And from the street they've moved up to fancy offices. The trouble in Wall Street is that the sales function is paramount. Everything has to be ground into a sales and merchandising machine. So you have a heavy dose of boosterism built into the system. As a result, negativism has to be subterranean. Only the positive is overt. So that when you see a stock listed in a broker's letter as having been changed from a 'buy' to a 'hold,' it is the broker's delicate way of saying 'Sell'—without using the dirty word. It has to be a cheerful business. Everything that runs counter is unfashionable. So they don't like me."

Unlike Phil and Jerry, he never sold a stock short. And he does not buy any stock before writing about it favorably. "The one thing I got out of the years with Leslie Gould is that you've got to play financial journalism straight. That's the least you owe your readers."

3. "Just Send Fifty Cables to Anyone."

Fools have always been exploited, and that's as it should be. The day they ceased being exploited, they would triumph, and the world would be wrecked.

—ALFRED CAPUS

Phil and Jerry once talked about the men who had influenced them most in their curious careers. They ran through several names, but the two that remained were Bryan Newkirk and John Christopher Doyle.

Jerry got his start in the business working for Newkirk as his ghost and publicity man. He had once gotten a Canadian magazine to do a piece on Newkirk: "The Mining Midas Who Can't Stop Making Money."

"I think he took a shine to me," Jerry recalled, "because I went to college in North Carolina. He was born there. Then he made a fortune in the Florida land boom of the twenties. He moved up to Canada and became a mining promoter. I remember we had a piece in the New York *Times* in 1957: SOUTHERNER DIGS NORTHERN GOLD—AND BRINGS OUT NOT A LITTLE URANIUM, COPPER AND OIL. He had become a Canadian citizen in 1935. He had only two years of high school but was an absolute genius at promotion. In 1932, he got his big break when he interested Harry Oakes in financing Giant Yellowknife in the Northwest Territories, which turned out to be one of the greatest gold mines in history. Then he got badly squeezed in the 1937 market drop but made another comeback in 1942 when he started picking up mining properties in Quebec, in the so-called East Sullivan area. They looked for gold but found copper instead. Then lithium in Quebec and oil in Saskatchewan. Once, in the late fifties, he called me to get a nice Christmas present for his grandchildren. 'The hell with the present. Let's get them a whole department store so they can pick their own.' He didn't get it, but that's the way he thought. He bought a 112-foot Navy craft and spent $300,000 converting it into a luxury yacht, the *Louvicourt*. Everybody got hospitality on the boat."

Newkirk, Jerry recalls, was about 6 feet tall, lean, and trim until his later years, when he began putting on weight. He was courtly, generous, and affable. "And he knew tricks of promotion that gave me a whole university education."

One of Newkirk's favorite devices for promoting a stock was the cable gimmick.

"We were eating at the Roosevelt in New York one night, and he says, 'Let's send some cables.' He was pushing Valor Lithium, a complete fraud. At one time Lithium stocks had been hot. Quebec Lithium had jumped from a buck to $18 on the Amex. Valor had come out at a dime and was now $1.50. He sat down and wrote a cable that read something like this:

COMPLETED MY DEAL ON VALOR. BOARD OF DIRECTORS HAS AP-
PROVED ACQUISITION. ACCUMULATE QUIETLY. REGARDS.
BRYAN

"He said, 'Jerry, my boy, I want you to send out fifty cables just like that one.' Who to? I asked, wide-eyed. 'Who cares?' he says. 'To *anyone*.' I still didn't get it. 'Look,' he says, 'I'm sending this one to Colonel so-and-so, in Paris.' I said—boy, was I stupid!—I don't know anyone in Paris. Finally, it got through to me. And so I sat down and wrote out fifty cables to people I didn't know, names I made up, in Paris, London, Montevideo, Zurich, Geneva, Milan. All the same cable.

"Of course, the cables weren't delivered because the people we sent them to didn't exist. But Newkirk operated on the theory that if you sent fifty cables, every cable was going to be seen by at least six or seven people and one or two of them would spread the word on Valor. They did. Of course, all the cables came back, 'Undeliverable.' "

That period in New York, Jerry went on, was one of New-kirk's lowest. "He had become a lush and he had been dead-drunk most of that week. He owed me salary and the hotel was going to evict him soon. I'd never seen him flatter on his ass than that month. I'm sitting with him in his room, figuring what the hell I'm going to do next, when we get this call from Canada. They'd been drilling up in the Quebec muskeg, in one of his East Sullivan claims, and they hit it. The Canadian mining stock business is one vast, whispering gallery and the news was out in a day. His East Sullivan stock went from 30 cents to $7 overnight. He was on his feet again and started all over. He paid me my back salary and gave me a bonus. You know, at one time this great con man's mining stocks made up 10 percent of all the volume on the Toronto Stock Exchange. He used to tell me he didn't have to worry about any govern-ment actions against him. He used to get little boys for one of the men in the Ontario Securities Commission.

"The cable gimmick sometimes had a minor variation. He'd send it to a bunch of nonexistent brokers at real brokerage firms in various cities. Something like:

BUY ME 100,000 SHARES CONSOLIDATED GOLD, PAY UP TO $2. WILL PAY VIA BANK SO-AND-SO, ZURICH. STOCK DOUBLING NEXT WEEK. KIRK.

Of course, there was no one at the brokerage firm with the name he'd put on the cable, but a lot of people in that office would see the cable and some would spread the word. Some-

times he needed another guy in on the deal. So he'd send a
cable to his partner in the deal who really worked for a major
brokerage. It would go:

IMMEDIATELY AT MARKET BUY NO LIMIT XYZ.   NEWKIRK

"Well, his partner in the deal knows he's to disregard the
order. But at least a dozen others in the brokerage office, from
the receptionist to the secretaries and God knows who else,
know that a fantastic order has come in for XYZ. By the end
of the day the word is out to at least one hundred people. Hell,
once, at 3 P.M., I got a call from somebody in that brokerage
office about XYZ. Very hot tip. Of course, I knew Bryan had
sent the wire that morning.

"Newkirk had a little Jewish fellow in Miami who was his
bagman. The one who collected the payoffs and things and
brought it up to Canada or the Bahamas. He had another function, though. Newkirk would send him phony confirmation
slips deliberately faked in several brokerage offices Bryan controlled in Canada. The slips would show that Newkirk had
bought 100,000 shares at $1.50 or $2 of some bust-out mining
stock. His bagman, he was Orthodox, would cover several syna-
gogues and after prayer would show the slips to all his retired
friends down there. And, of course, they'd buy. After all, they
knew the great Bryan Newkirk had just bought 100,000 shares."

Jerry left Newkirk at the end of the 1950's, when the promoter
suddenly announced he was stepping down from directorships
in some sixty mining and development companies. He said
he was quitting because he was sick. In 1965 he was indicted
by a U.S. federal grand jury on a charge of conspiring to evade
income taxes on the sale of $5,000,000 worth of stock in three
Canadian mining companies. "They can go to hell," he told
reporters in his Toronto office. "I'm a Canadian citizen and
they can't touch me." They couldn't—it wasn't an extraditable
offense—and he lived long enough to die in London in June,
1966.

"It was pretty sad toward the end," Jerry recalled. "He sank a hell of a big bundle in a Florida resort development, Duck Key, 95 miles south of Miami. He was nearly busted and had to start hustling stocks again when he was seventy. What a way to end it."

The other major promoter in their lives was John Doyle. Phil has curiously mixed feelings talking about Doyle because he once ran out on Doyle when the latter needed him most.

"Doyle," Jerry began, "is *the* promoter of our time. He's first, and the second is 100 miles back. He came from the South Side of Chicago and used to tell me about getting a science degree from the University of Chicago and one from Illinois Institute of Technology, but I wouldn't put a bet on it. He got a job as a $125-a-month salesman for his father who owned a medium-sized coal wholesaling operation. After his father's death, he sold the firm and took over a Canadian coal firm, Boon-Strachan. He built up the firm to the point where it was selling 10 percent of all the coal sold in Canada. In 1951 he became friendly with Newfoundland's legendary Premier, Joey Smallwood. As a result, Doyle, for a down payment of $2,500, got an enormous concession in Labrador. He had exploration and mineral rights on *24,000 square miles*. He spent a lot of money on exploring and drilling.

"He looks like a handsome Irish Tammany pol type," Jerry says. "Matinee idolish in fact, until he started putting on weight. But always very impressive. He was well read and also given to making up facts on the moment. One day we were talking to him and he suddenly said that the Japs had to buy his iron ore because Australia's iron ore is carbonized. He just made it up. That kind of thing. What made him bearable was that he could kid himself. He'd joke about his stupidity and his big, fat ass. He used to love sitting on the crapper, opening the door and giving orders to his batch of girl secretaries. He loved eating, and dinner with him for five people never came to less than a $300 tab because of the champagne. He was a disgruntled Catholic and dreamed of becoming Canada's Andrew Carnegie.

"He flew around in a DC-6. You never saw a plane furnished

like that one. Marbletop tables, sconces, silk-tasseled curtains and four sofa beds in a yellow print with leaves and cherubs. He used to love to take us to the front of the plane, the office, which had a map gimmick, with the approach maps and directions for landing at the leading airports. He'd come up front to the pilots' cabin, push a button on the gimmick, and say, 'Gentlemen, we're approaching Detroit. Let's see what we have here.' You look down at the gimmick and expect to see maps and landing patterns. Instead, you're looking at a list of local broads available in Detroit—plus their pictures.''

One of the reasons Doyle was able to get the incredible concessions in Labrador for so little was that while lots of mining firms knew there were large low-grade iron ore deposits there, no one ever thought they'd be worth developing. Doyle did.

Jerry: "He had this mine, Jubilee Iron Mines, which he had brought out at 50 cents a share and run up to $5–$6 on the over-the-counter market. He loved all his mines to begin with a *J*, for John. So he had Jubilee and Julian and the big one, Javelin.

"On this Jubilee thing, we met him in his suite at the Drake Hotel in New York. Jubilee was then $4—we called it Cherry Pie among ourselves—and he wanted to blow off 300,000 shares. He would pay so much a share. We moved 100,000 shares for him, and the next week we met at the Drake, and he pulled out the big, green strongbox he carried around on all his travels and paid us. What we didn't tell him is that we were back-dooring the stock. Everyone we brought in we had get right out a few days later, through different brokers. So our people moved out at 4¼, 4½, and we could never figure out who lost on that deal.''

They made a good deal of money once because Doyle was inherently skeptical of anyone else's mining promotion.

As Jerry recalls it: "We were having dinner with John once in New York, and it was the time when Texas Gulf Sulphur was acting up. From a low of 12 it was up to 16–17. I asked John if he knew anything. He said he'd just gotten a call from a prospector in Canada who wanted to borrow $10,000 from him to buy Texas Gulf stock. They were drilling like crazy over in Timmins and they may have a big discovery. But John wouldn't lend him the money. 'Ah, he's a drunk and he's in trouble with some whore up there. A bad risk.'

"I said, 'John, the stock is acting wild; something's going on.' He wouldn't buy it. *We* were falling for somebody's promotion. Well, we had to prove he was wrong, so Phil and I flew up to Canada and made some on-the-spot investigations. Mostly, we found that a helluva lot of helicopters were flying over properties owned by Texas Gulf up there. But it smelled *big*.

"We came back and wrote a market letter—this was when we were still at Lieberbaum—and said categorically that Texas Gulf was playing down the size of the ore body and that the company could earn $3.50 a share. The SEC jumped all over us, but *Barron's* quoted our letter on its front page. Well, we put a lot of people in the stock and we took big positions, and we got out at 49⅞. Too soon, of course, but we weren't too rich at the time and our profit was great. We bought at 17–18. And it all started because we had to show Doyle how wrong he was."

John Doyle was his own best tout, Jerry continued. He'd tout everyone: bellboys, waiters, manicurists, elevator men, cab-drivers. He never stopped. "He once persuaded me to do a plug in my market letter on Javelin. Then he insisted that I send copies of the letter, with subscription forms, to everyone listed in the *Statesmen's Who's Who*—every prime minister, every cabinet minister. We sent out thousands on that, I think, and most of them, I'm sure, couldn't read English. He was his own best PR man for pushing his stocks. When things were quiet with Canadian Javelin and he wanted a little market action, he'd get in his plane and start making his European circuit. He'd fly to Germany and talk to someone friendly at some major steel producer. A few days later, there'd be an announcement that the steel company and Javelin had entered into a provisional agreement for 10,000,000 tons of ore that the steel firm would take from Javelin. Why would a big steel manufacturer do it? Well, you could always find an executive at a big company who would be tempted with John's offer. He'd say, 'Look, my friend, my Javelin stock is quoted at 8 in today's Paris *Herald Tribune*. All right, now I'm going to give you a call on 1,000 shares of stock. When it rises, as a result of the good news you are going to announce for your company, why, you can sell and make a few points.' Hard to resist that kind of offer when all you have to do is go along with a press release. Then he'd go down to Italy and pull the same stunt. A good trip could get the Javelin stock up 4–5 points. Later, the steel companies would announce that after lengthy negotiations, the deal just didn't go through. Meanwhile, John would have gotten rid of a lot of stock. It was Doyle's perfect kind of stunt. He always came on strong, the first few times. Here was a man with charisma, with authority. But after you got to know him, it vanished and he emerged as just a promoter with a gimmick."

I sensed that somehow the Javelin story was being skirted. The subject seemed a little sensitive. Phil admitted it. "Listen, Phil," said Jerry, "we can't leave out the Javelin story. It was a big thing in our lives."

Phil nodded. "Yeah, you're right, but no matter how you turn it around, I don't come out so good. A bit of a shit, in fact. Still, it wasn't my fault and when they squeezed me, I had no alternative. Okay, here's the story:

"I was young and enthusiastic, and still with Bache back in the fifties. A guy I worked with at Bache named Stanley Sanders had been studying a new thing called Canadian Javelin. He told me this was one of the big ones. He filled me in with the details of the enormous concession they had; how many zillion tons of iron ore they had blocked out at a place called Wabash in Labrador. True, there was a little trouble with the SEC and John Doyle, promoter of Javelin. Seems that Doyle had paid off an old-time cocker named Frank Payson Todd, who ran a market letter called 'The New England Counselor.' In 1955 they made a deal with Todd. He got 17,500 shares—on money Javelin lent him—the company got his IOU's. He touted the stock real good and even sent out hundreds of telegrams to his favorite subscribers, telling them to get in on Javelin. The

SEC got to Todd in 1960 and put the letter out of business. And I figured they still had something against Doyle. For every bribetaker there had to be a bribegiver. So before I put my clients into Canadian Javelin, I wanted to be sure that the SEC miasma no longer hung over Javelin.

"The way to find out was to talk to the SEC. So one day I arranged a lunch with the chief investigator of the SEC, a man named Eddie Jaegerman, who has played a big and miserable role in my life. There was Jaegerman, myself, Stanley Sanders, and an important client. We asked a lot of questions about Canadian Javelin and the SEC. Mr. Jaegerman answered our questions. Mr. Doyle, it seems, had signed a consent decree with the SEC that he would no longer do what he had been doing, in violation of SEC rules. Jaegerman assured me that the future of the company seemed bright; that there'd be no further prosecution of Mr. Doyle now that he was minding the terms of the consent decree. We checked with other ore and steel companies. Javelin's future seemed very, very bright. Great. I proceeded to accumulate stock of Javelin for my clients in the $9–$12 range. Maybe 300,000 shares held for long-term investment.

"I got to know Doyle, and he suggested I get together a group of analysts and some more important clients, and he'd fly us up to Labrador to look at the property. He treated us royally, gave us the 'A' tour, and we went through one of the greatest ore mills ever. This was going to be an incredible $300,000,000 project. Everybody came back genuinely enthusiastic and my clients bought a lot more stock. Jerry was on the trip, of course, and he came back so enthused he wrote an eight-page report on Canadian Javelin. The stock moved up nicely with all this interest, and it was up to 18⅜.

"Things were going so well, so smoothly, I began getting nervous. We met one of Javelin's attorneys because I wanted reassurance that there was nothing against Doyle pending. This lawyer, ———, a no-good if I ever saw one, told us everything was fine; there was nothing hanging over Javelin or Doyle. Then we got hit. Hit? *Annihilated!*"

The government now disclosed that it had a sealed indictment against Doyle and Canadian Javelin for mail fraud. The indictment had been prepared at the time of the consent decree, seventeen months before. It was kept secret because they didn't know when Doyle was going to be in New York so they could grab him.

"Naturally, when the indictment hit the papers, the stock dropped to half in less than two weeks. I had a big personal stake in Javelin by then, and I was wiped out. So were most of my clients. Sure, we got some stock at lower prices but also a lot more near the 16–17 mark. And most of us were on margin. There was little trouble with the New York Stock Exchange, which gave me a reprimand, not for manipulation but for imprudence. I was personally involved in a stock which I had been recommending enthusiastically to clients. So now we were broke, and even worse was ahead.

"I had told Doyle of my luncheon with Jaegerman, who had informed me and several others that there would be no further prosecution, civil or criminal. Doyle now wanted me to testify to this effect when the mail fraud trial was held in Hartford, where the mail fraud was supposed to have originated, since a Hartford resident bought a few hundred shares of Javelin.

"Jaegerman called me: My future in the securities business would be very cloudy indeed if I were to testify for Mr. Doyle. One day he called me to meet him and an assistant U.S. attorney. Eddie left the room, and the U.S. attorney explained that he would be one of the prosecutors in the case and it would be wise if I didn't testify for Mr. Doyle. I was young, promising and had a wife and child, and my future in the business would be in serious question if I testified.

"So I chickened out; told Doyle I couldn't testify for him. I wouldn't take Doyle's calls. But he romanced Jerry, and finally, Jerry persuaded me I should see Doyle at his suite at the Drake Hotel. I went over one evening and we had dinner, and he had me meet one of his attorneys, a sharp character who had also represented Jimmy Hoffa.

"The lawyer, a little 280-pound barrel, said: 'Look, Phil, all we want you to testify to is that Eddie Jaegerman told you flatly there'd be no further prosecution, no indictment.' I explained that between the SEC and the U.S. attorney, I could be out of the business tomorrow.

"The lawyer said, 'We could subpoena you and force you to tell the truth.' I said he couldn't. This was pure self-preservation.

" 'Okay,' he said, 'just for the fun of it, let's try it on for size. Sit down and let's pretend we're in court and I'm cross-examining you as a witness under subpoena.' All right, I'd play his game and answer his questions. Then, after a few minutes, my early warning system got a red light and I heard a peculiar, rhythmic *pfft* sound somewhere in the room. I started walking around. The sound seemed to come from a credenza at the end of the room. I got on a chair and there was a tape recorder going. I picked it up and tried to throw it out the window, but there were bars on the window. So the next half hour Jerry and I were simply stuffing the used tape, yards and yards of it, down the toilet.

"Naturally, Doyle's lawyer wanted to use this as evidence I was being coerced by the United States, which, in fact, I was. Eventually, his lawyer did subpoena me and I went up to Hartford to testify. And that day Doyle pleaded guilty to a minor charge of selling 50 shares of unregistered stock in Canadian Javelin. Apparently, Doyle thought he had a deal going, to plead on this one count and he would get a suspended sentence. Instead, the judge fined him $5,000 and gave him three years— and all but three months would be suspended. Still, he wasn't going to do three months in any prison, and he fled to Canada while out on bail, pending appeal. He's still a fugitive because there's no extradition on that kind of fraud charge.

"The mine is producing 10,000,000 tons of ore a year, and Javelin is selling for $15. Doyle is a brilliant man and a stupid man, too. He loused up the company for a couple of million when he could have earned many, many millions legitimately. I don't think he ever expected to have a real live mine up there in Labrador. Javelin's still a great company, but its reputation has taken a beating. A few months ago, he met Jerry and was very bitter that I had run out on him. If I had been ready to testify freely, he wouldn't have pleaded guilty and would have beaten the case, and so on. Maybe. But he's gotten other troubles since. In August, 1970, he lost an appeal on a tax case. He has to pay Canada $3,400,000 in back income taxes. And an estranged wife sued him for $850,000 in back alimony which she said he hadn't paid for ten years. And there are lots of stockholder suits against him. In 1968, he paid Javelin $2,600,000 as a result of a stockholder suit. Still no one's going to have to run any benefits for him."

Several attempts were made to visit John Doyle in Montreal at Javelin headquarters and get his side of the story. But his lawyer persuaded him not to talk. Not so Phil's traditional enemy, Eddie Jaegerman, whose name means "hunter" in German. Phil said he had seen Jaegerman for the last time in 1969.

"I was involved in another mining deal. Eddie came in and said, 'Phil, I know you're promoting so-and-so, and I want you to tell me who you're using to promote it.' I said, 'Eddie, I don't know what you're talking about.' 'What brokers are you using?' he asked. I told him what he could do with himself. A month later, I found out he had contacted one of my clients and asked him for the name of the brokers I was supposed to be using. The client called me; I taped his story; and I called Jaegerman and accused him of blackmail and a lot else. He said, 'I'm going to see you indicted.' And maybe he would have if he hadn't left the SEC to go to work for Charlie Plohn, a Big Board firm, as the so-called compliance man for the firm, the one who makes sure the staff is minding all the SEC rules."

Phil had all sorts of dark reasons why Jaegerman had gone with Plohn, who had recently been fined $150,000 for violation of some New York Stock Exchange regulations. It was the largest fine ever meted out. "Jaegerman and I are mortal enemies," he concluded. "I hope he has a disaster at Plohn."

A few weeks later in April, 1970, I talked to Jaegerman, who was then chief executive and managing partner of Charles

Plohn & Company. The firm was undergoing severe strain in the market drop. Jaegerman was fifty-eight, gray-haired, and tired. There were pronounced pouches under the eyes.

For many years, he had been the chief investigator for the SEC. There was a staff of thirty investigators in Washington and another thirty in the regional offices. He had joined the SEC as one of its first employees in December, 1936, when he was fresh out of Yale Law School. He and his partner at the SEC, John T. "Tim" Callahan, had been one of the more colorful remnants of the New Deal, the Rover Boys of the SEC who investigated many of the key stock swindles of the past thirty years. When Callahan retired in 1965, Jaegerman carried on—until he got the offer of the Plohn job.

"The New York Stock Exchange asked me to take the job," he said. "And my boss at the SEC, Hamer Budge, thought I ought to take it. I was offered four times what I was making at the SEC, plus a partnership piece of the action. In a job like this you get more tolerant. Now I can see that the customer isn't always right, as I suppose you might tend to think from the SEC side. Now I realize that a lot of customer charges about evils and shenanigans by the brokers are unfounded or grossly exaggerated. Until I came to Plohn, I never owned a share of stock in my life. Partly psychological: After you've been with the SEC a few years, all stocks seem worthless and inflated. You get brainwashed; everything seems a swindle or a puff job."

He was surprisingly lenient about Phil and Jerry: "Jerry's a fine writer, but he just didn't know how to conduct himself and so he got indicted. Phil's a very clever man, very enthusiastic and very eager." He said he was glad to hear the boys were now well fixed.

Disaster came a few months later, and in July, 1970, Eddie Jaegerman severed his connection with Plohn, then a very sick brokerage firm. In August the firm was summarily suspended from exchange membership and the SEC ordered a receiver appointed for the firm. Plohn had to sell his wife's magnificent collection of old silver for nearly $600,000.

Later, when Phil was told about the comparatively nice things Eddie Jaegerman, his traditional enemy, had said about him, he laughed: "Very interesting, but I don't believe a word of it. That guy hates my guts, just as I hate his. You don't expect me to say I'm sorry all these terrible things happened to him at Plohn, do you?"

Terrible things also happened to Eddie Jaegerman at the New York Stock Exchange. On June 11, 1971, the exchange announced that the former SEC chief investigator had been permanently barred from association with any member organization of the exchange because of some securities violations while he was with Plohn. Among other charges they made was that he had used his position as managing partner to have Plohn prepare favorable recommendations of an outside corporation's securities without disclosing that he, Jaegerman, had a financial interest in the company.

Jaegerman provided a phone number for his ex-SEC partner, Tim Callahan, who retired in 1965. Callahan, who doesn't look his seventy-five, is tall, white-haired and freckled. He had once captained Yale's football team in 1919–20 and was an All-American guard in 1920. He never married and now lives with a sister in Queens.

"My pension is $12,000 a year and I have some government bonds. I never owned a stock in my life. And I never gambled, drank or smoked. And unlike some government investigators, I never used a stoolie in developing SEC cases. The trouble with stoolies is that they have to be on the clip side. If they do you a favor with some information, they'll want protection for their own shenanigans, and I was never ready to deal that way."

He knew Phil and Jerry, of course, but wasn't as friendly in his comments as Eddie Jaegerman had been. "None of the promoters I ever met ended up with money, but they lived very well during their short promotion careers. Phil and Jerry started younger than most of them. For some reason, some promoters get going only in middle age. Most of them go broke trying to run their own markets; trying to support their crazy stocks.

They become believers in their later years and that's what eventually destroys them. An interesting kind of poetic justice."

When Phil and Jerry heard about Callahan's "poetic justice," Phil grinned broadly. "I got a good one for you. The time I tried to *sell the SEC some stock.* Maybe it was a case of your poetic justice.

"A few years ago a guy comes to us from Canada. He had a company that controlled, among other things, a mercury mine in the Oregon. A legit mine, but the stock was selling for 35 cents–40 cents up on the Canadian OTC market. Now this is crazy. A mine producing *anything* doesn't sell for pennies. Non-mines sure, but not *real* mines. There has to be something wrong here. Things were a little slow, so Jerry and I get on a plane and fly out to Oregon. We rent a car, and, by God, there's the mine. Trucks and grinders and miners. Real stuff. We go wild. They show us the red mercury veins. A handsome German is running the mine. We fly back to New York and I buy 58,000 shares. Jerry gets 50,000 shares. We figure it's just too good for the public, so we only take in ten, fifteen friends, all pros, who've traveled with us before. We got in at the 42 cents–46 cents level. Most of them also bought about 50,000 shares each. We sit back rubbing our hands, knowing that this has to go to $3–$4 or even $5, once the public hears what this little mercury mine is doing.

"Nothing happens and I figure maybe I better take another look at their last report. Gradually, it hit me. The reported production was way under what the place was geared for, when we looked at the mine. We get a little investigation under way and we discover how we'd been had. Our handsome German mine manager was pulling the old tolltaker's chant: One for me and one for the road. He'd put a flask of mercury on the truck to the dealer and another aside for himself. When a mine gets stolen blind, even if it is producing, it can't make money.

"So we're stuck. What were we going to do? Start a stockholders' suit? We sold our stock and took a beating. I lost $30,000; Jerry the same; and altogether we dropped maybe

$200,000 on our crooked mercury mine. Yeah, the mine's still producing and he's still siphoning.

"Wait. It gets better. The SEC got wind of the heavy buying and calls me down. 'What's with this mercury thing?' So I threw the miserable stock certificates at them and said, 'Here, you guys want to buy it from me? I can let you have it real cheap.' You know, they didn't believe me, and for all I know, some poor SEC schnook still has us and that damn mine on his open-active file.

"On mining stocks," Phil continued, "you make your money on reserves, the stuff still in the ground, not on earnings. And another way. Years ago, when a couple of New York banks were the controlling shareholders—through their trust departments—of a couple of big producing mines out West, they had a cute gimmick. There'd be sudden news announcements that the value of the ore being pulled out that quarter had fallen greatly because it was low-grade ore. The stock would go down. Meanwhile, the insiders would accumulate the stock. Then the next quarter would come the good news: The ore taken out that quarter was very high-grade. The price would jump and they'd sell. Since they and the mine operators knew where the low- and high-grades were in the mines, they could control this beautifully. They did it for years. They made millions out of this simple manipulation of the ore bodies."

4. | Big Red

Speculator: a spy; a watcher.

—From Dr. Samuel Johnson's
Dictionary, 1755

    Market letter writers love writing about mines. The remoter the better. Peter Jeffrey, one of the most prolific market letter writers of the century, got his start touting some small Canadian mining properties.

    We met on a hot July afternoon in the back booth of the Sherry-Netherland's bar, which always has a morbid fascination for me. Late one afternoon in November, 1940, while I was having a drink there, Jesse Livermore, the great stock market plunger of the twenties and thirties, shot his brains out a few feet away in the men's room.

    I was somewhat prepared for Big Red by a briefing I got from Martin Orenzoff, a respected technical analyst who had just returned from Toronto and was now working for a New York Stock Exchange firm. Marty is thirty-six, tall, heavyset, getting bald, and only recently married for the first time. He met a pretty, young English decorator while he was in Canada. "I used to be a helluva spender, races and broads and clothes for me, $50-a-shirt stuff, and clothes for broads, and I lived beyond my means. I'm now reformed. Strictly a market man now. I figure it's time I started making money. I've been a technician for nearly twenty years, and I'm out to make a liar of the guy who first said that technical analysts never end up in Palm Beach."

He got a job working for a chartist named Jack Aberlin, who had bought a technical market letter, the "Owen K. Taylor Letter." He stayed with Aberlin ten years, learning the charting art, and later went to work for a new market letter, the "Dynamics Letter," which was run by two brothers, Peter and Grant Jeffrey.

"First, forget Grant. But Peter," Marty went on, "is one of the greatest characters in our business. Big Red. In Geneva, London, Paris or New York, you can spend an evening among guys in our business just telling stories about Big Red. Some of the stories are even true. When I worked for him at the 'Dynamics Letter'—I was doing charting part time then—it was marvelous to watch him banging out the letter. He'd start with anything to push a stock. Once I had gone to see a pacing race at Roosevelt Raceway and the two-minute mile had never been broken. That evening it was broken by a horse called Adios Butler. I told Peter about it and he started the letter with an account of the race. He could build anything into a selling point for the mooch, the subscriber. They fired me from the 'Dynamics Letter' because I got awful bearish in early 1962 and Peter was a bull—all the way. They had a good thing going there. Well above 3,000 subscribers at $100 a year. Then they got in a jam with the SEC and got closed down."

In its action against the letter in February, 1963, the SEC charged, among other things, that the letter was insolvent, owing $135,000, and that it had "employed devices, schemes and artifices to defraud clients . . . and engaged in transactions, practices and a course of business which operated as a fraud and deceit."

Jeffrey got up when I approached. He was Big Red. His 6-foot-2 frame was carrying more weight than he'd have liked, but his red-brown hair, blue eyes, and longish, graying sideburns added up to an attractive configuration. He had on a mod striped suit and dark-gray shirt.

"I've just had my forty-first birthday," he began, "and if half the things you've heard about me were true, I'd have to be one hundred and fifty. Or long dead."

He was born Peter Turner Jeffrey in Toronto. His father was a civil engineer of British stock. While still in high school, Peter became an almost professional photographer, making more money, as he put it, than his old man ever did. When he finished three years of high school, he tried to get a job with a Toronto paper but the lack of a college degree barred him. He went out into the provinces and got a job on the Hamilton, Ontario, *Spectator,* first as a photographer and then as a reporter. To supplement his wages, he used to play semipro football for $20 a game. Finally, he got a job on the Toronto *Globe,* a morning paper.

"I had a lot of time in the morning and early afternoon to myself, so I hung out a shingle as a publicity man and worked on the paper at night. My first client was a mining promoter. Then gradually, I drifted into doing market letters, which are a specific kind of publicity. I've probably written between fifteen and twenty different letters in my time, and there was a time when I was doing five simultaneously.

"It's the toughest product-development-area kind of writing. A market letter has to be torn down every week and redesigned. Therefore, you're really marketing a new product every week, fifty-two weeks a year. Also, it pays well."

He was a little vague about how well. "I can't function in a year in which I make less than $60,000–$70,000. Generally, it's been much more and my best year was 1959, when I made over $200,000. Right now I owe the Canadian Tax Department $130,000, and I could only have worked up into that bracket by having a few years of six-figure income."

He came back to 1959, which he recalled fondly and with some incredulity. He was writing five different weekly market letters on three continents that year. In person.

"The crazy schedule was this: Sunday night I'd fly from New

York to Lisbon on Pan Am. Monday morning, I'd connect with TAP to Tangier, where I'd write the 'American & Foreign Bank Letter.' Monday night to Madrid and play. They have interesting broads there. Tuesday morning to Zurich for writing *'Richtung'* (Direction). Originally, the private bank that published it had a long German name for it, but I got them to change. I wrote it in English and they'd translate it. Wednesday, I'd fly to Paris or London for a little playing around. Wednesday night or Thursday morning I'd fly back to New York. Then to Toronto, where I'd write the 'Jack Elder Letter.' From Toronto to Detroit, where I'd write the 'Cronenburg Report.' Then to New York Saturday morning for fooling around. On Sunday I'd do just the lead on the 'Dynamics Letter,' which my older brother, Grant, and I ran. In the afternoon I'd write the 'Owen K. Taylor Letter,' and then Sunday night I'd start all over again with the flight to Lisbon. I did this for a year and I probably made $200,000 that year. The only reason I had to quit was they were flying the piston planes that year, still. With the jets, I might still be doing that crazy schedule.

"But the pistons used to shake the hell out of you. I was flying 500,000 miles a year. I had to quit because my ass hole fell out. Literally. Early in 1960 I was in Mount Sinai Hospital in New York with a fistula cyst in my ass. I blame the shaking piston planes, but, you know, it could just as easily have been the damn cabs to and from the airports. In all, then, 1959 was my *anus mirabilis,* so to speak." He smiled broadly at his Latin pun.

He got onto the "Dynamics Letter," which he and his brother, Grant, owned and operated in New York. "We had something hot in that 'Dynamics Letter.' It was influential, but the SEC was right in closing us down. There was no firm hand on the tiller, and we ran it right off the cliff. The 1962 crash wiped us out. We even got the ultimate accolade. A reputable publisher brought out a book by Grant, *Science and Technology Stocks in 1961.* The jacket copy said the 'Dynamics Letter' was 'one of the most lively, indeed, controversial of the advisory services.' "

He thought that everybody who succeeded in the market letter business was, whether he admitted it or not, a speculator. "Many of the people who get into this business are often doing it as a last resort because there's nothing left for them to do in the securities business. A lot of bums have come down the pike and wound up with market letters. Not so much today, maybe. More difficult now. The zinger days, the payoff days, are dead. They can be spotted too easily, and the SEC is now paying a whole lot more attention to the letters."

The market letter business was dying, he thought. The old readers are largely gone.

"Most of them are the rankest amateurs, who are simply looking for hot tips on the way up and catharsis on the way down. It's a hideous audience, compared to the one that existed ten years ago. The only place where it's still a vital, growing field is Germany. There, you have an emerging, interested investment group such as the United States had after World War II. I do several offshore letters, which I'd rather not talk about, but one of them is a German letter. I sit in Toronto with a trained staff of chartists and analysts. I have two girls and three men working on charts, which gives me a sizable payroll and an overhead of $1,000 a week. If I'm not making at least $60,000–$70,000 a year, I'm in trouble."

Charts, he went on, are merely guides. "I won't do anything on a stock without a chart, but I also talk to the company first. I call four or five company presidents a day now. If you rely on charts alone, you're a blind man being led by the nose, and you must end up broke."

Like many other market letter writers and operators Peter Jeffrey loves gambling on anything. "I go to a casino and get $50 worth of chips and lose it. But I do make money on the races because, in some ways, it's like a stock. A stock goes down from 50 to 20 and then rests awhile. A good horse will do the same thing. By studying form, you can tell when the resting period is over and the horse is ready to win again. I don't think I ever had a losing day at the races. It's not an original concept, by the way. The guy who developed it was an American named

Richard Wyckoff, a market letter operator, who developed modern point-and-figure charting. You know, where the chart is filled with X's and O's marching up and down. Each X represents price gains; O's price losses; and each box on the graph paper represents a one-point movement. Well, Wyckoff developed point-and-figure for race handicapping. He got so good at it that the Pinkertons used to keep him away from the tracks. [There was another man who did it successfully, but it only worked once, Jeffrey said. This was the Earl of Glasgow, who lost millions of pounds betting on his own horses. On October 30, 1852, he announced that he would shoot the next of his horses that lost. That afternoon, all six of his entries at Newmarket won their races.]

"The only trouble with point-and-figure in horse races or stocks is the interpretation. There's a certain amount of guesswork. One analyst will look at a chart and say it's a top and then it will go down ten points. Another will say it's a bottom and it's going up ten points. And they both could easily be wrong. They usually are."

His difficulties with the SEC brought on other troubles in Canada. For several years, though, he was writing several letters out of Buffalo, New York. Mainly, he was doing "The Canadian Forecaster" for a well-known American promoter named Dick Angle.

"In 1967 when I got back to Toronto," Jeffrey continued, "they arrested me for tax evasion. I was fucked up for eight years with them. All I'm doing now is just paying off the interest on my $130,000 indebtedness to the Tax Department. I've become a fairly sober citizen now. Remarried. I've calmed down a lot. I'd drunk about $50,000 worth of twelve-year-old Bell's, but I haven't had a drink of it in two and a half years. No more penthouses in New York and elsewhere."

As he talked it was obvious Peter Jeffrey was very much a believer in the conspiratorial nature of history, particularly stock market history. He firmly believed that the 1962 market crash—which brought the SEC down on him—had been engineered by a few people, dupes mostly. He thought that the

Nicolas Darvas book, *How I Made Two Million Dollars in the Stock Market,* with its technique for using stop-loss orders—a dangerous trigger device in a falling market—and a piece Bernard Baruch did for the *Saturday Evening Post* on why we could have a repetition of the '29 crash were key elements in that crash. "It must have been a big manipulation. Somebody must have put all the elements together and made a helluva lot of money on shorting the high-flying stocks. Darvas was just a dupe, of course. And so was the *Saturday Evening Post.*" He wasn't so sure about Baruch, though.

"What I'd like is just eight real good trades, maybe just four. And I'll tell no one. Not in the market letters, not friends, no one. As soon as someone understands your pattern and knows what you're doing, then you become a potential source of revenue for him. To let people know how you make your money is the height of stupidity. I did it once and it cost me a helluva lot. Never tell your friends where you shoot ducks."

Wasn't there a real conflict here: the need for a market letter analyst to show people how smart he is in picking the right stocks? "Sure, there's that. But I've acquired discipline. The ego can go take a beating while I pull those four or eight great, quiet trades."

At the airport his return flight to Toronto was delayed and he got onto Dick Angle, another market letter operator about whom legends have accumulated. Peter Jeffrey had worked for Angle when the latter was operating a market letter called "The Canadian Forecaster."

"You know some of the market letter lingo by now," Peter began. "A *mooch* is a sucker-subscriber to a market letter that runs occasional *zingers,* paid-for items designed to generate buying in a crappy stock. Well, Angle is the only guy in the business who went from being a mooch to a manufacturer of his own zingers. Quite a rise."

Angle, he recalled, was of German and Norwegian stock. Very stocky, with reddish-brown curly hair. He grew up in Kansas City, Missouri, and the family was well connected politically with the Pendergast machine. Dick used to tell friends of the times he sat on the lap of Harry Truman, then just a rising politician. Truman was an old family friend. "When he left the Navy, Angle got into grain trading in Kansas City and did fairly well. One day he got a call from a man in Toronto who urged him to buy a fast-moving oil stock, Pontiac Petroleum. Apparently, Pontiac, drilling oil wells in Alberta, had found a big oil field. The man calling Angle was working for another character, Frank Kaftel. Frank was running several boiler rooms in Toronto, and Pontiac Pete was his big one. Well, Frank's salesman was hot and he got Angle in deeper and deeper. Meanwhile, with a little manipulation, Pontiac Pete kept rising and it was up to $3. Then one day they blew it off, and the stock dropped, in a couple of hours, down to a few pennies and got itself delisted by the Toronto Exchange in December, 1954. A big fuss, but nothing happened to Kaftel.

"Angle wouldn't take the loss of $40,000 quietly, though. It was nearly all he had and he was damn mad. You don't con a redhead *quietly*. Among con men, there's the classic story of J. Frank Norfleet, a short, skinny, redheaded rancher who once got taken in an old con game in Dallas. The operators told him how he could make a killing in the cotton market because they had inside information. Well, they got $45,000 out of Norfleet, but their victim decided to bring his crooks to justice. His wife managed his ranch, and he spent the next three years and another $30,000, and, by God, he ran down every one of the mob and helped get them convicted and sentenced. A great classic and, fortunately for con men and boiler room operators, very, very rare.

"Well, Angle, a redhead, was determined to get even. He drove nonstop from Kansas City to Toronto. By then, however, Kaftel and his crews had dispersed and Angle cooled off. Instead, he decided to make his money back the way he had lost it. Instead of being a mooch, he'd become a man pushing the zingers onto the suckers. By way of a market letter. He got friendly with Tex Mitchell, who was running a letter in Toronto, and he learned a lot of the tricks of the trade. He returned to Kansas City and began his letter. About 1956, I'd

say. Later, he moved it to Buffalo—where I worked for him—
and then to Toronto. It was 'The Canadian Forecaster.' He had
a helluva lot of good stocks, too. I remember in January, 1965,
while I was holed up in Buffalo and writing for the 'Forecaster,'
I called Ling Temco at $11 the most important buy in New
York. The charts called it. Arthur D. Little & Company and
some of the other pundits were predicting a major recession in
aerospace. So did 'Value Line.' But Ling Temco went to $110
and the 'Forecaster' got a lot of new subs. At the peak, I think
he had 3,300 at $75 a year. It was profitable, all right."

Later, Jeffrey left the "Forecaster" because he felt that Angle
was doing some very foolish things, like getting involved with
the Mafia and pushing the stock of a company he owned, Ganda
Mines, in the "Forecaster." What resulted was one of the
strangest and most extended set of trials in Canadian criminal
justice.

Ganda was a supposed silver mine that never produced much.
Angle got control of it in 1964 and, by touting it in the "Forecaster," ran it from 40 cents a share right up to $1.45. At that
inflated price, the stock began interesting several other promoters who knew enough about the mine to know it wasn't
worth 14 cents a share, let alone $1.45. So they began selling
short—borrowing the easily available shares—in the expectation that when the shares dropped heavily, they'd be able to
buy the shares back at a much lower price.

Angle was anxious to find out who was behind these short-
selling raids, and for that he called in a man named Albert
Volpe, whom he had used before in various inquiries. Volpe
and his brother Paul had been identified in 1963 before a U.S.
Senate hearing as two Canadian members of the Cosa Nostra
family of Stefano "The Undertaker" Magaddino of Buffalo.

At first, Angle, who had spent $200,000 supporting the stock,
paid Albert Volpe $2,500 to find out who was behind the bear
raid on Ganda Mines. On March 8, 1965, Angle had a meeting
with the Volpe brothers and a man he was introduced to as a
Mr. Palmer, who later turned out to be Pasquale Natarelli, a
lieutenant in the Magaddino Mafia family. There was also a

fourth man at the meeting, a solid 285-pound tough who banged a fork up and down on a table while Palmer-Natarelli threatened Angle. Unless Angle came up with another $17,500 for the Volpe brothers, he was going to have trouble.

"You better come up with it," yelled Palmer, "or blood will run in the streets of Toronto! I've got an army behind me."

Angle later testified that he was terrified. "I'd have sold my soul to get out of that room." He got out—after promising to pay the Volpes another $10,000.

Angle went to his attorney, Jack Gilbert, who recommended a well-connected Toronto attorney named Sam Ciglen, who said they should call in the police. The police, long after the Volpes, were most interested. They strapped a tiny recording device to Angle's chest and listened in on the meeting with the Volpes—after which Palmer and the Volpes were arrested and indicted.

The first trial ended in a mistrial when a juror said his English wasn't good enough to follow the proceedings. The second resulted in a hung jury; another mistrial came the third time out when a Toronto realtor who was an old friend of the Volpes tried to bribe a juror. The fourth trial resulted in a not guilty verdict. But the Crown prosecutor refused to give up and appealed to the Canadian Supreme Court, which ordered a new trial on the grounds the judge had misdirected the jury. During that trial, the Volpe attorneys got Angle to make several interesting admissions. For example, that he had recommended shares of Ganda Mines to subscribers to "The Canadian Forecaster" while secretly owning a controlling interest in the company. Actually, the mining company was owned by two offshore-Bahamas companies which Angle owned. Volpe's attorney said that such touting of stocks was "plain cheating." The attorney went on: "Since you've stepped into this country, you've employed devious and underhanded business methods."

"No," said Angle, "it's the general way things are done on the street." (Meaning Bay Street, Toronto's Wall Street.)

By the fifth trial the Volpes decided to make a deal. Two of them, anyway. Albert Volpe fled to Greece, where he ran a gambling casino in Athens; he's still a fugitive. But his two brothers, Paul and Eugene, pleaded guilty to lesser charges and were sentenced in June, 1968, to two years and three months, respectively. By then Palmer-Natarelli had been found guilty in a U.S. trial of conspiring to steal $500,000 in jewels from a Beverly Hills, California, hotel, and of conspiring to rob a Brink's armored truck in Beverly Hills. He got twenty years.

In 1968, Dick Angle surfaced in Spokane, Washington—just in time to become wanted himself. He had been indicted in Vancouver for issuing false prospectuses on Columbia River Mines. He returned to Vancouver, was found guilty, and given a suspended sentence of eighteen months. But his troubles weren't over.

The Canadian tax authorities had seized $120,000 belonging to a company Angle controlled—just as Angle was about to transfer the money to Bermuda. Angle, they said, owed the government $117,000 in back taxes. Angle appealed and lost.

Peter Jeffrey said there were several lessons to be learned for all stock promoters and market letter operators from the life and times of Dick Angle, his former employer: (1) Don't get involved with the Mafia; (2) pay your taxes; and (3) don't try to support a bust-out stock with good money.

Did he know where Angle was now? He thought he was probably dead. "The Mafia have long memories." But a few days later he phoned to say he had heard Angle was living in Las Vegas. He didn't know where. I found out. When Peter Jeffrey was told Angle was alive and well in Las Vegas, he said, "He's a lucky man, but I wouldn't want to have stock in his life insurance company."

5. | The Sultan

There is a certain cowardice, a certain weakness, rather, among respectable folk. Only brigands are convinced—of what? That they must succeed. And so they do succeed.

—CHARLES BAUDELAIRE

Of all the American writers who went to Paris to make their name and fortune, none succeeded as spectacularly as Frank Kaftel. Frank *who?*

In the winter of 1964–65, Kaftel, a New York high school dropout, wrote two thousand words of serial fiction, which he published and circulated to some five thousand devoted readers all over Europe. For this minor fiction—hardly even ordinary short-story length—he earned $775,000. Cash. Tax-free. His word rate—galactically higher than any ever paid other expatriate American writers such as Hemingway or Fitzgerald or Jimmy Jones—came to $387 a word.

The twentieth century has seen the development of two unique literary forms: the screenplay and the market letter. Frank Kaftel's métier was writing and promoting market letters. He also specialized in various numbers. As a friend put it, "Frank always played with big numbers, but the ones that got him down were little ones: twelve-year-old scotch and eighteen-year-old French."

Kaftel's name first emerged during a visit to the SEC in Washington, where Stanley Sporkin, associate director of the Enforcement Division, is in charge of checking on the activities of the four thousand Americans who had registered with the SEC as investment advisers. About one-fourth of them also issued market letters. Sporkin, a soft-spoken, harassed official, had heard of Kaftel. "A legend in his time," he said. Indeed, other SEC officials talking about Kaftel sounded like awestruck Europeans of the thirteenth century talking about a distant, legendary Kublai Khan, one they heard about but had never seen.

Finally, one SEC official, Irwin Borowski, a heavyset, dark Brooklyn lawyer who is branch chief of the Enforcement Division, said the man who knew most about Kaftel was, unfortunately, no longer with the SEC. His name was Peter Adolph, and he was now with the Department of Commerce in the Office of Foreign Direct Investments.

Adolph was amused that another writer was on Kaftel's track. "Well, that's two of us." He was interested because he was doing a book on the debacle of the Atlantic Acceptance Corporation, which had lost $150,000,000 and had sucked in many leading U.S. banks, pension trusts, and investment groups. Kaftel had a peripheral role in the catastrophe.

"I thought I had a line to Kaftel through a fellow, an American living in Canada, who was his bagman. This fellow used to bring him money from Canada to Paris or the Bahamas, wherever Kaftel was operating from. But I haven't been able to locate him." He described the bagman as about forty-five and very wily. "If you want the Kaftel story, you'll need the bagman. But he's going to be hard to find, and then if you do, I don't know how you'll get him to talk."

It was really no contest. I was already connected with a network that Peter Adolph couldn't hope to get tuned into. Phil and Jerry had bits and pieces about Kaftel. So did some of their friends. One of them had recently worked in Toronto, knew sources outsiders couldn't possibly tap. He dialed a number in Toronto and talked to the long-missing long-inaccessible bagman.

We met in the lobby of the Royal York Hotel in Toronto. He laid down only one condition: He mustn't be named.

"Nothing I'm ashamed of, you know. But I've just remarried. My new wife is the widow of an old friend of mine, and to tell the truth, I'm sure she never knew what I did for a living. Why tell her now?"

Joe—as we can call him—is seventy-five but looks considerably younger. But never the forty-five that Peter Adolph thought he was. He had known Kaftel since the late 1940's, when Frank had become the biggest operator of boiler rooms in Toronto, fleecing American suckers with telephone sales on bust-out Canadian oil and mining stocks. There were some fifty boiler rooms going then, which the salesmen called joints or houses. "It's a house when you're in it; a joint when you're not." It was a wild time, with anything going. Not until the summer of 1951 did the Ontario government, under pressure from the SEC, begin cracking down. All the boiler rooms were located in downtown Toronto on Bay, Adelaide, Queen, Simcoe, King, and Richmond streets. Frank was better organized than most of the others. He had his own four-story building on Simcoe and a big printing plant that specialized in printing market letters for the American market. He'd mail a million pieces at a time to every sucker list he could get.

Frank got his start, his first big money, by lucking onto a fat Greek mooch, a successful restaurateur in Edmonton. Frank practically commuted to Edmonton by plane to impress the mooch and finally took him for $100,000.

Joe went on: "Once one of Frank's boiler room salesmen got a check from a priest who said he was going to use the profits he was going to make for an orphanage. Frank happened to be in the office and saw the check. He sent the money back—but gave the salesman the commission anyway. Frank was very sentimental sometimes. He became a big sponsor of a Catholic orphanage near Toronto. Every Christmas he'd load up a truck with toys and take it over to the orphanage for a big party."

Joe met Kaftel through charity. "I heard about the Catholic priest bit, and I thought maybe I'd hit Frank for a contribution

to the UJA. I didn't think he was Jewish, but he sounded like
a man who would let loose a nice dollar for a good cause. So
I went to him cold and made my pitch. He explained that he
was brought up as a Catholic. His father had been an Italian
named Kulunderino and his mother was Jewish. So he gave me
$100.

"Meanwhile, he made some inquiries about me around town.
He must have liked what he heard, because he called me and
asked if I would work for him. Not as a salesman—that kind
of hot-box operation was behind me. He needed someone he
could trust, to pick up money and keep an eye on the boiler
rooms when he was out of town or in Europe.

"Frank had to trust you first. When he did, it was all the
way. When he first started using me as a fancy money messenger
to pay off the boys in the boiler rooms, he'd give me a bundle
of cash to pay the salesmen. It was all a strictly commission
operation: The men would get a percentage of the value of the
stock they sold—after the mooches' checks had come in and
cleared. And nice bonuses. The first time Frank sent me to pay
off the boys, I discovered I had $500 left over. I turned it back
to Frank. A few months later, the same thing happened. When
I turned it back again, I guess I passed the test. He could really
trust me."

When he first met Kaftel, Joe recalled, he was good-looking,
very dapper, with a neat mustache and well-fitting clothes. In-
clined to put on weight, he'd often go on crash diets to keep
his figure. "Dieting came hard to him because he was strictly
a quart-of-scotch-a-day man. Twelve-year-old. Frank was a great
spender, the fastest check-grabber on two continents. His nickname in Toronto was The Sultan.

"He was tough but fair. You fucked him once, and you were
dead. When he gave his word, that was it. He never backed out
of a deal. As I got to know him, he used to fill me in on details
about himself. Sometimes he contradicted himself, and it was
a little hard to tell what was and what wasn't. He once told me
that he had millions in a safe deposit box in Paris, which the
Nazis grabbed. But he had been in Paris only briefly, in 1937–

38, trying to push some stock. From the little I knew, it hadn't been one of his more successful jobs, so I could never figure out where the millions came from."

When things got too hot in Canada, Joe continued, Frank decided to move his operations to Paris. "He took a suite at the George V and looked around. He kept me on the payroll. Then he started his European market letter. He called it 'The International Financial Advisory Service,' and it was great, almost from the start. He had about five thousand mooches all over Europe and even England, and they paid him $65 a year each. You don't start a market letter over there quite as easy as you do here. So he needed a connection and a safe home base.

"The connection was a French Resistance hero, a doctor who had escaped from the Nazis three times and was badly beaten by the Germans. Kutner, I think his name was. Kutner knew a lawyer in Luxembourg who was able to clear permission for the letter to be published and mailed from there. Frank's French was pretty fluent by then, but I think Kutner did the translating. The letter was sent out in French only. Very classy."

Through the letter Kaftel pushed a lot of zingers for large payoffs. The money was brought in cash from Toronto or New York or the Bahamas to Paris by Joe.

"My deal with Frank then was he'd pay my expenses and $300 for my time. I'd go first class, of course, and he'd put me up at the George V and show me a good time in town while I was there a few days. Oh, yes, I had another rule: Every time I made the trip, I had to bring him fresh bagels, cream cheese, and lox.

"Frank was strictly a first-class rider, and he looked down on anyone in the business who cut corners in living. He always had a lot of women around. Until he was fifty-five or sixty, they were pretty young, usually eighteen. He'd keep them a year or so and get another one. But as he got a little older, so did the women. Frank got his first heart attack in January, 1961. The attack was mild, and he used to take pills and cut down on liquor. In November, 1967, I got a call from the

Swedish piece he was living with. He was very sick, and the doctor said the only place for treatment was the Lahey Clinic in Boston. He flew over with two doctors in a private plane, and I went down to Boston to see him.

"The doctors said it didn't look good. He had the works: the busted liver of a heavy drinker, the coronary, hardening of the arteries, and they suspected maybe a little lung cancer. I talked to Frank and he said he was broke—didn't know how he was going to pay his medical bills. I couldn't believe it because I had brought him a hell of a lot of money in '65, but with Frank it was possible. So I got back to Toronto to raise money for Frank. I called a lot of boys who had worked in his boiler rooms, guys who had made a real good dollar with him. And a few Toronto Stock Exchange brokers who knew Frank and hadn't lost by it. In all, we raised $18,000."

Frank Kaftel was buried on January 18, 1968, in an obscure cemetery on Staten Island, next to his brother, the doctor. His death certificate indicates that his father was Max Kaftel, and the deceased was a "broker" who was in the "Stocks" business.

On January 16, 1968, shortly after Frank Kaftel died in the Lahey Clinic, a federal grand jury in New York revealed that it had indicted Frank and his brother, Marcus, for manipulating stock of the Pentron Electronics Corporation listed on the Amex. (Jerry Allen also had been indicted in that case.)

The indictment said, in part, that two of the indicted conspirators, Mark Binstein and Alexander Brown:

> . . . did make cash payments to Marcus Kaftal for transmittal to his brother, Frank Kaftel, then living in Paris, France, who would and did in return, attempt to induce and induce other people, including the persons to be defrauded, to purchase Pentron common stock.

With their deaths—which the U.S. attorney hadn't known about at the time of the indictment—both brothers were dropped from the case.

Newspaper clips also provided some additional background

information on Frank. Back in 1932, when he was living in a
$10-a-week room at the Hotel Beacon in New York, he was
Jack Kaftal and had a small insurance and real-estate business
at 1775 Broadway. He had been arrested in April, 1935, for
trying to dispose of eleven Federal Farm Mortgage bonds worth
$3,700. The bonds had been stolen from a New Paltz, New
York, bank in January, 1935. Kaftal told the police he had
gotten the bonds from an upstate client. Apparently, the evidence against him wasn't too strong and the indictment was
later quashed.

Joe couldn't explain why Frank turned to his brother, the
doctor, to handle the payoffs in the Pentron case. Others
thought that Joe didn't want to come across to New York in
the early sixties. He had reason to think he might be grabbed
by the U.S. attorney for various SEC matters. Although he was
still an American citizen, Joe had lived in Canada for more
than twenty years.

There are some great mysteries about Frank Kaftel and some
of his fabulous fees that a Canadian Royal Commission hadn't
been able to fathom.

The commission was most curious about the climactic operation of Kaftel's touting career—the $775,000 payoff for pushing
just two stocks in his market letter in the fall of 1964.

The stocks were two Canadian issues called Analogue Controls and Commodore Business Machines. Great blocks of the
stocks were held by a Canadian named C. Powell Morgan, who
was then head of a vast financing operation called Atlantic Acceptance Corporation.

Morgan was a Canadian who went from chartered accountant to vice-president of International Silver Company of
Canada in 1948 and a few years later helped form Atlantic
Acceptance to finance door-to-door sales of the firm's silverware.
Atlantic Acceptance did so well it became a separate enterprise
with Morgan as its president. Meanwhile, an elegant French
financier, Jean Lambert, became interested in Atlantic Acceptance and began pushing it. The U.S. Steel Pension Fund
lent the firm money at above-average interest. So did the Ford

Foundation. Atlantic grew splendidly every year, broadening its financial operations and moving into small loan companies, too. The profits grew every year. Altogether a most estimable company that could easily get $10,000,000–$20,000,000 loans from leading lenders and banks. It also began absorbing various companies. Among them were Commodore and Analogue Controls. Morgan personally held a lot of their stock and now was anxious to get rid of the stuff at the best prices. He heard of Kaftel's great talents and knew that the way to reach Kaftel was through Joe.

In October, 1964, Joe phoned Kaftel in Paris and told him that he was bringing over some men with an interesting proposition. Joe flew over with Morgan and Rennie Goodfellow, a partner in a Toronto Stock Exchange member firm, Barrett, Goodfellow & Company.

On March 15, 1967, Frank Kaftel talked to Albert E. Shepherd, Q.C., counsel for the Royal Commission, then investigating the busted Atlantic Acceptance Corporation, the most disastrous failure in Canada's history.

"I flew over to Paris with Justice Sam Hughes, who was in charge of the Royal Commission investigation. We met first in the George V Hotel and then in Kaftel's apartment, a very nice place just off the Avenue Victor Hugo. As far as we could check, everything he told us was true, including the money he had received. There's no question he had been paid the $775,-000 for pushing the Commodore Business Machines and Analogue stocks. Whether his courier gave him all the money is another matter. The courier"—he gave me Joe's real name —"is missing. We thought he was in New York, but we couldn't find him. [In fact, "Joe" had been in Toronto all that time.]

"We talked about fifteen hours in all, over a two-day period. I got the gist of his comments down on paper; he read it, made a few changes, and marked it 'without prejudice' and 'no publication' and signed it 'F. Kaftel.' "

The statement, dated March 15, 1967, tells of his bagman and courier, "Joe":

He was known to me for many years and was employed by me when I lived in Toronto. He was a runner or courier. It was his job to pay salesmen and others and to collect moneys due. He was always paid a small share in profit equal to a full share taken by all salesmen. . . . He first introduced the Commodore Business Machine transaction to me.

After "Joe" brought Morgan and Goodfellow to Paris, Kaftel:

examined the financial statements, inquired about the holdings of shares and discussed the prospects of the company. I noted that the company had plants in Europe and I decided to go see them. . . . I was told the company was about to manufacture an electric portable typewriter and everything I heard about the company impressed me.

The terms of the agreement made were these: (1) I was to be paid $25,000 per week; (2) I was to recommend the purchase of the shares; (3) I was to cause 35,000 shares per week to be sold, on the average.

The assumption was that at least 80 percent of all orders for Commodore stock coming out of Europe would be due to Kaftel's touting in the IFAS market letter. Between October 15 and December 8, 1964, Kaftel pushed the stock in his letter, causing at least 315,000 shares to be sold to European mooches, who paid prices from 6 to 10, roughly an investment of some $2,500,000. When Kaftel pushed a stock, he *pushed.*

Frank's plugs for Commodore in the IFAS letters have a certain interest for the student of persuasive techniques. They are blunt and filled with half-truths and full concealments. But none of the catchy phrases that Jerry Allen used to get into his letters.

The first issue, devoted to Commodore, went:

DO YOU KNOW THE HISTORY OF INTERNATIONAL BUSINESS
MACHINES, BETTER KNOWN AS I.B.M.?
It is terrific, started very small, was traded as low as $3, reached a maximum of $607 and has been split 8 times

since its foundation, and is admitted to the Quotation on the N.Y.S.E. Can you imagine how much money you would have if you had bought 1000 shares at $3?

Now, we present to you a young world company, COMMODORE BUSINESS MACHINES, whose expansion has been enormous since its founding a few years ago. . . .

And on and on about Commodore's rosy prospects:

- This company has quintupled its turnover since 1959, and will increase its production annually. Its products are sold in 55 countries.
- It is placing on the market a revolutionary type of portable electric typewriter. Management states: "Orders for 250,-000 machines have been booked. First deliveries expected at the end of May."
- In our opinion these shares will be traded at $20 each by the end of 1965. This will be justified by the profits made by the company.

The conclusion was:

After all, a GOOD SPECULATION IS WORTH A TRIAL, and Commodore is a good speculation. It knows how to produce good products at low prices. . . . Remember that life is a game. Let us not allow today's opportunity to slip by. . . . Life is a good speculation. . . . Place your order with your bank or broker.

Understandably, Frank didn't tell his subscribers why, if Commodore were such a GOOD SPECULATION, the majority stockholders were so anxious to get rid of the stock that they were paying someone $1 a share to unload.

For his nine-week push Frank Kaftel should have received $225,000. He told Shepherd he only got $160,000 but the evidence is sound that he got the full $225,000. Frank stopped his push on Commodore on December 8 and then went to Rome and Bombay on deals no one knows about. In January, 1965, his satisfied customers, Morgan and Goodfellow, were back in

Paris anxious to push more Commodore shares. This deal wasn't as good, though: "I was to continue to support it in my bulletin. I was to receive $8,000 a week henceforth. I was to be paid for about four weeks."

Shepherd showed him six canceled checks made out to "F. Kulunderino" (a name he often used) and totaling $142,-000. Kaftel insisted, however, "I did not receive the proceeds of these checks and I do not know who did."

Later he made another deal with Morgan to push some 400,-000 shares of Analogue Controls, which Morgan had acquired for $2 a share. By the end of June, 1965, Morgan owed him $256,000 for these Analogue stock pushes in the bulletin, Kaftel insisted he never got this money. Later, he contradicted himself:

> It has been called to my attention that payments were made to —— [Joe, his bagman] out of the Royal Bank of Canada in Freeport, Grand Bahamas, substantially in excess of $300,-000. I did receive some of that money but not as much as half of it. —— [Joe] told me he paid other people and gave some cash to Morgan. I felt I was not getting my share. . . .

If Kaftel didn't get the money, who did? Shepherd, who lived with the Atlantic case for more than eighteen months, still thinks Kaftel got it. He doesn't understand why Kaftel would try to conceal all the payments.

Understandably, in what Shepherd calls "the half world of the securities business," there are some unkind characters who think that "Joe" held out and retained some of the money for himself. "Joe" vehemently denies this. He simply doesn't believe that Frank was paid $775,000 for pushing the two stocks. "Maybe half that, no more."

"Joe's" arrangement with Frank on the two deals was spelled out by C. Powell Morgan, who testified before the Royal Commission shortly before his death of leukemia, on October 17, 1966. The testimony in Vol. I of the Royal Commission Report goes:

MR. SHEPHERD: Now it was necessary, I take it, since the gross proceeds of sales which were made through the Royal Bank of Freeport [Bahamas] were deposited into that bank to get to Mr. Kaftel his appropriate share. Is that correct?

MORGAN: Yes.

SHEPHERD: Was this done through the agency of Mr. —— [Joe] who obtained the moneys in cash from the Royal Bank and took it to Mr. Kaftel? [In Paris]

MORGAN: Either he got it in cash or bought drafts in Nassau. . . . But he handled it out of Freeport. [Bahamas]

SHEPHERD: How did he [Joe] get it out of the Royal Bank?

MORGAN: . . . I'd give him a cheque and the Royal Bank would cash it for him or I would give him two cheques, one representing his commission, which I believe was ten percent.

SHEPHERD: What was Mr. Kaftel's profit on the transaction? [Involving just the Analogue Controls stock]

MORGAN: I would say approximately $375,000.

SHEPHERD: And would Mr. ——'s [Joe's] commission come off that or would it be in addition?

MORGAN: No, it would be including his.

SHEPHERD: Mr. —— [Joe] would be entitled to approximately $37,500?

MORGAN: Yes. The rest would go to Mr. Kaftel, out of which he paid whatever expenses were incurred. He was quite a world traveller.

"Joe" wouldn't get down to dollar specifics with me, but the authorities who investigated are convinced that he earned at least $75,000 as his 10 percent commission for bringing the two stock deals to Kaftel.

In Toronto, another veteran of the "half world" speculated: "Frank trusted 'Joe,' and 'Joe' made good money out of the connection. But who knows? After Frank had his first heart attack, 'Joe' *may* have decided it was time to lay something extra aside for his old age. Not nice to think that money could come between old friends, but when you have so much of it floating around, it would have to be an iron man who didn't get tempted even a little bit. Hell, I would have."

Later "Joe" had another idea on the money and what happened to it: "Toward the end, Frank had this Swedish piece living with him. Frank always kept a lot of cash around the house. She beat it when he got very sick. I bet she took a big bundle with her, when he was lying helpless on the sickbed. There sure wasn't any money in the apartment after he died."

INTERLUDE

Paris, March 9, 1970

I'm in Paris on some magazine assignments. Phil told me Jerry would be there at the same time on an overnight stop because of a plane foul-up, but he didn't know which hotel. "Let's see how smart you are," Phil challenges. "See if you can guess what hotel Jerry goes to."

I did, first call. The Ritz. It couldn't be the George Sank, because every stock promoter stays there. The Lancaster? Too quiet. Jerry isn't that quiet. No, it had to be the Ritz.

Jerry and his pretty, blond wife, Janis, are there in a magnificent suite. An enormous chauffeured Mercedes takes them around town. Jerry treasures a line from Marcel Proust, who once explained his liking for the Ritz: "I prefer to be where there is no jostling, where the staff is so obliging that I feel at home and less tired."

Jerry is dieting, so there's no liquor in the suite except Perrier water and Cokes. While I was in the suite, he made two transatlantic calls to Phil in New York.

Later, at dinner at the Tour d'Argent, Jerry expounds his philosophy on stocks.

"God bless the American housewife who plays the market. If she buys 1,000 shares of Consolidated Garbage, by the time she tells her friends it sounds like another IBM. Who is the con man? The man who set up the deal or the customer who touts it?

"Why is Wall Street the only place where people will buy a stock much higher than it was the week before? If a shirt was $5 a week ago, would they buy it now if it was $15? On Wall Street, everyone is so goddamned sanctimonious. I never heard an allied member of the exchange say to another one: 'You're a whore, Herb, look at the deal you just pulled.' This is one business where they will not admit what they are."

As we leave the restaurant, a dark, swarthy, middle-aged man nods coldly to Jerry. Jerry smiles back. Later, in the Mercedes, he explains. "Phil and I had a hot stock deal. We rode it up from 7 to 65, and then at the peak, we were able to unload on a couple of Lebanese gold traders. That was one of them. It was a crappy stock to begin with, but he's a pro and should have known it wasn't worth six bucks, let alone $65. There's only one thing you can say for Phil and myself: We operated in the jungle only with other jungle denizens. We didn't sell to widows and orphans. Only to other operators. Serves them right. It was a crappy stock all the way up. We made a bundle on that deal."

The next morning Jerry makes two transatlantic calls to Phil in New York to bring him up to date on various developments at their Swiss bank, which he had just visited the day before. On the way to Orly, Jerry fills me on the joys of Swiss banking operations.

"First, since there's no SEC, you can get away with almost anything. For example, Danish, German and Swiss banks, with their very thin margin requirements, can push their clients into a stock. Then they run it up a little and sell short. About a fourth of all their accounts are discretionary. So they can regularly work against their clients to make a fast mark and there's no one around to yell copper. The clients generally get a once-a-year summary only."

To really understand the Swiss setup, Jerry said, I'd first have to get my head cleaned out of all the garbage put there by magazine pieces and books talking about Zurich gnomes stacking gold bars in some cave or some Schwyzer-Deutsch in Homburgs Causing Cabinets to Fall by ruining their national currency.

"What the Swiss have is a beautiful game which they can't lose, or hardly ever if they play it by their rules. Sometimes they lose when they get real greedy and start playing it with

American rules. Switzerland is unique: one of the few sporting houses where the madam is in one place and the girls in the other.

"You're wondering—or should be—why I'm worth $5,000 a month to that private bank in Zurich? Since the indictment I've been over twelve times—first class, with a suite at the Baur au Lac, and they pick up all the tabs.

"They have a lot of wealthy clients, and our batting average on stocks is such that they've made a lot of money following us. Sure, we had a few dogs, but we got them out in time. I've known them since 1957–58 when we came to our present arrangement. In addition to the $5,000 a month, we get a percentage of the profits on our deals. And it also provides us with a nice little playpen where we can operate on very small margin for stock buys."

How could they know if they were getting their fair share of the profits of their Swiss deals?

"Good question, you never *really* know. We must trust them to pay us our agreed-on percentage. We have to trust them when they report they bought so many shares and made so much on our recommend. We get 10 percent of the profits. I know they won't cheat me. At least, not by much. I know if they buy 100,000 shares of the stock and make five points, I'm going to get $50,000. Basically, it wouldn't make any sense cheating us. We have to trust each other or the relationship isn't worth a dime."

There *is* a lot of cheating that goes on in some Swiss banks, Jerry added. "Say, you're a European and have 10,000 shares of Unilever. You go to your Swiss bank and say to them, 'The stock cost me $40 and I'll give you an option on my 10,000 shares. Anything above 42 you can keep.' Don't you think the banker suddenly has a great incentive to sell it to his own accounts and keep the nice profits? He does. They are usually the stockbrokers for their clients. You know, I've had Swiss bankers tell me that if Switzerland had our SEC laws, most of the bankers would be in jail."

What about the Swiss numbered accounts? "It's the old shell

game," said Jerry. "Everyone's watching the wrong thing. Sure, the numbered account is what everyone knows about on Swiss banks, but the real pro approach is the Liechtenstein setup."

He explained: "You go to a Swiss bank and they then form a Liechtenstein trust for you. For openers, it costs you $750, I think. The Liechtenstein consul in Zurich gets a fee for each corporation. The other $500 is theoretically the legal fees, which are split in various ways. Now the trust is set up. The officers and theoretical stockholders are two or three directors of the bank you're working through. As far as their records show, they have an account for the XYZ Trust and this trust is owned by two of their bank directors. You have the receipt from the bank, plus all sorts of legal paraphernalia that shows, in effect, they are your nominees. You get a copy of the trust agreement and a copy goes into their vault. As far as the bank employees are concerned, the XYZ Trust buys and sells securities, bonds, paintings, jewelry—anything. Your name appears nowhere on the trust and can't be traced to you. This is the *only* safe device because the only people you're relying upon are the three bank directors. You get the usual undated resignations from them. No bank known has ever reneged on such commitments, and they wouldn't because it would destroy the whole fabric of their banking operations.

"Any U.S. citizen," he went on, "who walks into a Swiss bank with cash can effectively lose this cash and any profits that accrue from the investment of this cash. I know about the new IRS requirements about disclosing an interest in foreign accounts. But I don't see how they're going to be able to tie you to a Liechtenstein trust if you don't tell anyone but the bankers about it."

The ultimate refinement is to have two accounts in Switzerland. One a Liechtenstein trust, and one an ordinary account in your own name which you can openly disclose to IRS. In fact, you want to tell about this.

"You buy stock through your trust account. You got a profit; you keep it in the trust. You get a clinker and you have your accommodating banker transfer the purchase and sale of the losing stock to your open-name account, get a confirmation on paper of the loss operation, and now you file this when you pay your tax. There you have it: solid evidence that you just lost, say, $80,000 speculating on silver. Or Fairchild Camera, or anything. Sure, you have to be an important enough account for the bank to be so accommodating. Of course, it's a white-collar crime here, but I'm all in favor of it."

The Swiss bank briefing, Jerry concluded at the airport, was designed to make me ask more intelligent questions when I met their Swiss bank friend next week when he came to New York. Fellow named Bluntschli.

I said he had to be kidding: Bluntschli? The chocolate soldier in George Bernard Shaw's *Arms and the Man?* Jerry laughed. "Just our code name for him. You'll see why when we meet him next week. At the Waldorf."

6. Bluntschli

The Swiss are offended at being called gentlemen.

—BLAISE PASCAL

Banking establishments are more dangerous than standing armies.

—THOMAS JEFFERSON

Bluntschli is a tall, ramrod-straight playboy of the Western world. Handsome, smiling and rather saturnine in appearance. He made it clear that I couldn't use his name because he expected to live—and profit—among Swiss bankers a long time. He's thirty-six and a U.S.-dollar millionaire.

"Back in 1921," he began, "one of your great financial journalists came to Switzerland and gave a talk to the Swiss bankers. He was Clarence W. Barron, publisher of the *Wall Street Journal*. He told them: 'In Switzerland one can get a better financial view of the whole world than from any other point. If I were a Swiss citizen I should think I owned the earth.' "

Bluntschli grinned. "Couldn't have said it better myself."

He has only a slight accent—he speaks four languages fluently—and comes from one of those conglomerate European families. When he was fifteen, he was apprenticed for three years in his first bank job. Then, at nineteen, he did his obligatory Army service. The present job is his fourth. He's been there seven years. He's married and has three children. His wife is distantly related to a minor, and now defunct, royal house.

A little background, he said. "In Switzerland, first come the five big public banks with all their branches, the ones whose ads you see in the Paris *Herald Trib*. Then come the private banks. There are perhaps twenty important ones. Our bank is one of the more important of those twenty. Now, I'm in charge of the U.S. end of the bank. Our job is to reinvest money people give us. All banks over there pay employees like myself —and I'm only an employee, not a partner or anything—a straight salary and a bonus. (Incidentally, no one knows who owns these private banks.) So there's no need for us to churn accounts or pull tricks to generate more business. In 1969 I made about $12,000 in salary and bonus, but that year I also made myself $250,000. We have no capital gains taxes in Switzerland, but there are penalties for nondisclosure of hidden funds. Fortunately, every now and then there is a nationwide amnesty. We had one last year in Switzerland and I came forward and disclosed. So I paid my regular income tax and a fee, under the amnesty, for previously undisclosed funds, so now I'm all clear with them.

"There are certain rules all Swiss bankers operate under. Nothing like the SEC or anything, but our own self-imposed rules. For example, no honorable Swiss banker will buy stock for himself until he's completed the client's order. The reason is a selfish one: If you did that too often, it would come out and you'd get a bad name. But when a client comes to you with hot inside information and asks you to execute an order, why you can always ask him to set aside 2,000–3,000 shares for you. Nothing wrong with that.

"Virtually every Swiss banker has a numbered account at another bank. I have five such accounts."

Now, why does an *American* open a Swiss account?

1. First and foremost, tax evasion.
2. Stock manipulation.
3. Lower margin on stock trades.

Bluntschli explained the last item. "You go to a Swiss bank

and put up $100,000 in collateral, and they'll give you another $100,000 as margin for your operations. In effect, a 50 percent margin as against 80 percent in the U.S. There are some shitty private banks that will even let you operate on a 20 percent margin."

About half of all Swiss banks' trades in U.S. securities are for insiders. They Know Something and want to take intelligent advantage of that knowledge without disclosing it to the SEC, which they would have to do if they bought and sold directly through a U.S. broker in New York.

Most of Bluntschli's special clients are insiders, guys who really know. Still, not all of them work out. He thinks perhaps only four out of seven, on average. Insiders will sometimes overvalue the news they possess; or the market may be dropping; or the information leaks out to others and the price is prematurely driven up.

When an insider comes to Bluntschli for his banking skills, the arrangement is 10 percent of the profits for Bluntschli for overseeing the buying and selling operations. Actually, the usual Swiss fee is 5 percent, but Bluntschli can get 10 percent because he is known to be completely trustworthy and doesn't double-cross. "For my 10 percent they get a very professional handling and complete secrecy and trust. They're going to get the money coming to them within $1, and they know it. With others, sometimes you can't be so sure, so I'm worth the extra 5 percent to them."

There's a major myth, he went on, that Swiss banks are great judges of stock values. Not true. "Actually, we only know what the insiders are doing through us. Nothing more.

"An insider who has an account with our bank and uses me on these deals comes to me. He has some hot dope on his firm and wants me to pick up 100,000 shares for him. I got to hide my hand here. We don't want whispers starting prematurely. So, out of the forty major U.S. stockbrokers in Switzerland, I might select ten different ones to do the purchasing of this 100,000 shares. Or I might be even more careful and place 10 percent of the purchases through a London broker, another

10 percent through a German bank, and then I might spread the rest around twenty U.S. branch brokerage offices in Switzerland. Or I might space it out with only 1,000 shares a week to any one of them. Sure, there's an extra cost here for the insider. How much?

"Let's say I have his order to buy 100,000 shares at $10 a share. Swiss stock commissions are anywhere from a half to three-quarters of what the New York Stock Exchange rates are, but since we have to use the New York brokers anyway, that means a higher set of fees. On this deal, for example, it would come to something like this:

> $8,500 to the Swiss bank
> $17,500 to the New York brokers through their Swiss branches

Or about $26,000 plus taxes.

"Now, let's say this insider really has it right. The stock doubles. He makes $1,000,000 on paper, less my 10 percent and the fees for buying and selling. But wait a minute. He's going to be making a whole lot more because he's not going to pay any taxes on his capital gains.

"Naturally, we use U.S. brokerage offices in Switzerland that work with us. We give them the commission business of our clients, and we expect them to recompense us with hot issues. And, of course, there are some bank managers who just have private arrangements with some of these brokers. He gives the broker his bank's business and, in return, gets private payoffs. Or they might disguise it as 'research service' which the bank is supposedly doing for the broker."

He supplemented what Jerry had already said about the Liechtenstein trust setups. "There are about twenty lawyers who handle these. We have one right on our payroll. He forms the corporation, the trust, without knowing who owns it. Only two of our bank staffers technically own the corporation, and I turn over the papers and undated resignations to the real owner—and one stock certificate. But when you get right down to it, I become the only one in the bank who knows him. You see why I'm worth my 10 percent, no? At any given time, he can swear and be technically honest that he doesn't own any Liechtenstein trust.

"You do have to post $5,000 capital, which you get back. The tax law agreement with Liechtenstein comes to anywhere from $100 to $500 a year and the lawyer gets $500 a year. So the annual carrying costs are $1,000 a year. So unless you're really going to *use* it, there's no sense fooling around. It's not one of your status symbols that you talk about or show off. You certainly wouldn't talk about it in the United States, and you'd be foolish to even talk about it in Switzerland. I'm afraid your Internal Revenue Service has begun getting to a number of trusted Swiss bank employees. Yes, disclosure of information on a numbered Swiss bank account is still a criminal act, but for a sizable bribe . . . it happens, I'm afraid."

(IRS bribes to Swiss bank employees acquired new significance when the Swiss Supreme Court early in January, 1971, ruled that the court *could* supply Washington with information on the Swiss accounts of U.S. citizens suspected of tax fraud. But the information would have to be legally obtainable under Swiss law and only a very few special categories fit that. Routine prying is out, however, as in the past. In short, before the information would be furnished to the United States, the IRS would have to have considerable knowledge as to the tax fraud. Whether a bribed tip from a Swiss bank employee comes under that category remains to be tested in the courts.)

Since he also deals with rich men of many other countries, Bluntschli has his own estimates of relative honesty and shrewdness.

"The English are most correct. Fantastic. The crookedest? Believe it or not, the Swedes. Because the Swedish tax laws are the severest, most confiscatory on the continent. So what they do is literally bankrupt their businesses slowly with false invoices for orders from abroad. The money is drained out of the business and into their accounts in our banks. Every year at least two thousand Swedes, mostly businessmen and professionals, leave for tax havens abroad."

The shrewdest? No contest: the Rumanians and Hungarians. Émigrés? Bluntschli relished this one. "No, the Rumanian and Hungarian Iron Curtain bureaucrats. We've been building a remarkable business with them. And several Russians, too.

"Very simple operation. The Hungarian bureaucrat is in charge of ordering certain kinds of steel from abroad: Germany, Sweden, anywhere. His suppliers arrange to overcharge his country 5 percent, and that money goes into the bureaucrat's numbered account. What does he do with it? Most of them feed the money through the account to relatives in the United States. I can only assume that they plan to skip their countries sooner or later and have a nice stake to start over again in America."

Suddenly Bluntschli began laughing at a private joke. "They start out as good Communists, end up good capitalists, and they might even go to work for your CIA or DIA as stock market experts."

What was he talking about? On the plane over, he'd been reading a paperback, *The Super Spies,* by Andrew Tully. It's a terribly admiring puff for the U.S. Department of Defense Intelligence Agencies, the natural enemies of the U.S. Central Intelligence Agency. On page 96 Tully tells of the adventures of Sergio, a DIA agent planted in Jordan:

> For four years Sergio offered the DIA no intelligence of any substantial value . . . his job was to cement his relationship with the Jordanian high official so that some day the Jordanian would tell him something worthwhile. . . . Sergio ate with the Jordanian and drank with him and womanized with him. *He gave the Jordanian tips on the stock market, furnished by DIA experts, that made him richer.* . . . [Emphasis added]

I assured Bluntschli that regardless of what books said, he and his fellow Swiss bankers probably knew more about the U.S. stock market than all the experts at the DIA put together.

7.

How One of the World's Fifteen Best-Dressed Men Made His Fortune and Got Hit by the SEC

In the late fifties and sixties hundreds of cheap stock issues blossomed in the paper slum of Wall Street known as Reg A Land. Reg A stocks—the reference is to Regulation A in the SEC rules for stock underwriting—were for issues $300,-000 or less in total value, generally distributed on the basis of 150,000 shares at $2 or 100,000 at $3. To help the small businessman get his stock issue out at smaller expense and through minimal red tape, the SEC deliberately let these issues come out with less scrutiny and required them to go through fewer obstacle courses. (In January, 1971, Reg A limits were raised to $500,000.)

Most of those early issues are now dead or languishing. But some of them had spectacular life-spans. In May, 1967, you could have bought shares of Nylo-Thane Plastic for $3. In seven months it had risen to $85. Inter-American Industries came out at $1.50 a share and a few months later was selling at $20. They died later.

Among the kings of these cheap new Reg A issues which

were traded strictly on the OTC, the over-the-counter market, was Charlie Plohn, the man Eddie Jaegerman went to work for. Another big man in the Reg A market was a close friend of Phil and Jerry's. At one point in the sixties he and his firm were grinding out four and five near-worthless Reg A underwritings a week. The underwriter usually got 10 percent of the proceeds and a lot of fancy options.

I had assumed that he would talk to me freely because I knew he had been barred for life from being a broker-dealer by the SEC and had had nothing to lose in talking. But some lawyer had talked him into making a plea to the SEC for reinstatement, and though his chances were admittedly dim, why take a chance? He'd talk, but no names.

Neil Milton, as I'll call him, is a gray-haired, blue-eyed, rather impressive six-footer who's been married "to the same woman for twenty-seven years." He has three children.

"I've never been in trouble except the SEC, and I've never appeared in a court of law. I served honorably in World War Two and a few years ago I was selected as one of the Fifteen Best-Dressed Men in the World." He forgot to mention who selected him.

After the Army he went into a successful family business in steel fabrication. He worked there until 1952, when he developed a rare kind of cancer.

"I was very lucky. Survival rates for this kind of cancer are very low. The treatment was radium, and I got these radium burns over my body. I had to leave the family plant because I had to spend a few hours each day at Memorial Hospital in New York. I now had to find a quiet, sedentary job. I was down to 105, a walking stick. When I got up to 120 pounds and the outpatient treatment ended, the doctors said I could try working a little. Well, I studied finance in college, and I figured maybe it's time I looked into Wall Street. So I got a job with a minor outfit. I was a contact man which meant I sat in a little office and went through the Yellow Pages in, say, the podiatrist category, calling prospects on a stock called Sunflower Oil coming out at 15 cents a share. It was quite a prospectus they got up on it. I still shudder. It went like this: Of the $300,000 to be raised, the company will end up with $60,000 and the rest of the money goes to the promoters and underwriters. I did pretty well and they invited me downstairs to the main room where I became a customer's man. The only trouble was I didn't get along too well with the head of the firm. So I left to go with another outfit which was selling a new issue of a stock called New Mexico Copper at 50 cents a share. The deal was the salesman got $20 for every 100 shares he sold for $50. For selling 1,000 shares a week you earned $200."

The week Neil joined the firm they ran a full-page ad in the New York *Times* on a stock called Great Sweet Grass Oil. It was offered at 25 cents a share, and as a result of the ad the firm received 12,000 inquiries.

"The great response made the boss cocky, and he called all us salesmen in and said we'd only get $1 a 100-share lot sold, since the firm had done all the preselling through the ad. Well, everybody bitched and screamed. There wasn't enough commission for them and so on. Me, I quietly went to the boss and said: 'Give me all 12,000 leads and two secretaries and I'll work for the $1-per-100 commission.' He agreed.

"We waited until all 12,000 had gotten their prospectuses. Then I'd get on the phone: 'Well, sir, are you interested in acquiring 10,000 shares of Great Sweet Grass Oil?' If he said no, I'd say thank you and hang up.

"How did it go? At the end of the first week I made myself $6,000 commission. This went on for five weeks. I was averaging $5,000 a week, and I was wondering how long this beautiful life had been going on. Naturally, I couldn't let the other salesmen—the ones who had turned down the $1-per-100 deal —know about this gold mine I found. Hell, they were averaging $400–$500 a week on other stocks. On Friday when we got paid and they'd ask me how I was doing, I'd say I made maybe $180."

Meanwhile, a friend of Neil's was going to open his own brokerage office at 39 Broadway and asked Neil to come in with him. Neil agreed, but he would stay at his old job until he had exhausted all the Sweet Grass leads.

"When I finished our leads, I had made $60,000–$70,000 on them. At the new place a very interesting thing happened. This was 1952. The stock I had sold, Sweet Grass, went from 25 cents to $1 and was now listed on the American Stock Exchange at $1.50. Great. A man I had sold $2,500 worth of Sweet Grass now had stock worth $12,000. Boy, he loved me. The only thing in life he really remembers now is the name Neil Milton, magician. And this was 1952, mind you, when a $10,000 profit meant something. So I was a power. I had a genuine winner."

The firm got another deal in something called Texas Adams Oil. Neil sold 200,000 shares of the 300,000 issued—at $1 a share.

"The stock went to $2 and I did something peculiar for the business. I knew my boss had gotten most of his Texas Adams stock at 10 cents a share and the stock was getting hot. The drilling reports looked better and better. The stock moves up to $3. But I liked the idea of Neil Milton, magician, who puts his customers only into winners. So what I did, which was absolutely forbidden in the trade, was to call my customers and tell them to *sell* at $3. This is 'back-dooring' and men have been killed for less. If your customer's stock started coming back to the firm, they'd just have to resell it. So I told my customers to sell through other brokers. I had about 150 very loyal customers then, and they'd only made money through me. Sure, the whole thing was a boiler room operation, but through some luck the mooches were way ahead.

"Well, you can't keep a back-dooring operation quiet very long. When the firm found out, a lot of harsh things were said and I was invited to leave. But that year I had made $100,000 in commissions, which meant I earned four times what my uncles were making in the steel-fabricating business. One of my uncles called me and said, 'Neil, my boy, I don't know what the hell you're doing at 39 Broadway, but you'd better stop. Someday you're going to get in a lot of trouble.'

"The funny thing is that I agreed with him. Here I was working maybe four hours a day and I'd go home at the end of the week with $4,000–$5,000 and I'd take it and throw it up in the air and scatter it all over the living room and my wife would say: 'I don't know what you're doing, but you'd better stop. I'm getting nervous.' So was I."

He left his job and went with an old-line over-the-counter trading firm that had a few stocks listed in the pink sheets, the voluminous daily listing of low-priced stocks. They dealt only with other OTC brokers.

"It works this way. You're listed in that morning's pink sheets for XYZ stock at 5 to ½. That is, you'll buy the stock at $5 and sell it for 5½. You buy 100 at $5 which means that you won't pay that for your next buy for the day, so the stock automatically becomes 4¾. If you get hit at 4¾, why, your next move is down to 4½, of course. If you have to *buy* the stock only, you keep doing down."

Neil admires the OTC brokers he dealt with around the country. He found them honorable and trustworthy.

"Say there's a dispute on a stock price between me and a broker in San Francisco and the amount is under $2,000, which was 'a small number' to us. Over $2,000 it went to arbitration, but under that it would be decided this way. The man in California would say, 'Okay, I'm flipping a coin, Neil. How do you call?' And I'd say heads and he'd say, 'Okay, you win.' You know I've won many more times than I've lost on those tosses by out-of-town brokers."

Honor among thieves? "Perhaps. But these are men who live up to what they say on the phone, which is a lot better than many customers will do. Sometimes customers will try to weasel out of a trade when the stock has fallen. Boy, how many times has a customer told me to sell 1,000 shares at 10 and if at the end of the day it's gone up to $13, he'll call and say, 'I never told you to sell.' This has happened hundreds of times to me. *Customers!*"

Neil was earning a lot less in the OTC trading business but felt he was acquiring a valuable education. "I felt comfortable with the sharp drop in my earnings. I had acquired a partner. We had picked up three new men who came to us from Bache & Company and they were retailing our stocks. My partner and I were trading the stocks with other brokers, and we had a treasurer who used to come in two days a week to discuss policies and to get me on the right track. I used to get off easily."

Neil laughed. "Phil has probably told you that they used to call me the most arrogant prick on Wall Street then. I had a bad temper. Once we did an issue on a minor drug company at 3 and the stock went to 8–9. The president had a bad disagreement with us. We had a final meeting with him at Oscar's Delmonico Restaurant where I threw a glass of water in his face. But I also gave him a napkin to wipe himself off and then I walked out."

"Don't get me wrong," Neil said. "I can get rough, but I was a good, honest salesman for our stocks. "I used to call a customer and say, I want you to buy 1,000 shares of this new $2 stock and he'd say, 'What do they do, Neil? What do they earn?' Ever hear such crazy questions? I'd say, 'Listen, this is a piece of crap but I'm telling you to buy it.' Later, if the stock fell from $2 to 50 cents and he gets a letter from the SEC asking what Mr. Milton told you about the stock when he urged you to buy it, why, he's got to tell them exactly what I told him. So the trick is to tell them it's a piece of crap— and still sell them."

Things kept getting better, and by this time Neil was senior partner in the firm. They had well-furnished offices on Pine Street with great views of the East River. One week they were doing an underwriting of a certain stock. The issue was 100,000 shares at $3, and the firm's commission was the usual 10 percent, or $30,000.

"The night of the underwriting we knew we had a live one. From the interest expressed by other brokers we knew the stock would open at 8 or 9. Now, I never skimmed off the top. Instead we got the stock to friends and others we wanted to make money for. That night three characters came into the office and the leader introduced himself like this:

" 'My name is Miller and this is Kemp and this is Russo. We'd like to get 10,000 shares at $3 and billed to Summit Securities in New Jersey.' I happened to know that Miller was also known as Morris 'The Weasel' Miller. Well, I was sitting at my big desk with jacket off and sleeves rolled up. I got up, smiled, and threw my glass of scotch in Kemp's face. He wiped the booze off and he said, 'You'll be hearing from me.' And they left.

"Then a friend of mine came in the office and said, 'Neil, you did a bad thing. You now have made serious problems for yourself because these are bad characters. You're liable to get hurt if you go down in the street tonight.' So my partners called a detective agency and hired a bodyguard for me. He lived with me for three weeks. A big husky 250-pound character who had two steaks for dinner and five eggs for breakfast. So I decided I had to get rid of him or the grocery bills would bust me. I called my friend and said, 'Okay, get back to the people I insulted and make up.' Eventually, for $3,500 everything was forgiven. That was the most expensive glass of scotch in my life." (The three hoods were subsequently indicted and went to prison.)

Neil was proudest of the time when he exposed an out-and-out crook. "I never got any accolades for it and I did a real public service."

One afternoon he was visited by a friendly analyst from Bruns, Nordeman, a Big Board firm. He told Neil he had a great little company and showed him the balance sheet of the firm, Bradford Audio.

"The balance sheet," said Neil, "read like this: Assets: $690,000. Liabilities: $11,000. Orders on Hand: $5,000,000. The analyst said he met Bradford and the firm was making baffles for hi-fi rigs. It sounded good to me. I picked up the pink sheets, and there I see the stock of Bradford is traded by the crème de la crème of the OTC houses. Outfits like Troster, Singer and Hanseatic. They were trading the stock at 1½–2. Right away I knew we had to get into the stock. So I put in an order for 5,000 shares at $2. It went through, and now I decided maybe I ought to look at that marvelous balance sheet a little closer."

Meanwhile, Neil had sold 1,000 shares to each of five trusted customers—in case he wanted to get the stock quickly.

Neil noticed particularly the incredible amount of cash that Bradford Audio showed in its balance sheet. "Cash is the one thing these little stocks never have."

The balance sheet had been certified by a Dwight Smith who had an office in Mamaroneck. Neil phoned him.

"Mr. Smith, are you a CPA handling Bradford Audio?"

"No, I'm not. I'm in advertising. But you're the fourth guy to call me about this in the past few months."

Neil tried other Dwight Smiths—in Long Island, in Connecticut. But no Dwight Smith, CPA.

"Now I start getting a little nervous. Have I retailed a phony stock? Have I sold somebody's investment stock, unregistered paper? I decide maybe it's time for a visit to Bradford Audio. I go to this brownstone building in East Thirty-eighth off Park. I push the bell. I go in the hall. I ring. A peephole opens. Someone looks out at me: 'What do you want?' I say, 'My name is Neil Milton and I'd like to talk to you about Bradford Audio. I own some stock.' He tells me to go away or he'll call the police. I started kicking and hammering at the door. And *I* called the police. Told them I'm a stockholder in a public company and I had to get in. They said I'd have to swear out a warrant. Well, this is now 11 P.M., not swear-out-warrant time."

Neil phoned the analyst from Bruns, Nordeman and told him what had happened. The analyst insisted that Bradford was a lovely man, but Neil insisted *something* was wrong. He said he'd come right down. He did—and brought the Bruns, Nordeman attorney with him.

The attorney persuaded Bradford to talk to Neil. As soon as Bradford opened the door, Neil started to push his way in, but "Bradford raps me a shot in the face and locks the door again."

The next day Neil went to the New York attorney general's office, since Bradford Audio had been a purely New York State stock offering.

"There I see Dave Clurman, the assistant attorney general in charge of stock frauds. I told Dave there was a helluva fraud here. Meanwhile, I had sent out wires to each of the five clients I had given 1,000 shares to and told them not to pay for the stock, to forget the confirmation. And then I sold the 5,000 shares at the price I had paid: $2. So I was free and clear.

"The next day Dave Clurman calls me. They had Bradford down and he seemed a perfect gentleman. The thing looks absolutely legit. But they'll continue to look into it. But before he hangs up, Clurman says, 'Neil, if you're wrong on this, you're in for such a libel suit your brains are going to get scrambled.' "

Neil was vindicated. There was no Dwight Smith, CPA. Bradford, himself, had been printing the balance sheets. He got eight years, since it was his third offense. He served only two years and died of a heart attack soon after his release. He was seventy-two.

The first New York *Times* story on the case, BROKERS CALLED VICTIMS OF FRAUD, quoted the New York State attorney general's description of Robert Leland Bradford as "one of the most artful and dangerous confidence men in modern financial history," who had duped some of the country's leading brokerages into handling illegal stock.

Neil is still saddened that his name was never mentioned in the story—the man who had exposed the operation and got the attorney general interested. "And I didn't have a dime's worth of stock to protect, either," he concludes. "No medal from the AG, no commendation from the SEC, nothing."

Neil had another bout of *pro bono publico* in 1961, and he still thinks that this one really undid him.

"There were twenty-two brokers called down to Washington and interviewed on how the SEC could cure the hot new-issue market and various other ills of Wall Street. I went down with my lawyer, an honest and delightful man. I enjoyed the limelight of being invited down. I described some of the issues we did, and since a lot of them had been winners, I had a good time. At the end of six hours of testimony by all of us I was to give an hour of recommendations. My lawyer whispered, 'Neil, let's just catch a plane.' Oh, no. There was something I had to get off my chest. I brought with me the sad details of a stock called Transitron which had been underwritten by Merrill Lynch. I got classy on this one and started out with the words '*Sic transit gloria.*' I said if you want to correct Wall Street's faults, don't bother with the little stealers, the little brokers. Maybe I made myself $150,000 a year, but I was a little broker. I told them to shake the tree at the top, not the bottom. I said take Transitron and Merrill Lynch which brought it out at 36, 1,000,000 shares and the stock went to 70 and they did another 1,000,000 shares and the stock collapsed to $10. It was now around $4. I guess I was talking pretty strong and my lawyer keeps nudging me under the table, 'Let's go, Neil, let's catch a plane. This isn't your ball game.' It wasn't, but I didn't learn that until later."

Neil's thriving brokerage empire collapsed in May, 1962—along with many others.

"What happened was I tried to support my own issues. I wanted my stocks to look good. Remember that old picture with George Arliss as old man Rothschild and all he keeps saying is 'Buy, buy, buy'? So I bought and bought. My first mistake and I got killed."

Jerry, who was sitting in with Phil, breaks in with an updated version of an old street joke. "A Reg A underwriter goes to heaven and finds that the little corner reserved for his group is already full. He assures Saint Peter that he could easily make room for himself if he had a soapbox. Saint Peter is curious and gets a soapbox for him set up in front of the place where the underwriters hang out. The newcomer gets up and tells them about a fantastic mine just discovered in hell and that stock is available. They all get hysterical and run out to get the shares. Saint Peter is nearly tripped over by the guy on the soapbox, who starts running, too. He says to him: 'I can understand why they're running. But why you?' As the man runs, he shouts back: 'Maybe there's some truth to the rumor!' "

It gets a tired laugh. Neil finishes: "I didn't go bankrupt. I got rid of what investment stock I had left over and paid off everybody. My firm went out of business, but clean."

Neil, Phil and Jerry went broke with the same stocks. They were so busted they could only buy $1 worth of gas at a time. Neil got a break by going into a totally alien field.

"We had once done an underwriting of a minor car rental outfit. One of the partners in it took pity on me and said, 'Neil, listen, why don't you try selling franchises in one of our open territories in the Midwest? We have forty leads. Here's your plane ticket.'

"I get to this city and check in at a nice motel. Now, I never sold a franchise in my life. I got on the phone to the leads the firm had provided. I made appointments. That night, in come four Turkish brothers with their WASP lawyer. I told them I wanted $80,000 for the local franchise. They call back the next day and say eighty is too much. Ten minutes later I get a call from their lawyer. He's gotta see me. He comes around and lays it on the line: His clients are ready to approve the deal at $80,000—if he gives his okay. And I can have his okay for $5,000. I leave town with their certified check for $80,000—and quietly hand the lawyer his $5,000. In another city I sell a retired police chief a franchise for $30,000. Then another franchise in a nearby city for $30,000. A retired school-teacher. In all I made $30,000 in commission and I'm on my feet again, thank God. I got back just in time to prevent Long Island Lighting from letting our house go dark."

Neil looked around Wall Street and found a partnership with an older man who had a lot of money but was very tight. "We were on William Street and we had an office that was worse than a pigsty. I was so ashamed I wouldn't even let Phil and Jerry come visit. My partner and I shared profits, but he was a hard man with a buck. If I made a $15 phone call, he'd get hysterical—even if it meant a sale of a few thousand bucks' worth of stock. If he had to write a check for more than $100, he'd have an apoplectic fit. But it was a working combination, and at the end of our first month we made $20,000."

Phil takes over: "Well, Neil is finally solvent again. Jerry and I had gone into cocoa without any money but the backing of our friend, Rink, and suddenly we had an enormous cocoa profit. Only one catch. We had sat on it five and a half months parlaying it beautifully to where we had $250,000 worth, but we had to wait our six months and a day for our capital gains.

"Now Neil comes to us with a great little issue out of Philadelphia called General Numismatics. Neil was supposed to do 30,000 shares, and he wanted to keep 15,000 shares for the three of us. We loved the concept, a private mint with the designer of the Kennedy half-dollar on the board, good people, but we still had ten days to go on our cocoa positions. By September 13, 1966, we'd have been clear and home free with a fat capital gain. So cocoa fell out of bed in the next few days and we were busted again. Except Neil. Now he put up our gasoline money and paid our electric bills.

"We started making a little money here and there. Meanwhile, we keep an eye on General Numismatics and look for a chance to get back in it. By now they had changed their name to the Franklin Mint. They needed more money for big special coin presses. But they needed big money which we didn't have then. But still we managed to pick up for clients about 43,000 shares in the open market at about $23–$30. Meanwhile, we arranged a meeting with Unterberg, Towbin, a high-class Big Board firm. They met us in Massoletti's or Eberlin's restaurant—not their offices. They don't ordinarily associate with people like us. We interest them in the Franklin Mint. They send their men out to the company in Pennsylvania. They like his report and they decide to go into the stock, big. Unterberg buys 32,000 shares at $23 for partners and clients, and they give the company $759,000 for investment stock. Now the stock starts moving up in a straight line and soon the stock is 80. Unterberg, Towbin brings out a secondary stock issue at 80. Then from 80 it moves to 270 in the next year. All of us made a lot out of Franklin Mint. But Unterberg, Towbin made $3,000,000 for their partners and clients on it. Meanwhile, they had me down as a finder on the deal and arbitrarily decided I was worth exactly $3,000 for bringing the deal to them. Well, I may be something, but I'm not a $100-a-night whore. That $3,000 check they sent me is still sitting in the Unterberg, Towbin offices. We're suing them, of course. Franklin Mint was the biggest single winner anyone had in those two years. From 21 to 270 and split three times. If we could have closed out our cocoa positions five days earlier, we'd have had it all. Still, we did all right on it. So did Neil."

What kind of makeup does someone need for this kind of feast-or-famine existence? Neil replied: "You have to have very big balls and you have to believe in something, up or down, but *believe.*"

Neil's firm once brought out a leasing stock which was run by two brothers. "We did 250,000 shares at $2 a share. The stock opened at $4–$5. I ended up with 20,500 shares which cost me $2.20 each. I sat with that stock two years. Then I was solicited by a go-go mutual fund. The stock was then selling for $30 and they gave me a deal to take the whole package for $17. They gave me a certified check for $348,500"—he flashes a Xerox copy—"and that was very nice. Why did I sell a $30 stock for $17? Well, if you put 20,000 shares on the market in a thin issue, you can drive the price down awful fast. Besides, my stock was investment stock which had to be held a certain time and a lot of funds were loading up on investment stock, bought at bargain prices in those days. God help them. The leasing company stayed at the 27–29 level for four months after I sold it and then it collapsed. Turned out the president of the firm had reported wildly incorrect earnings."

The leasing firm also made money for Phil and Jerry. One large block of private investment stock that they sold off was to the Lebanese Jerry and I had encountered at the Tour d'Argent in Paris. It was recently quoted in the pink sheets at 6 cents a share. The firm is now bankrupt.

Neil's troubles with the SEC started over the stock of a now-defunct company.

"What they had was something called a correlator. It was a gimmick that told you if there was oil in the ground or if you had cancer. We brought out the stock at $4, but it fell to $2 and stayed there for seven months in the 1960–61 period. I sold all my stock at crappy prices because I couldn't get along with the brothers who ran the firm. Naturally, I felt like a great jerk when the stock got up to $20. The brothers got rid of most of their stock at $15.

"The SEC got interested because they felt the stock had been oversold. Could be. We had a customer's lady, now dead, who was very enthusiastic over the stock. I think she had fallen in love with an executive at the company who wined and dined her lavishly.

"Joe Daly, the chief of SEC enforcement, told me that he was going to recommend a one-year suspension for me. I said, 'I'll take it.' But Washington turned him down. So there's a long hearing in Washington running to eight thousand pages of testimony and the SEC hearing officer hands down a decision that said I seemed to be an honorable and forthright man but perhaps I used bad judgment in hiring this saleslady. And he thought a six months' suspension was right for me. But the SEC brass decided that wasn't enough. Eight months later, the SEC, overturning the ruling of its own examiner, decides that the only right penalty for me is to bar me for life from the securities business. I appealed in the Appellate Division of the New York Supreme Court but lost and that's it. Sure, I'm bitter.

"What do I do now? Well, I'm in the field of mergers and acquisitions. And I was for a couple of years president of a small listed company, an outfit with nothing but losses. I got into it with three partners. We bought 150,000 shares at 50 cents each for an investment. The stock opens at $2, even though there are no earnings, no nothing. My attorney gets nervous at this price rise. So we get out a letter that we can't understand why the price has risen since there are no earnings or prospects at the moment. What happens? The stock goes from $2 to $4. We get out another letter to stockholders: We're still losing money, please don't buy or sell without using great caution. The outfit does precision molding up in New England. So now the stock goes to $5. So I tell my lawyer, don't worry I'm going to send out the balance sheet given us by Ernst & Ernst showing that we have $40,000 in assets and $90,000 in liabilities and the stock will drop like a piece of crap. Instead the stock stays at the $4–$5 level. I figured out that if I sent ten negative letters, each gloomier than the previous one, I could get the price up to $100."

Neil got so uneasy he resigned as president of the firm, although still retaining his stock. It has since merged with another firm.

(Great minds often come to similar conclusions, even though they start from different vantage points. Back in May, 1959, *Fortune* magazine did a wry little editorial comment, "How to Handle Suckers," which concluded: "Actually, the sucker is often *encouraged* to speculate by all these warnings about rising stock prices, for they serve as a harsh reminder to him that others are growing filthy rich in the market; and the sucker mentality, being what it is, construes the warnings as a sign that the 'insiders' want to keep him out of a good thing. A bit of reverse psychology might be called for here. The New York Stock Exchange might, say, issue a statement calling on small investors to empty their savings accounts and buy heavily into cheap stocks. The suckers would see right through *that*.")

Neil concluded: "It's a great business for little thieves. Sure, I'd go back in the business if they let me. The greatest soft take in your life. Still, I think there's room for everyone to make a dollar legit in this business. Also, I've not broken one rule: I've never lied to anyone on a stock. I can still speak to the same people I spoke to twenty years ago about buying stocks."

After Neil left, Phil said: "He could have been franker about his great little Reg A stock issues. The funny thing is that the sum total raised by the thieves for operations that *survived* is far greater than the money lost in the bust-out stocks."

On these Reg A issues, which were exempt from certain SEC requirements in order to make it easier for the small business-man to raise money—in theory, anyway—there was a restriction. The promoter couldn't do any preselling of the issue. In that case, Phil went on, how could the entire issue of 100,000 shares be sold out in a few minutes on the Monday morning it came out?

"It was done this way. You called in ten of your broker friends and said: 'Phil, how many are you taking?' and I'd say 20,000 and Harry would take 30,000 and so on. And in fifteen minutes the whole issue was distributed. Neil usually got any-where between 10–12 percent for promoting the issue. He gave us 4 percent for our selling efforts. Everybody got a cut for taking the stock in big blocks. And in addition you got some of the promoter's options on the stock. As long as you had a bull market it was a great operation. Neil's trouble came when he tried to support his stocks after the market bust in 1962. That's like trying to hold up Boulder Dam after it's been dynamited. Eventually he owned all his stocks and they weren't worth anything, so he wasn't. But he went broke clean. The SEC did give him a bum rap, and sometimes if you hear me refer to an organization in Washington called the SS, you'll know who I mean.

8. | RINK: David Ricardo Is Alive and Well and a Member of the NYSE

If Neil Milton is mad at the SEC, he's no match for Rink, a multimillionaire member of the New York Stock Exchange.

Neil Milton said it was a great business for *little* thieves. There's nothing little about Rink's operations. He's made more than $20,000,000 in the market, a major operator by anyone's standards. Like everyone else in the street, he has his wound stripes. Not the humdrum ulcers, high blood pressure, colitis or migraine. Rink has a special psychic wound that Phil warned me about.

"I don't know what kind of impressions you're forming of Jerry and me," Phil said, "but the chances are you're probably thinking we're a little paranoid. Everyone against us: the SEC, the stock exchange, the NASD [National Association of Security Dealers] and so on. Maybe. But you got to understand that Rink *really* feels the establishment is *all* against him. Him and his twenty million bucks. But they don't really give a crap about him.

"He can be conned, but he's also had some great ideas. He once hired five young analysts and gave them each $50,000 to invest for three months. Then he charted their records and fired the bottom two and hired two more . . . and so on. The gimmick worked and he did well with it. Then he latched onto Sam Stedman, one of the smartest—maybe luckiest—analysts who ever hit the street. After that he didn't need any other help."

Every decade turns up its outstanding financial analyst. Samuel Lee Stedman, a small-town lad from Sedalia, Missouri, hit the street after World War II. He worked for Loeb, Rhoades & Co., and in the fifties *Fortune* magazine said of him that he was among "the most powerful ten men on the Street," even though he was largely unknown outside it. He became known and highly respected because in January, 1958, he picked a group of nine stocks: Polaroid, Diner's Club, Brunswick, Zenith, IBM, Merck, Fairchild Camera, Thiokol, Crowell-Collier. He said these would do far better than average. In the next eighteen months the Dow-Jones index rose 48 percent. Stedman's selections jumped nearly 300 percent. Rink was in on every one of the issues and a few more. Stedman died in September, 1961, of cancer. He was only forty-five and very prosperous but not nearly as rich as Rink had become.

Phil, who has no idols, is a bit skeptical of Stedman. "Just say he died before the market could make a liar out of him."

Rink went into cocoa with Phil and Jerry and lost a lot. There was a period of bitterness between them because Rink thought they made him look silly. "Rink is something special in our lives," Phil went on. "What it comes to is that we still have this love-hate relationship with him. At times I think he's a prick, but it's like a pretty woman who spits at you: better than a smile from a dog. Okay, we *envy* him. He had access to backup money, which meant he could make five, six big mistakes and still have enough to keep going for another try. With us, one or two big mistakes could wipe us out."

Rink—a childhood nickname—lives in a fourteen-room duplex off Fifth Avenue. A month before, it had been featured in the New York *Times* Home Furnishing section. The editors called it the home of a "young, adventurous couple." Only half-true. Rink is forty-seven, but his second wife is much younger. He has three sons by his previous marriage and a two-year-old boy from this one.

We talked in the library, with its red-velvet walls and a great collection of Currier & Ives prints and lots of fine bindings. He was in pajamas and a bathrobe and sat in a rare *Bürgermeister* chair, swinging his long legs back and forth. The chair was nearly as high as a tennis umpire's seat.

He laid down the ground rules. I couldn't give his real name, of course. The things he was going to tell me were damaging in some ways. He was very bitter against the SEC, which he pronounced SECK.

Rink is 6 feet 1 and getting heavy; he speaks freely with great, exaggerated hand gestures and, every now and then, with curious speech throwbacks—"having yourself a jim-dandy time" —or curious pronunciations—his facts were often "*preg*matic."

His family is well-to-do. His mother, a great beauty, was re-married to a very wealthy manufacturer. His father, a prosperous salesman, is a handsome glad-hander who plays near-professional golf. Rink's sister is married to the head of a fair-sized insurance company. A relative is on the Board of Governors of the New York Stock Exchange. "I am, as they say, well-connected. But in this business that doesn't help too much, regardless of what the boys tell you," he said, smiling with the relish of a man who knows what others are jealously saying behind his back.

(As Rink was to tell me later, he had no lingering bitterness for Phil and Jerry. The cocoa thing was over, and besides, he had once promised himself to follow a rule laid down by one of the great speculators of the twenties, Jesse Livermore. "Never," said Livermore, "speculate in cocoa." "Besides, any fool can see that, by and large, commodities are rigged and crooked. Why should you expect them to be nice and honest?")

After World War II service in the Air Force he went to the University of Michigan; then into a trucking concern; as a buyer for Gimbels; in ladies' lingerie—his stepfather was a major manufacturer—but he had an itch to go into business for himself. With a loan from his family, he bought a seat on the New York Stock Exchange for about $40,000.

"Those were the great days. We'll never see them again. A lot of horseplay. BB's in your shoes; talcum powder sprayed all over you if they heard you were engaged or getting married. And the big thing to look forward to was the exchange's annual golf tournament. Saturday was mistress day. Everybody had to be at work at 10 A.M., Saturday mornings. Until noon. So you had the whole afternoon off. The happily married brokers went to their mistresses—that's how they stayed happily married—and the unhappily married took it out on the golf ball. Yes, sir, the whole character of the exchange changed when they ended those Saturday sessions. Most of us loved them. For people who like their work, the weekend is a big bore. The average wealthy man can't stand the weekend with his family."

Rink was a $2 broker. He bought and sold stocks for smaller member firms that didn't want—or couldn't afford—to have their own brokers on the floor all the time to execute trades.

"On a Saturday in those days, I might clear maybe $60–$70 and on a regular trading day maybe $200. I used to get a lot of business from a bunch of *arbitrageurs* in Canada, guys shaving points on differences in the convertibles and the regular stocks of a company. They liked me because I ran faster than most other $2 brokers."

Few $2 brokers die rich. Rink made his money in the fifties and early sixties because he followed the star of Sam Stedman.

"He taught me. He got me into Syntex, U.S. Smelting, Xerox, Fairchild, Polaroid. The most brilliant man who ever hit Wall Street. Pure, unadulterated cerebral power. He made me and fifty other guys millionaires before he made a big dime himself. He was the dominant analyst and there just aren't any more like him."

Rink had his first spot of trouble with the SEC in the early sixties. "They slapped a twenty-day suspension against me. Something to do with a lousy 1,500 shares of ———. I sold it at 8 or 9 and bought it back at 12. Big deal. The trouble is, when a small operation like mine is suspended, you're out of business for that time. I figure the SECK has probably invested $400,000–$500,000 in seeking my destruction."

He wasn't smiling. "SECK is a dirty word. It's like a drawbridge. To get over it, you have to pay a fee. First, by hiring a very expensive lawyer. An ugly lawyer boy who couldn't make it on his own goes into SECK, makes a pest of himself, and then gets hired. The kind who wasn't good-looking enough to marry a rich girl. Why does SECK pick on little lawyer boys for these jobs? Very sad, these SECK lawyers. Immobilized, ugly, despised by their families, so they go down to SECK and there do their pesty work until they get a good job offer from a law firm in Wall Street."

During his troubles with the SEC, he went on, as a muted snarl whirled around his words, "I had two approaches, not so subtle, from the SECK investigators. One told me about his son who had to work so hard on his vacation in order to make his way through college. Very sad. I didn't sympathize."

He felt that the SECK's worst fault was giving the public the impression it is protecting it when it is not. Still, he felt the SECK was necessary.

"They should prosecute out-and-out fraud. They should provide for uniform prospectuses on stocks. The prospectuses should be like a debate. The SECK should list all the bad points and weaknesses, and the underwriters all the strong ones, and let the public decide. And they should insist on a single, uniform system of accounting and reports for all corporations. They could save U.S. investors millions by forcing honest accounting methods alone."

Rink is pessimistic about the future of the New York Stock Exchange. He thinks the seats will be nearly worthless in ten years.

"It's been a good show, but the time has come to start walking to the exit. When I came to Wall Street, there were many characters around and after a while I was one of them. There were great, colorful personalities and they're disappearing.

Why? The massive, dead hand of the government, of SECK. No bright guys should go down to Wall Street anymore. I plan to be out of it by 1972."

What will he do? He's already started teaching economics and finance at a small college. Occasionally he's thought how nice it would be to be a U.S. Congressman. He talked of "buying" a seat in Washington as one would buy a seat on the exchange.

His wife, an attractive, slender blonde of mixed British-Scandinavian ancestry, came in, and he introduced me. He explained that her British ancestors were prominent Quakers and suddenly it all fell into place. I said unexpectedly, "Ricardo."

He said, "What?"

I said, "David Ricardo." The great eighteenth-century economist of whom Keynes said "he was the greatest mind that found economics worthy of its powers."

Every other graduate economics student dreams of emulating the Great Lord Keynes. He sits up in bed every morning and coolly plots moves on foreign exchange. Makes a few phone calls, and before the day is out, he's a few thousand pounds richer. Or he cleverly speculates on the stock exchange and makes more money. He writes brilliant books that influence the whole Western world. He becomes the fountainhead of more effectively used economic approaches to finance and unemployment and money than any economist before or since. He marries a lovely Russian ballerina. Entertains the most brilliant people of the age. Writes wittily. Rises high in British government as the adviser on monetary policy. A splendid life blemished slightly, for some students anyway, by the revelation that he had been a homosexual back in his Cambridge days. Also, there was the fact that he very nearly went bankrupt as a result of his foreign exchange speculations. Keynes' biographer, Roy Harrod, describes the grim days of 1920:

As the later days of May ebbed away, it became clear that he was ruined. Between the beginning of April and the end of

May he had lost £13,125. [Then about $65,000.] A small syndicate, for part of the resources of which he was morally responsible, also lost £8,498. [About $42,000.] . . . It would indeed have been a disaster if the man who had so recently set world opinion agog by claiming to know better than the mighty of the land had himself become involved in bankruptcy. One can imagine the banner headlines.

He was rescued by an unexpected loan of $25,000 from a famous financier who admired Keynes. But it was a near thing for a while. Still, a great life to emulate.

But how did Rink resemble David Ricardo?

Ricardo came from an old Spanish-Portuguese Jewish family. He went to work in his father's London stock brokerage business when he was fourteen. At twenty, in 1792, he fell in love with a Priscilla Ann Wilkinson (and like Rink's wife), a Quakeress. His family was against the marriage, so he left home, married her, got a small stake and proceeded to make a great fortune on the London Exchange. He bought an immense estate of 6,000 acres, Gatcomb Park, in Gloucestershire, became a sheriff, and then went into Parliament. He did it the way Rink planned to: by buying it. He lent the Irish Earl of Portarlington, who owned the seat, £25,000 at 6 percent and paid him £4,000 outright for the seat itself. Perfectly normal then.

In Parliament he became one of the most active proponents of reform. And he started turning out his influential essays on economics.

Rink insisted he no longer planned to buy a seat in Congress and didn't know just how brilliant or influential *his* economic writings would be. But he savored the comparison. "Ricardo, eh?"

There were some pitfalls, too. Ricardo had brought about a revolution in economic thinking in the early 1800's by advocating more attention to the distribution of income among social classes, a viewpoint that decades later greatly influenced

Karl Marx and in fact made Ricardo his favorite economist. By now the analogy had grown dimmer. After all, Rink is a Republican who gave $25,000 to the Nixon campaign.

Rink once violated the traditional Republican admonition: Don't sell America short. Rink sold a tiny segment of it short and found it a most uncomfortable experience.

"Early in 1970, when the market was tumbling, I looked around for high multiple stocks to go short on. So I picked on Eli Lilly and you never found a more embarrassing short. I sold 1,000 shares short. Five days later I get a call from the firm I clear through, and they are very embarrassed; they could not find *any* Eli Lilly stock in customer accounts that they could lend me for a fee so that I could go short on it. This was crazy: There are 33,000,000 shares outstanding and none in the hands of brokerage firms? I figured that all the Lilly stock was being handled by banks, insurance companies and trusts. *No ordinary people in America owned it.* Even Merrill Lynch, the giant supermarket, didn't have any. Finally, the specialist in the stock on the exchange did me a great favor and let me have 1,000 shares out of his own stock. Sure, I lost. There are some stocks you must never go short on. Lilly and maybe Avon.

"I'll go further. Don't go short in general. You never want to be in a race where there's only one or two winners. You want a race where the first 400 out of 1,000, say, take home some kind of a medal, winnings. And in going short, only one or two can win. Too many short sellers in the same stock would defeat this purpose. In going long, a lot of guys can win. There never died a rich bear."

He had some general advice for investors.

"Find yourself a bright *young* broker. Listen to his stories. Some of them are going to be bright *and* rich. Middle-aged guys don't get rich in Wall Street anymore. If you're gonna do it at all in the street, you make it in your first five or six years. The young ones have got to be bulls; they can make it only by finding something at a buck that's going to sell, in time, for $20. String along with them.

"One other possibility. Find yourself a nice little old lady. Do what she does. I mean it. Little old ladies do fabulously well in the market. Why? They buy and hold cosmetic stocks, little-old-lady stocks, fabulous textile stocks. They know consumer products. I've seen some of their accounts. Little old ladies like to own things they can *touch*. No razzle-dazzle Fairchild Camera for them. They can't touch or even understand *that*. They're nice, but I don't want them for customers; they give you no business because they *never* sell. I bet you don't know a man who owns 100 shares of Wrigley's. My old ladies do. They also own and hold Kellogg's, Ralston Purina and Hershey. They're terrible clients, but they always own the right things and they bought them at the right time and they're a living reproach to 95 percent of your male clients. So find yourself a nice, smart little old lady—and do what she does in the market. Even if it kills you to do it."

And there are some people, he went on, who shouldn't be in the market, even if they have a smart young broker or a shrewd little old lady to follow. "I don't know why it is, but there *is* a born loser. No matter what, he just can't make it in the market. When he gets into a stock Things Happen that haven't happened in one hundred years and will never happen again. But for him They Happen. The psychologist who figures out a surefire test for the born loser may make a fortune—or get shot by a born loser who doesn't want to know he's in the club by birthright."

He had a name for the loser syndrome: the Tarini Effect. Giovanni Tarini was an eighteenth-century schnook from Genoa who bet ten ducats on the local lottery, which was like a parlay where your winnings on the first drawings go into the second, and so on for five drawings. After all the drawings, he emerges as the winner at odds of 44,000,000 to one. Naturally, they didn't have enough to pay him off—it would have bankrupted the whole city—so they did the only logical thing. They declared Tarini insane *for accepting such crazy odds*. Since he was crazy, his winnings were forfeited to the state.

How did he feel about some of the tricks of the promotion

trade? "What's wrong with them? Sure, I'm paid for plugs in tipster sheets. Never cash. Always stock or options. Why in hell should it be any of SECK's business if a market letter owner takes a payoff? What's he supposed to be: some kind of charity or something?"

PART II | *The Middlemen*

9. The Brokers

I do not regard a broker as a member of the human race.

—Honoré de Balzac

Is it not odd that the only generous person I ever knew, who had money to be generous with, should be a stockbroker?

—Percy Bysshe Shelley

The art of getting rich, wrote Ralph Waldo Emerson, who never mastered it, "consists not in industry, much less in saving, but in a better order, in timeliness, in being at the right spot."

Ever since, many men have agreed that one of the best spots, possibly *the* right spot (Rink's pessimism notwithstanding), is on the floor of the New York Stock Exchange. For the privilege of being able to get on the floor, some 1,366 carefully selected Americans have paid sums of up to $515,000 each. (And as little as $17,000 in badly timed 1942 when it was very difficult to get rich, even on the floor of the exchange.)

Members of the exchange have surprisingly few surface kudos: no initials after their names, no honorifics in front. Not many even rate *Who's Who*. And as everybody knows, they don't have seats. True, they alone of all of us have the right to walk the floor of the exchange to buy and sell any of the 3,500 traded stocks and bonds for others or for themselves and their partners, without paying sizable commissions. They also get the right to join the Stock Exchange Luncheon Club for $400 yearly dues. On their death, their widow or next of kin will receive a $20,000 gift from the exchange's Gratuity Fund. And a memorial service in Trinity Church.

At the end of 1970, after a severe market drop, the classic and potentially profitable privileges of exchange membership were undergoing snide scrutinies. Some members felt they were being hectored and lectured unduly by the Securities and Exchange Commission, which wanted them to cut their commissions. When a trade journal, *Institutional Investor*, ran a gloomy article, "Can the Stock Exchange Survive?," a few seat holders privately agreed that it couldn't. There *are* powerful, new forces that could kill the exchange. Computers, talking and bargaining with one another around the world, could probably match most of the buy and sell stock orders without human intervention, without the necessity of going through that fairly expensive tollgate, the exchange. Major institutions such as banks, insurance companies, and mutual funds—which paid out about $700,000,000 in brokerage commissions last year, some 27 percent of *all* buy-and-sell order commissions exchange members received—want the right to have membership so as to save most of this commission money. Instinet, a new computer service which matches buy and sell orders, had signed up thirty clients—mainly banks, insurance companies, mutual and pension funds—and at a cost of only one-third of stock exchange commissions. And, finally, the men on the stock exchange floor, the privileged 1,366, have lost much of the cachet they once had in the eyes of their less privileged partners, the upstairs partners, the allied members of the exchange. Floor partners are considered men who do as they're told, such as what to buy and, roughly, how much to pay.

None of this dismays Alexander E. Chapro, a short, sober, pragmatically cheerful member of the exchange who proudly wears his plastic badge, No. 980, as he walks swiftly—never running—from one trading post to another on the 33,000 feet of first-grade Michigan maple that makes up the physical floor of the exchange.

On the floor, Chapro is the very able representative of his firm, Cogan, Berlind, Weill & Levitt—a young group that started operating only ten years ago. In the 1969–70 fiscal year, Chapro bought and sold $700,000,000 worth of stocks and bonds on the floor of the exchange and thereby earned his firm $10,000,000 in commissions.

For his daily long-distance walking on the exchange floor —some pedometered floor brokers have clocked up to eighteen miles a day—and for his savvy in getting the best possible prices for his firm's customers on buy and sell orders, Chapro is well paid. He earns $55,000 a year, has the title of senior vice-president—one of seven—and has accumulated a $180,000 stake in the firm.

Chapro differs from his typical colleagues in several important respects. He's younger. The typical floor member today is forty-nine; Chapro is thirty-nine. Unlike many of them, he didn't attend a posh private school and one of the Ivy League colleges. And he's foreign-born. Exchange membership rules call for an applicant to be merely an American citizen who is at least twenty-one.

In some ways, Chapro is peculiarly adapted for the seventies, a decade another broker thinks will be "the most troubled years in exchange history." Chapro comes from a family that has successfully adapted to trouble and changing conditions in four countries.

He was born in Paris in 1933. His father, a fairly prosperous gasoline dealer, had been through a Nabokov-like hegira: prewar Russia, postwar Berlin, between-wars Paris, and then in 1939 came to New York, which the family didn't like. They moved to Beverly Hills.

At Stanford Alex majored in economics, graduating in 1951. After two years in the Army, he went on to get an MBA from the Columbia Graduate School of Business, graduating No. 2 in his class. Soon after marrying in 1959, he got a job as a trainee with a stock exchange firm, rising to registered rep, a salesman. He averaged about $8,000–$9,000 on commissions.

"I didn't like it. My wife's brother, who was the floor broker on the American Stock Exchange for a new firm, Carter, Berlind & Weill, was promoted to be their floor broker on the Big Board, the New York Stock Exchange. My wife persuaded me to try for the job he was leaving. All the partners interviewed me. I suppose I got the job because the other man they'd considered was too fat to get around the floor fast. The fact that I had a slight accent still, and sometimes lisped a little, didn't bother them.

"It was a whole new world. My brother-in-law took me around for two weeks to break me in. Volume on the Amex was low then—this was March, 1965—and I had lots of time to learn. In order to get the Amex seat I had to be an officer of the firm. I was made a vice-president and given a 1 percent partnership, which cost me $4,000. I was getting $12,000 a year, and my first summer I was buying and selling maybe 4,000–5,000 shares a day only. It was slow, but I loved it from the start."

The Amex is smaller and chummier than the Big Board, with its own customs and pranks. If you appeared on the floor with a frayed collar, some of the more sporting members might tear it off. ("A disgrace to the exchange!") On a rally following a market drop, those who had been selling short might find their underwear shorts yanked out above their trousers. ("Getting the shorts by the shorts.")

Meanwhile, his firm's floor broker on the Big Board, Richard Davimos, wanted to get off the floor. He had owned his own seat.

"The firm asked me if I wanted to move over. I was only a little reluctant," Chapro recalls.

His firm then bought a seat for $200,000, in what the exchange calls an ABC deal, under which a firm puts up most of the money for the seat to allow its floor partner to use it, even though his share of the purchase price is nominal. Since Chapro's interest in the firm was now 2 percent, he had, in effect, put up only $4,000 for the seat, although it is listed in his name.

Chapro had to go through the normal routine: He needed

two sponsors, underwent the usual rigorous personal investigation of his background and business dealings. These reports, made by a private firm, take two to three weeks and cost the exchange several hundred dollars each. And like all applicants, he underwent a thorough physical examination which cost him $50. The commonest diseases afflicting active floor brokers are hernias, varicose veins, and coronaries. He also had to pass a three-hour written test—which you can take three times, if necessary. Chapro did it nicely, the first time. Then he appeared before the Board of Governors, who questioned him for fifteen minutes, mainly about the percentage of the seat he owned and whether he required outside financing to raise it. He had not.

(Many applicants are turned down; a shady past, dubious commercial dealings, financial irregularities, even poor health might lead to a polite suggestion by the exchange's Membership Committee that the man should "withdraw his application.")

Once he was admitted to membership, Chapro again went through nearly a month of guided apprenticeship with Dick Davimos as his cicerone.

"It took getting used to. The trading floor was at least five times bigger than on the Amex. The noise level was much higher, the comings and goings more frantic. And the floor was much dirtier at the end of the day. Sure, I got kidded about my accent at first, but I guess I was lucky that the old horseplay days were over. A clerk would give you an order on a stock. Try as you would, you just can't seem to buy it. You get frantic and sweat bullets and then they tell you there's no such stock. It's a gag. And there used to be water pistol fights. No more. Thousand-dollar fines ended that. Very little horseplay now. Mostly, when a man is getting married, some broker will douse him on the floor with talcum powder or some cheap cologne."

In the twenties, the floor partner of the firm was usually the senior man. It was a proud job. Today, many firms call the floor partner "our mechanic," and he has little seniority.

"What happened," Chapro explains, "is that the floor became less important as the exchange relaxed a lot of rules. And at the same time, it became more and more important to have the senior partner back at the office to make vital decisions. Sure, if you're only doing an ordinary retail business, buying and selling 100- and 200-block shares for your firm's clients, I guess it *is* pretty mechanical. But my job here is to take care of the big blocks of stock—usually 5,000 shares and over—and there's nothing mechanical about that. On a block of 50,000 shares of a $40 stock, if you don't get the best possible price, if you miss it by a quarter of a point, your client is out $12,500."

Reinforcing Chapro's feeling that he isn't a mere "mechanic" on the floor is the fact that he is on the firm's policy committee, sitting in on all its major decisions. These meetings, which are deliberately held at 4:15 P.M., enable him to come uptown after the close of trading at 3:30 to the firm's very modern offices in the new General Motors Building on Fifth Avenue and Fifty-ninth Street.

As a new boy working for a comparatively young firm, Chapro was assigned rather remote working quarters in the U section of the floor, in a far corner, from which he could hardly see the tape. It was hot, in spite of the air conditioning.

His quarters consisted of three narrow, open booths for which his firm paid $2,200 annual rental. The three booths had a total width of 66 inches and they were manned by two company clerks. They handle the two teletype machines and the phones, each with eight buttons. On the teletypes, the main office sends in the buy and sell orders for Chapro to execute at any of the eighteen fortresslike trading posts that dot the exchange floor. Each handles about seventy-five stocks through the specialists assigned to these posts. When an order is teletyped to the floor, the clerk signals Chapro on the three huge annunciator boards by flashing his number, 980.* He then walks quickly—running is illegal and fined $1,000—in a kind

* Pocket-sized radio receivers which give off a beeping sound when the floor broker is wanted were introduced in August, 1971.

of heel-and-toe rocking rhythm back to the booth to get the order.

Sharing the immense 33,000-square-foot floor with Chapro on a busy day are another 2,000 men. About 1,000 to 1,100 are likely to be floor brokers like himself. Another 900 are clerks working for the specialists inside the trading posts, broker-clerks, exchange squad boys, and trading officials.

There are further distinctions among the floor brokers. About 370 of them, like Chapro, are on the floor representing their firms. Some 372 are specialists who make the market in several stocks. About 80 are odd-lot brokers who specialize in handling fewer than 100-share orders. Some 55 are registered traders who are buying stocks for their own accounts or for their partners. Another 95 are $2 brokers who are, in effect, free-lancers buying and selling for any member firm. (They used to get $2 commission for every 100 shares they traded, but that has since been raised to an average of $3.40 per 100.) These brokers are used by small firms that don't have enough trading volume to justify having their own full-time floor trader. And by member firms when their own regular floor trader is sick.

In August, 1970, Chapro's firm took over most of a major brokerage house in distress, Hayden, Stone. The takeover got Chapro better-located booths, since he was able to use the ones Hayden, Stone had occupied. In addition, he now has two other floor brokers working with him, but since they handle most of the regular retail business, Chapro is still in charge of buying and selling big blocks of stock on the floor.

His working day starts with a 6:30 rising at his $100,000 ranch-style home in northern Westchester. He usually breakfasts with his ten-year-old son while his wife is still asleep. He drives down in his Buick Riviera and parks in a garage near the Battery. He walks to the dismal New Street back entrance of the exchange, goes down a flight of stairs to the cloakroom. There he takes out his work shoes, a pair of black rubber-soled oxfords—Murray Space shoes and crepe soles are popular with the floor brokers—and an unlined, gray-checked summer jacket which carries his badge. He then rides up to the seventh floor Luncheon Club where he has iced coffee while he skims through the *Wall Street Journal*. By 9:30 he's on the floor checking with his clerks on what buy and sell orders are in hand before the exchange opening at 10 A.M.

Just *what* does he do? "An order came down on the teletype this morning. A client wanted to buy 5,000 shares of Southern Pacific (SX) at the market, at the current going price. I went to trading post 2 where the specialist handles the SX stock. I asked him, 'What is it?' and he said, 'An eighth to a quarter, 2 by 5,000,' which told me the key fractions, since I knew that it had closed at 30. He also told me that 200 shares were wanted and 5,000 was offered. I said in a firm and loud voice, 'A quarter for 5,000,' and he said, 'Sold.' He put my badge number, CBWL-980, in his book opposite the entry for the broker who had offered the 5,000 shares for sale. I made the notation on a floor report for the P&S (Purchase and Sales) Department.

"The transaction must be paid for in two days. Meanwhile, an exchange clerk at the scene made a notation on a prepunched IBM card. He put it into a reader which transmitted the information upstairs to a computer tied into the high-speed tape. In a couple of minutes the transaction will come across the tape all over the country like this: 5000 SX 30¼." This transaction took Chapro about two minutes, and with it he earned his firm about $1,500 or 1 percent of the total transaction.

The biggest deal he's had so far resulted when an institutional customer of the firm wanted to sell 1,000,000 Pan Am shares. As it happened, another CBWL customer wanted to buy 1,000,000 shares. It happens. Since his firm is pledged to transact all its dealings in Big Board shares through the exchange facilities, it could not be done by a simple exchange of stock certificates at an agreed-upon price in some quiet office.*

* Why don't more institutional investors make these trades off the floor of the exchange and save themselves considerable sums in commissions? For one thing, they may want to reward a clever broker for successful stock research. Or a bank might have an understanding with a broker: In exchange for the

Brokers naturally love these deals, which they call a "cross." For one thing, they get the buying *and* selling commissions and also a certain amount of street acclaim for really big crosses. But crosses have to be done with considerable expertise on the floor of the exchange to prevent other brokers with Pan Am stock from getting into the act.

"On these crosses you have to see if it's a quiet or an active stock that day. If it's quiet, as it was that day, the prudent thing is to go to the Pan Am trading post. The specialist tells me the stock is $7/8-1/8$ 2 & 2, which means that there are 200 shares offered to buy in at $29 7/8$ and 200 shares to sell at $30 1/8$. No sweat. I can easily allow both other parties into my deal. This is cooperation. I include the seller at $29 7/8$ and the buyer at $30 1/8$, and it takes only 400 shares off my million. Since the total amount involved was about $60,000,000 and our commission was between $250,000 and $275,000, it was a very small sacrifice." (When the deal runs over 100,000 shares, the exchange permits negotiation on the amount instead of the usual 1 percent. Recently, however, the SEC proposed that negotiation on commission be permitted on all transactions involving $100,000 worth of stock or more.)

But when the market in a stock is active, Chapro wouldn't dare invite "cooperation." He has to, in his words, "big ball it." On this occasion, after inquiring from the specialist how the market was and finding that the range was $29 7/8$ to $30 1/8$, he would have called out in a loud voice, "Seven-eighths for a million and an eighth sold!" As he was making the bid, any other floor broker there at the time could have broken up his cross by offering to buy or sell his own block of Pan Am stock at the prices Chapro mentioned. So far, Chapro hasn't been caught. "It's a very nervous few seconds when you big ball it. Sure, you make some brokers unhappy that they couldn't get in on it, but the first responsibility is to protect the interests of your customers, no one else."

---

large commissions paid, the broker agrees to keep a large sum, interest free, in a checking account at that bank.

There are other protocols and niceties to be observed if a broker is to earn the trust of the specialists and fellow brokers.

"A broker comes to me and says, 'I'm a seller of Continental Insurance, but stay out of Boston.' He's telling me he's anxious to sell a big block of the stock, but I shouldn't go to any banks or mutual funds in Boston to locate a buyer, or we might run into his seller. If I was a son of a bitch, I'd run to the phone and have the office try to smoke out the seller of the stock block in Boston and then find a buyer and we'd have the cross all for ourselves. I'd have gained a nice cross, but I'd have lost my reputation and that broker would never give me the time of day as long as I'm on the floor. And he'd spread the word around."

Chapro thinks that the recent brouhaha about the iniquities of the specialists, as detailed in the *Wall Street Jungle,* is "pure nonsense."

The specialist's job is to maintain a fair and orderly market in each stock he handles. When there is a disparity between demand and supply on a given stock, it's his function to buy and sell the stock for his own account so as to narrow the price changes between sales "and give depth to the market," as the NYSE officially puts it.

The job is a demanding one, calling for considerable capital and nerviness. There are times when he's called upon to take great risks, particularly in a falling market. Still, there are several specialists who are believed to net $5,000,000 or more in a good year.

"It's not a perfect system and we do have three or four outstandingly bad specialists out of the 372 on the floor," Chapro says. "They make poor markets: too much spread between bid and offered prices. They won't put you together with the buyer or seller, and they make it difficult for you to execute your order. They don't break the rules, but they're just not helpful. But apart from these few—and most brokers agree on who they are—the great majority are tremendously responsible men with a very high moral level."

Specialists have one minor advantage over other floor brokers.

Although there are no "seats" on the floor of the stock exchange—there were seats a century ago—specialists have at-
tached folding seats on the outside of their posts. These seats,
rather like the folding *strapontins* in French buses, are used
only when business is very slow.

On a typical day recently, Chapro bought and sold 90,000
shares of various stocks. It was a fairly easy day, and it gave
him time to run up to the seventh floor Luncheon Club for
a shrimp salad and iced coffee and a few cigarettes. (There's
no smoking permitted on the floor.)

Since things are a little slow on the floor—the rest of the
world is "upstairs" to brokers—he lingers at lunch, knowing
that he can hustle back to the floor in less than ninety seconds,
if needed.

Over another cigarette, he marvels at the level of democracy
on the floor. "There've never been racial or religious requirements for membership. We had a Negro broker for a while,
but the firm cut down when business fell off and he's no longer
on the floor. No women brokers, so far, although one or two
women own seats, I think."

In the all-male clubby atmosphere of the floor there is a
certain earthiness to the nicknames members give stocks. Pacific Southwest Airlines (PSA on the tape) is affectionately
known to floor traders as Pisser. Associated Spring Corporation
is ASS, and "How's your ASS today?" is a perfectly legitimate
question. Reading & Bates (RB), a high-flying stock that bounces
around a lot, is, inevitably, Rubber Balls. Simmons Company,
which makes mattresses, is better known as the World's Playground, and Continental Can is sometimes called Zsa Zsa
Gabor.

Chapro is proud that he hasn't missed a day of work since he
started with CBWL. "I go in with a cold; they're never bad.
And so far, thank God, no colitis, no ulcers, no varicose veins.
It's a good job to be young in, but there are men in their sixties running around the floor as vigorous as ever."

He sleeps well, but at the start of his job in early 1968
he had the same nightmare week after week: "I'm on the floor

and very busy. I have an order to buy 25,000 shares of a stock and somehow it seems to be taking forever and ever to get to the specialist's post. Suddenly, I look up at the tape on the wall and there I see that 50,000 shares of the stock I was supposed to buy had just been sold and I wasn't part of the action. I wake up in a sweat. But I don't have those nightmares anymore. I have more confidence after nearly three years on the floor. There must be about 200 brokers and specialists I know by name and face now. And I'm sure a lot of them know me, too. So far, I've not gotten into any feuds with any other brokers; I haven't called for any arbitration on disputed buy or sell orders and I haven't done any broker dirt."

There was a favorite comic colloquy Chapro had with foreign customers of his firm to whom he was introduced. "And you're the only member of the firm permitted on the floor?" they said. "Don't you get awfully tired running around so much?" "Sure," replied the 5-foot-5 Chapro. "When I joined the firm, I was 6-foot-2."

The seat Alex Chapro now holds originated on February 28, 1929, when the New York Stock Exchange decided to add 275 members. With seats then selling for $400,000, the exchange ruled each member would have one right to a new seat for which four rights would be required. In effect, the exchange had voted each existing seat holder a $100,000 bonus. He could buy three other rights and get another seat for his firm, or he could sell his right.

Walter John Rich, Jr., a twenty-nine-year-old college dropout, wanted and got a seat for $416,000. He kept it only sixteen months and sold it because of intense ulcers. Howard Filston, a twenty-seven-year-old Ohioan, picked it up for $260,000 representing a Midwest brokerage chain, which dissolved in 1933 when the seat was sold for $150,000. James A. Hogle, a mining engineer turned broker, acquired it, and it was sold after his death for $75,000. The new seat holder was Edward Gordon Hooker, a good-looking Ivy League WASP. His health started failing in 1966, and the seat was sold to Alex Chapro for $200,000. Hooker died a few months later.

Over the past forty years the Chapro seat incurred a loss on
its sales of $341,000, offset somewhat by the $125,000 Hooker's
estate profited. Along with losing money on their seat sales, the
prior holders also incurred a fair set of occupational diseases
such as severe ulcers and heart attacks. But with one exception
all of them *enjoyed* the experience of being active on the floor
of the exchange. And all made a good living while they held
their seats.

Technically, Francis Bartow Farr is just another stock salesman, a broker, a customer's man, a registered representative.
Now in mid-1971 there are 51,000 like him who work for the
571 member firms of the New York Stock Exchange that deal
with the public. But such statistical lumping is misleading as
well as slighting; in his own way, Farr is a rarity, and when he
left his firm recently, there was spirited bidding for him. I
first met him during the dread bear market of 1970.

Farr's earned income was then based solely on the commission he got when his customers bought or sold stock; and like
that of other registered representatives, his 1970 income was
cruelly cut to a third of what it was in 1969.

In some ways he and the other registered reps, the RR's,
were hit even worse than America's 31,000,000 stock owners,
who found that the stocks they bought a few years ago had
declined in 1970 about 30 percent on the average—even while
the cost of living had risen more than 11 percent.

In 1970, though choking waves of dismissal hit back-office
help in dozens of Wall Street firms and even partners took
substantial cuts, the firms kept most RR's, dispirited and dis-
tressed because they weren't on salary and all they cost the
firm was desk space and phone bills. And there were now
pressures in some firms: RR commissions were cut from a pre-
vailing one-third to 28 percent and some were even assessed
for their phone calls. As a result, vigorous unionization moves
were going on in several of the larger brokerage-firm branch
offices, particularly in Chicago and Detroit. Other RR's simply
dropped out.

Most of the larger firms spend several thousand dollars training their newer RR's. In many cases the new men were kept on salary for six months or even a year until their commission earnings caught up, so brokerage firms have a considerable investment in them. "When they start firing RR's," says a veteran Wall Streeter who also invests in plays, "the show is so bad you can't even paper the house."

What distinguished Francis Farr, a slender, russet-haired fifty-year-old, from the mass of dispirited stock salesmen in the 1969–70 bear market was that he was—and still is—a Very Big Producer. Until 1970, his annual income from commissions hadn't fallen below $225,000. In 1970 it dropped to only $75,000, so he still earned about seven times what the average RR made. In 1969, a typical RR averaged between $13,000 and $20,000.

Farr was always choosy about his clients. "I've always avoided customers who take too much of my time or like to spend a lot of time hanging around the office chewing the fat. Frankly, I'd rather my clients *never* came to the office. After a while, you develop an intuitive sense about the kind of client he's going to be."

Wall Street doesn't go in for the favorite life-insurance company device of saluting its top salesmen with serried photos and encomiums in full-page ads. The street doesn't broadcast the incomes of its star salesmen—would customers make sour comparisons?—but where it counts, the big producers are fairly well known. The best estimate is that Farr is one of perhaps twenty-five top-earning registered representatives.

For a man who gets along on a drawing account based solely on commission, Francis Farr has managed to live like the very rich. He and his third wife live in a traditional, comfortable eighteen-room duplex at 960 Fifth Avenue, with a domestic staff of three. His neighbors in this very social building include Douglas Dillon, the former Secretary of the Treasury, and Mrs. Joan Payson, owner of the Mets. The Farrs also have a much-photographed 2½-acre place in Southampton. He is chauffeured to Wall Street every morning, and until recently

his annual office phone bills—gladly paid by his employer—
used to run up to $18,000. He dresses unostentatiously, Ivy
Leaguish, in $325 double-breasted suits which he has been get-
ting from Sills since 1949, when he became an RR. He's in
the Social Register, belongs to the Racquet Club, and considers
himself a Nixon Republican.

Like the ancient Romans who used to display an empty
coffin at the wedding banquet to remind the joyous participants of the inevitable, Francis Farr lives with his own sober
realization that good fortune in Wall Street is never permanent. His own symbolic reminder is a crepe-hung figure 4.

"When I got into the business," he said recently, "I expected
that I would have to start almost all over again four times.
When the market breaks, all the big producers know they're
going to lose lots of good clients.

"Nineteen seventy was my third bad break, but I only
lost about 20 percent of my clients. I had some luck here: in
June, 1969, I got most of my European clients out of the market, and in the past few years my biggest domestic clients have
been banks, mutual funds, and insurance companies, and they
go into the market for different reasons. So although 1969–70
was a terrible market, what with stock values falling off about
$50 billion, I wasn't so bad off as I was on the previous two
breaks."

That is, as far as clients go. On his own stock holdings, he
remains determinedly uninformed. Farr has about $200,000
invested in the market, but it is handled for him by a friend,
an investment counselor who gets a small percentage for his
services.

"Our deal is he mustn't tell me what he's going to buy or sell
until well after. This business is tough enough without having
to live with market schizophrenia: me telling my clients I think
XYZ looks good and then finding out the same day that my
investment counselor is very bearish on XYZ. Right now I
don't know how my portfolio stands. I haven't talked with him
in a couple of months now. I'm sure it's come up as the 1971
market did. Maybe a bit better."

A few of Farr's clients in 1970 made a large amount by short selling, borrowing certain stocks for a small fee, and then replacing them in a few months when the stock had fallen still further.

"In a falling market you think more rich people would go in for short selling," Farr says, "but it just doesn't happen. About 75 percent of investors just don't feel comfortable with short selling. Maybe it goes against the national grain of optimism. Most of my short sellers were foreign clients."

Farr made no pretense of knowing how far the current debacle would carry the Dow-Jones averages when clients asked him during 1970. He'd tell them:

"All we can go on is past experience. When the move up gets under way, the first to benefit are the blue chips, then the cyclical stocks such as coppers, aluminums and meat packers, and then come the more speculative stocks."

But the past isn't always a very accurate guide for the future, and occasionally Farr thinks ahead to what he would do if business fell off even worse than it did in 1970. "If my income ever fell down to $25,000 or $30,000, I'd probably decide I'd had it as a registered rep," he says. "I'd probably go into public relations or something."

But even in '70 he could see this was a fleeting gloom. "Things *always* come back, and basically, I really like the business, always have. There's excitement and tension and a great kick when you are able to spot a good situation and get your people into it early."

He remembers the best deal he got his clients into. "Resorts International around 7, and it eventually went to 62 but I got them out around the high 40's." (It was around 7½ in June, 1971.)

His worst deal for clients was in 1962, when he put many into E. L. Bruce, a hardwood firm, at 30—partly because he had gotten to know Eddie Gilbert, its president. Gilbert became a client and through Farr—as well as four other brokers—bought great chunks of Celotex stock. What Farr and the other four brokers didn't know was that Eddie Gilbert was financing his purchases by illegally raiding the E. L. Bruce treasury for about $2,000,000. When Gilbert fled to Brazil in June, 1962, the Bruce stock fell to 15 and trading in it was suspended. When trading was reopened in November, 1962, the price was down to 8¾.

"I met Eddie Gilbert at a party," Farr recalls. "I sized him up as a very bright son of a bitch. But I liked him. Lots of guts."

Two years ago Francis Farr had a reminder of the Gilbert affair. Gilbert came out of federal prison at Danbury in April, 1969—after serving less than two years—and a few old friends planned a welcome-home party for him. One of them invited Farr. Reluctantly, he decided not to go.

A friend who *did* go thinks that Farr wouldn't because while he still liked Gilbert, he just didn't want a fresh reminder of how much his clients had lost in the stock.

Another unpleasant reminder of the period was that it was the only time Farr was ever called in by the Securities and Exchange Commission, which was then checking on Eddie Gilbert's many transactions. Farr was merely questioned about his stock purchases for Gilbert, but no RR likes to be called in by the SEC.

In the early sixties, the SEC began paying much closer attention to the temptations faced by registered representatives. Too many, the SEC found, didn't resist opportunities to take advantage of their clients.

The most obvious way is by "churning" an account. If your client has implicit trust in you or has left the choice of stocks solely up to your judgment—a discretionary account—the RR has great power. Since every buy and sell order he puts in for a discretionary account adds further commissions for him, the temptation to churn the account with numerous—and pointless—transactions is great.

Farr has always avoided taking discretionary accounts. He prefers to let his clients make the decision to buy or sell.

The other major temptation for an RR is to push some low-priced stock for a special fee from those wanting to get rid of a large block. Farr has had several of these overtures.

"On my level they're pretty subtle. I'm sure it's a much more naked proposition with a lot of other RR's. With me, it's generally a call from a medium-sized listed corporation. 'Why don't I come down and look at the firm?' Then comes the very discreet hint that they're prepared to make some mutually cooperative arrangement. What they mean, of course, is if I'd push their stock on my clients, they'd give me generous options on a large block of the stock at a low price. I stop the proposition cold just by saying: 'Sure, if you think you have something special worth looking at, I'd love to come down but I'd have to bring two of the firm's security analysts with me,' and they'd have to agree. That's the end of the proposition. They're prepared to fix an RR, but if they also have to get an okay from two tough analysts, they know the deal is dead."

To prevent RR's from engaging in such activities, as well as account churning, most New York Stock Exchange firms have created a new position on their staffs, the compliance officer. It's his job to police the RR's, as well as the firm's other activities that might bring it afoul of SEC rules.

Wall Streeters probably carry a disproportionate number of civilization's wound stripes. Farr bears his share; he had painful ulcers in 1949 and then again in 1959. Most weeks he gets a couple of bad headaches which last three to four hours each. One of his permanent desk adornments is a small bottle of Tylenol, an analgesic. And he almost never sleeps more than five hours a night. To help him get to sleep, he goes through two suspense books a week.

Unlike most of his friends and classmates in Princeton '43, Farr didn't really know what he wanted to do after the war. His class voted on the traditional superlatives: the handsomest, cleverest, wittiest, and so on. Farr was chosen as one of their three biggest "Party Boys." The party was interrupted by military service in the ETO, where Farr rose to captain in the artillery and was captured, briefly, in the Battle of the Bulge. After the war he married.

For three years he worked in his father's sugar brokerage firm, but by 1949 he realized that the line of succession put him too far behind. In all, 1949 was a tragic, yet decisive year for Francis Farr. His first wife died, leaving him with two small sons; he had his first ulcer attack; and he became a registered representative for Harris, Upham. They gave him six months of training and paid him a modest salary during the course.

He threw himself into his new job with great energy. But he is the first to admit that hard work alone isn't enough to get a man up into six-figure earnings as a stock salesman.

"Social connections are a big help here. I'm lucky in that I was born into the Social Register. You need connections if you're going to become a big producer; without them, you're almost surely doomed to being a small or medium producer. I can go into any office in New York and be well received— thanks to some connection or other. It's a big help."

Farr is quick to point out that most of his clients are *not* old school-tie connections from Kent and Princeton. Only 5 percent of his clients fit that category. He tells how he got one of his biggest customers.

"He was one of the richest men in Cuba before Castro. I called him cold. Maybe he knew our family name vaguely from sugar trading, but he didn't know me at all. Yet I got him as an important client just with that one phone call."

The 1956–57 period marked two crises for Farr. He had remarried in 1951 and was divorced in 1956. (His second wife's alimony is directly based on his earnings, so with his then-current sharp cut in commissions she was another of the millions of Americans directly affected by the bear market of 1969–70, even though they haven't any stocks or mutual funds.) His other crisis, in 1957, was the sharp market drop after the Soviets had launched their successful Sputnik. It was Farr's first major loss of clients.

"It was a terrible period," he recalls. "Your earnings fell off sharply and so did your clients. So you try to make new clients. Who can you get?" Smiling thinly and popping some favorite jujubes into his mouth. "Well, people have lost money during a downturn and naturally they look for scapegoats. The easiest one to find is your registered rep. It's the old story: If the client makes money, he attributes it to his sagacity. He loses—naturally it's the RR's advice that's to blame. Well, when a lot of other RR's get blamed, a certain number of key investors are looking for new RR's, and I try to get my percentage of them. Just as other RR's are trying to latch on to some of my clients who may be dissatisfied with me."

In 1960 he left Harris, Upham for McDonnell & Company. He was able to bring all his clients with him. At McDonnell, he got 35 percent of the 1 percent the firm received as its commissions for buying and selling stock. Other big producers were able to negotiate deals that gave them up to 40 percent, but Farr was given some unusual fringe benefits. McDonnell provided him wth a full-time assistant and an executive secretary and paid for *all* his phone bills, including overseas. Since these easily ran $15,000–$18,000 a year, it was a generous arrangement.

After the 1962 market crash, he lost many of his clients but again gained new ones. From 1963 to 1969 was his greatest earnings period, averaging about $225,000 a year. He had built up an important European clientele as well as a number of American jet setters, which meant that he usually started work at 8 A.M. and had breakfast at his desk. The first thing he'd do was place his transatlantic phone calls. On a typical day, he'd have four to ten such calls, during which he'd simply keep the important clients posted on how their stocks were doing and he'd occasionally recommend a stock. But usually they'd ask him.

"Many RR's usually have a batch of stocks to recommend," Farr says, "but I've always made it a policy to pick just one. I tell them I like A, not A, B, C, D or E."

In 1963, Farr remarried. Like himself, the new Mrs. Farr, the former Lydia Buhl Melhado, a divorcée, brought two sons to the new family. She is a granddaughter of the man who had shrewdly backed the Fisher brothers in their venture in autos and ended up as one of the largest stockholders in General Motors. As a result, Mrs. Farr is a multimillionairess. Her two sons, Peter and Christian Melhado, also have very large trust funds. Farr deliberately avoids handling the money of his step-sons or his wife, just as he refuses to make investment decisions on his own money.

In mid-1969, Farr got his first hint that McDonnell & Company was in great trouble. The firm, founded in 1905 mainly as a family investment business for one of the wealthiest and best-known U.S. Catholic families, was facing a major crisis. Not only had business fallen off, but the back office was in a hopeless muddle because of a computer failure. Worse still, the chief administrator of the firm, Sean McDonnell, died suddenly while jogging. He was thirty-three.

Farr had long been friendly with T. Murray McDonnell, who had been running the firm until 1966, when he decided to concentrate on selling. One of the firm's more important accounts was the Catholic Church.

"Murray called me in," Farr recalls, "and told me things were bad. He asked me not to leave them in the lurch. He thought they could work things out somehow. We had been good friends for years, and I decided to hang on, even though I had been getting quite a lot of flack from clients about serious errors the back office had made."

Later it was found that there were 4,000 errors in McDonnell's 47,000 customers' accounts, and dividends uncollected by the firm for its customers totaled nearly $900,000. Economies were introduced: Salesmen who weren't producing at least $50,000 in commissions were fired; the executive dining room was closed; upper-echelon executives took a pay cut; Farr lost an assistant; and many branch offices were closed.

"It was pretty sad all around," Farr recalls. "But I hung on. I'd had some very good years with them."

The end came on March 13, 1970, when the firm decided it would gradually close down because of insurmountable financial problems. But a month later, the SEC shut it down *permanently* for serious violations, including churning of accounts, making false and misleading statements to clients about some cheap, speculative stocks, and failing to keep accurate customer accounts. Farr wasn't involved in any of the charges.

Early in March, Francis Farr started getting offers. "All the firms asked me to name the draw I wanted, and one of them offered me a full partnership. But that would have meant I'd have to take a real pay cut. Anytime you become a partner in a down market, you lose. Of course, if you want to look ahead and take your chances on building up equity in the firm, a partnership isn't a bad deal, but it definitely means cutting current income."

He finally chose Jas. H. Oliphant & Company, a seventy-two-year-old firm known for its excellent research staff. "I wanted a small firm with good research. They have nine top-flight analysts here and five of them are partners in the firm." His arrangement called for a 40 percent commission on his clients' buy and sell orders. In addition, the firm paid the salary of his secretary whom he brought over from McDonnell.

There were adjustments to be made. "It's the first time I'm physically back in Wall Street. Life is more frantic down here. Unless I'm lunching with a client, I don't bother going out. I used to be able to walk to my uptown office, but now that's out, so I'm using a chauffeured limousine service that the firm pays for.

"The client situation is no different. Some of my private clients—about thirty-three pretty rich Americans and Europeans—have been sitting on the sidelines since I suggested they get out in June, 1969. Well, maybe that's too strong. The way I put it to them was that I no longer thought the odds were in their favor, so why play? And being a pretty intelligent bunch of investors, they knew I meant it was time to just sit and see what happens. Some didn't sit; they took nice flyers in Australian and Japanese stocks. But mostly now I concentrate on my institutional customers: banks, mutual funds and insurance companies."

The selling process for these clients is more intricate, more of a gamble, and potentially much more lucrative. Which is why so many ads in the *Wall Street Journal* are for "institutional sales specialists." An RR who can persuade a mutual fund to buy 100,000 shares of a medium-prices is, naturally, infinitely more valuable than an ordinary salesman who can persuade a Teaneck doctor to buy only 500 shares of some $10 stock, even if there are more doctors than mutual funds.

One of the Oliphant analysts, Ulysses Yannas, a black-haired Greek with a slight accent, had spent several expensive months studying the relative merits of Kodak and Polaroid. His conclusion was that Polaroid was a better buy at this time.

The start of the selling process was for Yannas to convince Francis Farr. "I had been in and out of both stocks over the years with my clients," Farr says, "and I knew them pretty well. I threw all the curves I could at Yannas because I was damn sure he'd get them during the presentations. Then when I felt he had all the answers, I lined up a series of meetings with many of my institutional clients."

One of the first was with a major and prestige-laden bank to which Farr had long had cordial entrée. "They had two of their senior analysts present, and a couple of their top investment people. I introduced Yannas and he took over for about ninety minutes. He's very bright, but that alone wouldn't impress anybody. What he had to do is come up with stuff about Polaroid they *didn't* know, and that isn't easy. He had facts about the new Polaroid wallet-size camera due out in late 1971 and a lot of details about their pilot plant for this new camera. He had spent months on this and even personally checked out hundreds of recent Polaroid patent applications. At the bank they listened carefully all the way and asked a few questions. Then we left. The next day I had a similar presentation to an insurance company. This time, they asked him dozens of questions, and he fielded them very well. My own hunch is that the insurance company will buy Polaroid; the bank is iffy."

The *benefits* to Farr here become a little tricky. "At this level there's a lot of indirection, a lot of waiting. For example, if the insurance company decides to buy Polaroid as a result of our presentation, they wouldn't necessarily call me and ask me to pick up 100,000 Polaroid, which would give me about $15,000 in commission. They could just as easily buy the Polaroid through someone else and instead ask us to buy 100,000

General Motors and with the order might come a little note, 'For your help during the past month.' We'd know exactly what it was for. And Oliphant would credit me with the commission."

Late on the afternoon following his bank presentation, he was stretched out, relaxing on a narrow bed in his study on the upstairs floor of the duplex apartment. He pointed to a picture of his two handsome, grown sons who are now twenty-one and twenty-four. He is a little sorry but not surprised they aren't at all interested in Wall Street. The older one, a Vietnam veteran, wants to be a rancher; the other, a recent NYU graduate, wants to go into journalism.

Reviewing his twenty-one years as a registered rep, with its three major bear markets, he became atypically introspective. He mused on what he would do if he could do it all over again.

"I think I'd go into a small manufacturing company and build it up. That would have given me a much greater sense of accomplishment. There isn't much of that in the street. Here you're just making money, which is okay when you can, but there should be more than that."

He thought a while. "Still, it's made me quite a lot of money, and there have been many satisfactions. A man could settle for a whole lot less."

In May, 1971, when the Dow-Jones was up to 932 and the terrible days of 1969–70 were almost forgotten, I looked in on Francis Farr again. Things were much brighter and he now expected his 1971 income to be somewhere in the $150,000–$200,000 range. He was almost glad that it wouldn't get up to the $225,000 he used to make in the great days of the sizzling sixties. "That was an outrageous sum; no reason at all why I should have been earning it. Why, it's more than a GM vice-president. I think I'd be downright uncomfortable going back to the old days."

The Oliphant firm's presentation on Polaroid had a considerable impact. For one thing Polaroid rose from 60 at the time to more than 100, while Kodak, which they had advised selling, went down to 51 and only recently had come up to 82. "We're now authorities in the photographic field. We're the firm that called the shots on Polaroid. In the long run that series of presentations is going to earn millions for Oliphant. For us."

He accepted a partnership offer in April, 1971. "My whole orientation is now toward the institutional client. Sure, 15 percent of my list are still private investors, many foreign, but they've been fairly inactive. Oliphant has turned into a great research firm, and the institutional clients value that. So now I spend most of my time making these presentations on stocks to banks, mutual funds and insurance companies. Right now we're pushing some airline stocks that we think are due for a good rise."

He thought many Wall Street firms wouldn't be around when the seventies ended, but he was sure Oliphant would be. "Hell, the stock exchange itself might not be here two years from now. But there's always a great place in the street for a research outfit that can call the shots correctly. That's where the big payoff is."

INTERLUDE

Miami, April 17, 1970

I was in Miami and Jerry invited me to drop in on his family at their apartment in Miami Beach. It's a large twenty-first-floor, two-bedroom apartment with an enormous L-shaped terrace. The style is adaptable Spanish, out of Barcelona.

Jerry's two sons are there, too. The younger one, Glen, is sixteen and a promising musician. The older, Gregory, has his fiancée, Diane, along. He's in City College, interested in becoming a songwriter. He makes one of the few references I've heard to the indictment hanging over Jerry's head. "One of my friends was kidding me about having to go visit my father in Atlanta." It didn't put anyone off, not even Jerry. I notice that Jerry almost never raises his voice or gets angry, which Phil does from time to time. (Phil would have exploded if anyone had pulled that kind of crack about him.)

Jerry explains: "The one thing I've always tried to do is to be honest with myself. I know what I am and what I do, and that's the way things are. I don't try to dress it up. Sure, there are occupational hazards here and you have to live with them." He tells me the story of another promoter he knows slightly. One day the man came home and found his wife raising a storm. Her father, who had made some accommodating deals for her promoter-husband, had just been served with a subpoena by the SEC. She yelled at her promoter-husband: "Listen, I don't need that kind of paper around here!" The promoter was unperturbed. "Look, honey, for $127,000 in a nice bundle, you get that kind of paper."

Jerry fills me in on one of their Vegas ventures. Together with Joe Arden, their special assistant, Jerry and Phil had worked out a system to beat the crap tables. They spent hundreds of hours at it, and it looked good. Finally, Joe Arden and Jerry went out to Vegas to try the system. Joe played twenty straight hours and had a minor breakdown—complete exhaustion. But the system didn't work; they lost $5,000. Later, in a postmortem by Phil, they found one curious item: On their trial runs with the dice they averaged a seven only once every six times, but in Vegas once every five times. How come? Phil asked. He's still suspicious. "Who's repealed the probability tables in Vegas?"

I asked if they'll ever go back to doing their own market letter. (I had momentarily forgotten the indictment hanging over Jerry's head.) "They wouldn't let me unless I can beat this rap, which doesn't look too possible. Anyway, market letters have had their day. Sure, there are some guys running it as ego satisfaction, and there are probably some who run it on the up and up; no payoffs, no zingers, no sendouts. Nothing. But today, fixing a market letter is the hard way of getting rid of 100,000 shares of Consolidated Moose Pasture, at $5 a share. There's a better way: unload the stuff on a friendly mutual fund. You have a fund manager making, say, $40,000 a year. You slip him $40,000—a year's salary—to take the crappy stock on his books and he can always explain that the stock was depressed and looked interesting. After all, no one expects *all* his buys to work out."

We talked about the first *known* case. In April, 1970, in Boston, Frank D. Mills, a former officer of the Boston-based group of Fidelity investment funds, pleaded guilty in U.S. District Court for taking a payoff in order to take a weak security into one of the mutual funds he was managing.

"It's happened dozens of times," Jerry said. "God knows how he got caught, poor bastard. There must be damn few fund managers who haven't received some kind of 'gratuity' to buy or sell a certain stock position. Sometimes, the manager may take in a pretty good but little-known stock and get a nice fee, anyway. The promoter figures that if this big fund takes in a big block of his stock, it's free advertising to the thirty thousand people who are holding that fund. It generates a kind of 'if it's good enough for them, it's good enough for me' kind of thinking."

There had also been, coincidentally, the first known case of an SEC employee indicted for utilizing inside information for his own benefit. Jerry was, naturally, scornful that it was the first.

"I know every SEC employee signs a statement that he won't buy or sell any stock he's working on for one year. But what's to prevent you from telling me to buy it for you, or do it through a bank in Canada, where it's fashionable to buy stock through a nominee's name so that it can't be traced?"

10. A Timely Tip for Colonel Wilson

The lie is a condition of life.

—FRIEDRICH NIETZSCHE

On a June night in 1970, Colonel Henry B. Wilson, USAF, retired, tells how he became the first American victim of a stock market tipster to recover his losses through a lawsuit.

Now fifty-four, Colonel Wilson has steel-gray hair and a spare 5-foot-9 frame. His salary from teaching elementary physics at Delaware Technology and Community College in Wilmington, plus his half-pay pension from the Air Force, enables him to live fairly comfortably with his wife and four children in a four-bedroom colonial in Newark, Delaware.

He was in the Air Force twenty-three years after getting out of West Point, Class of 1938. During the Second World War, he flew twenty-five missions as a bomber pilot before he was given ground duty—teaching Spanish at West Point.

Why twenty-five? "We usually had 4 percent losses in each flight, so they figured by twenty-five missions you were probably dead. If you weren't, it was time to let you live longer on the ground," he explains. "For us, Catch-25 was the lifesaver." After the war, he had various assignments, including running an Air Force base near Athens, Greece, and teaching Air Science and Tactics at St. Louis University. He knew that he was finished in the Air Force when they assigned him to recruiting duties. He took the hint and retired in February, 1961.

Some $10,000 had been saved from his service salary—he didn't marry until 1953—and he inherited another $20,000, so he decided to pay more attention to the stock market. He began subscribing to various market letters such as "Value Line," "United Business Service," "Spear's," "Investograph," and "Forbes Guide to Common Stock Profits."

He had been investing in the early forties, but mostly in General Motors. He did well and by 1960 had about $50,000 worth of stock in a margined account. He was then earning $975 a month as an Air Force colonel.

He was a fairly active trader and between 1955 and 1963 had 125 stock transactions involving some 40 different stocks. But 1961 was the deadliest year. From one of the market letters he got a tip on Avnet at 56, which was pretty high for a stock that had been as low as 12 the year before. He lost a great deal on Avnet, about $11,000. Then, on April 26, 1961, while reading the current issue of *Time* magazine, Wilson became fascinated by a one-column article in the business section. In it, he learned about a small over-the-counter firm called Technical Animations, Inc., of Long Island, which had developed a new industrial training system that animated still pictures by polarized light. The development—called Technamation—is a method of applying transparent plastics to still pictures so that they appear to move when ordinary light, projected through a revolving disk of polarized plastic, is thrown on them. Motion can be controlled so accurately that a Technamated cutaway drawing of a jet engine shows the fuel flowing in and burning, the turbines and gears turning, the gases rushing out the rear, all in the exact timing of a real engine.

The *Time* piece was filled with promise. The firm's sales, according to the article, had risen in five years from "$7,000 to $600,000 this year. The company went into the black this year, but is spending its small profits in research." They were developing methods so that the technique could even be applied to textbooks. Students would see, for example, how the blood actually moves through the body.

Colonel Wilson was impressed. The next morning he phoned his broker, Edwin C. Hogan, at the Merrill Lynch office in York, Pennsylvania, and ordered him to buy 900 shares of Technical Animations, over the counter. It was then selling for 13¾, a remarkable price level for a stock that had been selling for only 4¾ a month before. It rose to a high of 15½.

Somehow the magic seemed to have gone out of Technical Animations, and soon after his buy it started dropping steadily. By November, 1961, when it was down to 4½, he sold—for a loss of $8,625. Colonel Wilson didn't cancel his subscription to *Time,* but he was disgruntled.

Norman Poser was merely curious. In 1962 he was a bright, thirty-four-year-old lawyer working for the SEC. Harvard College and Harvard Law. Sharp. The SEC was then beginning a major study of some of the abuses in the securities market, particularly among OTC stocks. Poser, who is now vice-president of the American Stock Exchange in charge of compliance —the Amex's cop—recalled recently how he got interested in Colonel Wilson's loss.

"I had an idea in early 1962, when I was at the SEC: Let's look into the effect of publicity on these OTC stocks. So we gathered a lot of clips about OTC stocks and one of them was about Technical Animations. Let's do a study, I said, of the effect of publicity on this stock, which had a sharp rise in a brief time. So we started working backward. We looked in the pink sheets for the brokers who had been making a market in Technical Animations. We got lucky first time out; we went to a Big Board member firm, Wineman, Weiss, which cleared through E. F. Hutton & Company. My first thought was, we'd go to the customers who bought Technical Animations through them and sit down with them to find out why they bought the stock; perhaps, which piece of publicity influenced them most. That kind of thing. Well, we talked to a few purchasers of the stock, and all said it was the piece in *Time* magazine. Then, one morning I got an interesting idea. God knows where it came from. I said, let's check through the whole customer list of Wineman, Weiss & Company. Let's see what their customers do for a living. And about 10:30 that morning, we hit the jackpot. There was this lovely customer card showing that one of Wineman, Weiss's most active investors was a man who worked for *Time* magazine—as business editor. Joseph Purtell.

"Well, we had his trading account pulled out, and a number of interesting coincidences began emerging. This business editor would buy a stock of an OTC firm, not just 100 shares, either. Several hundred usually; sometimes 1,000 shares. A few days later, there'd be a nice write-up in the business section of *Time* magazine on the stock. Then a few days after that, the business editor would sell his stock, which had usually risen several points on the basis of the publicity *Time* had given the stock. We added up his trades, and, by God, he'd made himself a nice package; as closely as we could figure out, he made about $65,000 on these curious stock deals. Very nice.

"Now, he wasn't running a market letter with paid subscribers, and, of course, he wasn't a registered investment adviser with us, so there was no immediate cause for action on our part. But still, this was most interesting for the big SEC study, and we called him in for questioning."

When Purtell came to the New York offices of the SEC for questioning on August 28, 1962, Poser quickly discovered that Purtell was a *former* business editor of *Time*. He had been fired on May 3, 1961, "for unsatisfactory performance as head of the business section," according to *Time* publisher Bernhard M. Auer. In short, he was fired right after the issue containing the article on Technical Animations appeared, that of April 28, 1961.

"Between August, 1957, and April, 1961," stated the SEC report, which Norman Poser helped write, "Purtell had transactions in the securities of 64 companies, of which 27 were written up in the business news section of *Time*." The report continued:

In each of the 27 cases he purchased the stock a few days or a few weeks before the date of publication of the article concerning the particular company, and he usually sold the stock within a few days following the date of publication.

Most of the companies were small and little known, and Purtell made "considerable profit" trading in them, the report went on.

On Technical Animations, for example, Purtell bought 2,500 shares at 6⅛ to 6¾ through his favorite brokers, Wineman, Weiss, on April 13 after he had attended a demonstration of the company's polarized-light device. On April 18, he assigned a *Time* writer and researcher to the story. Benjamin Weiss, his broker, had told him about TA. Naturally, when Purtell bought, Weiss and four of his regular customers also joined in and bought some 6,000 shares between them. Meanwhile, word of the forthcoming *Time* story leaked out and salesmen in two other brokerage houses were spreading the word, so when the *Time* article appeared, the price had climbed to 9¼. Three days after the article was out, Weiss and his four customers sold off 4,700 shares at prices ranging up to 13¼. Purtell waited until May 4, when he sold 1,000 shares at 11⅝. He sold the remaining shares, 1,500, six months later at 5¼, so he had a small loss on this batch but an overall profit on TA. He made much more on some of his other stocks, which he had written about in the business section of *Time*—Barnes Engineering, Dynatherm, Grolier, Inc., Digitronics, Acoustica and Technical Operations. Benjamin Weiss also usually bought stock in these firms about the same time Purtell did. Purtell also passed the good word on to a friend of his, Fred Rosen, a prominent and prosperous New York public relations man.

Later in his questioning by Norman Poser, Purtell got a little indignant:

> *P:* My major investment during this period was not in these stocks you mentioned; it was in . . . Seeburg Corporation.

Q: Has *Time* magazine run any articles concerning Seeburg?

P: I think we mentioned them in passing. We may have done one a long time ago, years ago.

Q: Wasn't there one in the issue of October 27, 1958?

P: There may have been one.

Q: I show you a tear sheet from *Time* magazine . . . dated October 27, 1958. Did you sell any shares shortly after the article appeared?

P: I don't have a recollection of it. . . .

Q: If I tell you that you sold 500 shares of Seeburg on October 23rd, would that be in conformity with your own recollection?

P: No, I don't have a recollection of selling it, frankly.

Q: I show you a photostat of your brokerage account. . . .

Purtell finally admitted that maybe he had sold the 500 shares after the article appeared.

"He was a pretty evasive witness," Norman Poser recalls, "but we had the evidence and there was no way of squirming out of it."

Had any other staffers at *Time* played Purtell's marvelous selections?

"Yes, there was some evidence that a few others would invest, but they didn't get the tip from Purtell. They'd simply see a story in the business section scheduled for the next issue. Based on past performance—after all they were pretty sharp —they knew such stocks had a nice little run-up after publication. So they bought. We weren't concerned with them. And there was one really sharp character, we're convinced, who was one step ahead of everybody else up there. He not only bought and took a quick profit, but he also then went *short* on the *Time*-mentioned companies, acting on the assumption that after a couple of weeks the stock would fall back. As they usually did.

"Of course, *Time* management didn't know anything about this. It was embarrassing all around. The public relations on it was terrible for them. I think in June, 1961, they issued a confidential memo to their staffers, pointing out the impropriety of staff members of Time, Inc., owning stocks in which they are editorially involved."

The SEC also absolved Technical Animations. The firm hadn't solicited the publicity in *Time,* nor was it responsible for some of the misstatements as to its prospects. But the public relations man for TA, Harold A. Wolff, profited from the stock's run-up. Because he was incurring heavy medical bills at the time, he exercised his option on 1,800 shares of TA stock. He was doubly embarrassed. It appeared that he had been one of the main profit takers on the stock and yet he'd had nothing to do with getting *Time* and Purtell interested in his client, Technical Animations.

When the news of Purtell's shenanigans broke in April, 1963, following publication of the five-volume SEC report, it inevitably came to the attention of Colonel Wilson, who was then living in California, where he was getting a master's degree in business administration at San Francisco State College.

"I figured I had some kind of case here," Colonel Wilson recalled. "But I never used a lawyer, so I went to the Air Force Judge Advocate and he suggested a San Francisco firm. I went up, told them what happened, and they thought I had enough of a case to take it on a contingent fee basis—that is, they'd get nothing unless I won the case."

His lawyers filed the complaint on June 19, 1963, in the federal district court in San Francisco. In it, Colonel Wilson claimed damages of $18,000—his actual loss, plus exemplary damages of $10,000. In addition, his complaint said, since there were at least 300 other readers of *Time* who had bought the TA stock on the basis of the *Time* story, Colonel Wilson's lawyers were also suing in their behalf: their actual losses on the stock, plus $10,000 each. (This figure is a little murky. The SEC sent out a mail questionnaire to 160 purchasers of TA stock in 1961. Some 101 said the *Time* article was a determining factor in purchasing the stock.)

The suit, which was filed against Time, Inc., Benjamin Weiss, and Wineman, Weiss & Company, alleged that the defendants "employed a device, scheme and artifice to defraud; made untrue statements of material facts and omitted to state material facts in order to make statements made by them misleading." Then the complaint detailed what the misleading and untrue statements in the *Time* story were:

a) that sales of Technical Animations, Inc., "have risen in five years from $7,000 to $600,000 this year" when in actual fact sales of Technical Animations, Inc., for the year . . . totalled only $449,000. . . .

b) that T.A. "went into the black this year" when in actual fact the company incurred a loss for the year referred to and each and every year from the time of its incorporation.

c) that "one big selling feature of Technamation is its relatively low cost, e.g., the Air Force spent only $1200 to build a Technamated system for missile training . . ." when in actual fact no such Technamated system had been built by the Air Force or for the Air Force, and no such Technamated system had ever been built for only $1200.

Colonel Wilson himself unearthed that last item. In 1963 he went out to Sheppard Air Force Base where the TA system was supposed to be in use.

The case was quiet until March, 1964, when it was ordered transferred to the federal court in Manhattan at Colonel Wilson's request. By this time the San Francisco law firm had transferred the case to a young New York lawyer, Martin N. Leaf, a partner in a new firm, Leaf, Kurzman and Duell. Leaf, a tall, rather handsome young lawyer, talked about the case.

"I looked upon it as a strict liability situation, as far as *Time* magazine was concerned. They present themselves as a magazine of fact, and the article was shot through with major errors. *Time,* of course, was embarrassed by the case and I could see their position that they hadn't known of the business editor's extracurricular activities and I'm sure they didn't. Still, my client had been damaged and so had a lot of other readers of the magazine. Several other lawyers, representing some of these other victims, wrote me, but none of them followed up with suits. But you had to be realistic. If this got to trial, you had to be prepared for a long siege of appeals, and so on. In addition, Purtell, the real culprit, was kind of broke. He bought a Westport, Connecticut, paper, but it was now out of business. He was also unemployed. He also had a stroke. The Wineman, Weiss brokerage firm was out of business. So, when the *Time* lawyers started talking about a settlement, I was receptive."

On July 18, 1966, *Time* settled for a payment of $4,000 to Colonel Wilson. In 1969 Purtell settled his suit by paying $2,000 to the colonel. When he finished paying attorney Leaf, Colonel Wilson had a net recovery of $4,000.

While readily providing the details of the case, Colonel Wilson admitted he had hesitated at first because he was wondering if the publicity might not be embarrassing. "After all," he said, "I come out as a sucker. Somebody who read an article in *Time* and then went out and bought stock on the basis of that write-up." When it was pointed out that more than a hundred other *Time* readers had done the same, and that after all he had no way of knowing about Purtell's sideline operations, or that the article had certain key inaccuracies, Wilson said: "Well, I'm cured now. I haven't been back in the stock market since 1967. It's a little too tricky for me."

11.

Gimmicks, Techniques, Formulas—and Profits?

There are dozens of superstitions, surefire systems and silly syllogisms that are supposed to have made money for some people in the stock market. They are invented—or followed—by kinky kooks, frenzied fanatics, sober scholars, and they have persistence far beyond mere logic or proven profit. Some of them are:

- Never buy stocks on a Monday morning.
- Contrary Opinion: Observe the psychological status of the crowd and do the opposite.
- Don't buy airline, camera or TV manufacturer stocks in May; that's when they attain their seasonal high.
- Buy only stock warrants; they're cheaper and move faster.
- Chrysler and GM stocks always turn up in June, down in November.
- Buy only stocks that are rising on unusually high volume.
- December 15 is the great annual bargain day for stocks. More stocks seem to hit their all-year lows that day.

- Buy only convertible bonds; you get solid interest and a claim on the stock's future.
- Airline stocks go up in December, down in May.

All these have some degree of validity in some years and under certain circumstances; but this kind of knowledge alone isn't going to make you rich. One of the few certain ways to profit in the market is to find where the *bias* lies, where there are real price discrepancies you can exploit. The classic examples are provided by the Wall Street *arbitrageurs* who are happy with a profit of ¼ or ½ point on the price differences in a stock between New York and the Pacific Coast Exchange; between New York and London; between a convertible bond and its stock warrants. The best example comes from a kindred form of gambling, roulette. Its discoverer was a Scottish engineer named William Jaggers who gave Monte Carlo the only real nightmare it ever had. He carefully studied roulette wheel construction for months, looking for the bias, the weak points. Each wheel rested on a steel cylinder with a hollow upper end. A small metal pin fitted into this socket under the wheel. Jaggers realized that if this pin got worn, certain numbers would be favored because of the bias, the deviation. So he stationed men at every table to record winning numbers for five weeks. Then he found at one table that certain numbers were coming up oftener than others. He was now ready for his move. In just four days he made 2,500,000 francs, which would be like $2,500,000 today. The casino was scared white. At night, after closing, they got their croupiers to play Jaggers' favorite numbers—and they came out 50,000 francs ahead. So they switched the wheels around. But Jaggers had been expecting that. He had noticed that his favorite wheel had a little scratch on the brass handle. He found his wheel, played his numbers again, and won. They were ready to cut their throats. Finally, of course, another engineer beat Jaggers. He suggested they change the partitions around the little slots in the wheel. It worked. Jaggers knew they had beaten him, and he left Monte Carlo but he was still way ahead, maybe a 1,500,000 profit.

Finding the bias in Wall Street, the exploitable discrepancy, is much harder because every pro is looking for it, too. But occasionally an amateur from left field will come down the street with his own bias just at the right time—and clean up.

Jeb Wofford, for example, known in the sixties as Jeb, the Boy Bear.

Jeb's market exploits have been told in tantalizingly vague details in a thin little volume published in 1964. It was written by Elizabeth M. Fowler, a New York *Times* financial writer, and titled *Ninety Days to Fortune: How to Make Money in a Bear Market*.

The author introduces her hero, Jeb (for John Edward Brown) Wofford, thus:

> Although Jeb made a small fortune in Wall Street, he was strictly an amateur, which makes his successful career more astonishing. . . . He is the son of a cavalry colonel . . . who devoted most of his time and money to competitive riding. Jeb became an excellent rider, so good that he won a place on the U.S. Olympic equestrian team in 1952. He might have been a member of subsequent teams except for fights with officialdom. . . .
>
> Like a young and modern Don Quixote who enjoys crusading on his own, Jeb Wofford later decided to make a foray into Wall Street. . . . A wealthy young man in his early thirties who did not need to work and did not like the confinement of an office, he had nonetheless the self-discipline, the determination, and the grit that comes with being an expert rider. He applied these characteristics to his study of the stock market. . . .

Jeb made his "small fortune" in 1962–63 by buying "puts," or sell options. Puts and calls are the market's insurance premiums. And like much high-risk insurance, the premiums aren't cheap, usually running about 10 percent of the share value, for which the purchaser is granted the option to buy or sell the stock at a later date at the present price. Still, they serve a useful function. Puts and calls are sold by any one of several members of the Put and Call Brokers and Dealers Association of New York. *They* always make money.

(A profitable but complicated business, puts and calls. The late Herbert Filer, a prominent dealer, once told MIT Professor Paul Samuelson, one of our great economists, that Samuelson would "never understand the put and call business; it takes a European kind of mind to do so.")

In a 1961 survey of the put and call market, the SEC found that the public paid $1,500,000 for calls on some 361,000 shares of leading stocks in June, 1959. On this, the public lost $647,000. But a small group of these option buyers made a 150 percent profit. The SEC concluded that "most persons bought options for the opportunity it afforded them for speculation on a small amount of capital."

Through puts and calls, you can bet your hunches and pay only 10 percent of the stock's price for the privilege. The 10 percent goes in part to the put and call broker and part to the stock owner who is willing, for a variety of reasons, to rent out his 100 shares of stock for a fat premium. Since put and call option buyers guess wrong most of the time, the stock owners don't stand to lose very often. Still, it happens.

Convinced in early 1962 that the market was headed down, Jeb began buying puts on leading stocks. In a typical deal, he bought a put on Xerox on April 16, 1962, paying a premium of $1,148 for the right to sell 100 shares of Xerox at the then price of 154 through June 4. The market broke on May 28, but he waited until the afternoon of June 4 to sell at 106. He made a net profit of nearly $3,000, or more than double the money he had risked.

Puts, or sell options, are worthwhile only if the price of the stock is going to drop *considerably*. For example, on the Xerox trade the price had to drop more than 121½ points for it to be worthwhile for Jeb. His premium on each share was $11.48, plus another point to cover brokerage commissions and taxes.

He did much better on 20 put options, covering 2,000 shares of IBM. He spent about $31,000 for these options, and his net profit on them, after IBM dropped from 550 down to 300, the year's low, was $63,000. He also bought puts on Radio, U.S. Steel, American Motors, American Viscose, Zenith, and a dozen others. He lost on three; the stocks didn't drop enough to clear his put costs. And he made his money in about ninety days, hence Miss Fowler's book title.

How much had he made? There was some understandable vagueness:

> Wofford, who kept his records informally on scraps of paper, did say modestly that his gain probably amounted "to several hundred thousand dollars." But because of his future income tax considerations he said his lawyer would not let him say much more.

There were also other losses on gold stocks. Again, a certain vagueness:

> He bought a large number of calls—the opposite of puts—on stocks in gold producing companies. Some Wall Street firms have been advising clients for many years to invest some money as a hedge in gold stocks just because the U.S. might someday devalue the dollar. . . . With that in mind he acquired "calls" on gold stocks, believing that they would surely rise in the Fall of 1962. Unfortunately some of his "golden eggs" got cracked by economic developments . . . so Wofford lost on his gold calls.

Miss Fowler hadn't seen Wofford for years; a few put and call dealers remembered the Boy Bear, who used to come down to their shops to bargain on puts, in his sports jacket, open shirt and sneakers, but had no idea where he was now, although one of them said: "I think he went nuts."

Then one day a current clue turned him up. Wofford had been living in Eastchester under a nurse's care. In late 1970 I met John Edward Brown Wofford, the Boy Bear, now approaching his fortieth birthday, to hear about his stock market adventure and its aftermath.

He is 6 feet tall and has the husky, unlined face of a lad

half his age. He's wearing a blue sweater, yellow shirt and tan jeans. His green eyes look out at you in boyish wonder.

"When I was twenty-one, I came into money. My grandpa, Warren Brown, was very generous; in fact, he gave away most of his money before he died. Primarily, to my mother and my aunt, but also to his six grandchildren, including my brothers and sisters. At one time, my grandfather was the largest single stockholder in the Santa Fe Railroad.

"My net worth was around a million, plus a lot more money in trust for me. I came into it in 1966; I now get an income from the trusts amounting to $90,000 a year. The trust income is spasmodic; some years over $100,000, and some years less. I can dip into capital if I want to.

"When I study something, I do it very thoroughly. I became friendly with John Magee about 1960. [Magee, a well-known stock market technician, publishes "The Stock Advisory Service," for which he gets $500 a year.] I visited him in Springfield, Massachusetts, and got interested in puts and calls. I read a lot of books on the subject. I retain nearly all I read. Price-earnings ratios were getting high in late 1961, and I decided to go to New York for a little speculating. I'd visit the put and call dealers and get friendly. Because most people are bullish in outlook, they can sell calls easily. But a put is generally sold at a discount because there's less demand.

"Wall Street, as you know, has many different social levels. On the top are the investment banking firms like Morgan Stanley, and the put and call dealers are near the bottom. I'd come by at 9 A.M., wearing a sport shirt, old slacks and brown-suede shoes, and a lot of them thought I was some kind of nut. I wasn't trying to impress anybody. I was picking up a lot of put options, and before long, I was millions of dollars short in terms of the value of the puts I bought. From January, 1962, on, I was throwing around large chunks of money. I started closing out my positions around June, 1962, and I was pretty lucky. Just hit most of them right.

"I went to Switzerland during that period and traded there, too, to keep up secrecy and not let too many people know what

I was doing. I didn't want to drive up the price for puts. I kept large accounts there, for which I still haven't received a complete accounting. I've narrowed it down to three banks, and I'm going over soon to settle things."

What was he worth now? He gave several different answers. At one point, he thought perhaps $8,000,000–$10,000,000. Then again, he said he was pretty sure it was "in excess of a million." Then, "I've got $200,000. I've applied for a seat on the exchange, and that's what I was going to buy a seat with. I'd still have $50,000 left over."

His troubles really started, he continued, because he got involved in an over-the-counter stock called International Photocopy. He was to ante up $50,000. He did. Then he started studying the figures again and got suspicious. He felt the figures were faked.

"I finally confronted them and laid it on the line: I wanted my money back. They gave it back to me, but I wrote a letter to the SEC about International Photocopy, and the Attorney General's office, and the New York Stock Exchange—and they all ignored me. I received some threats from underworld figures in Chicago who were involved. I got phone threats to stop contacting the SEC or I'd be taken care of. Their attitude was: We paid you off, now shut up. I went back home to Kansas and I was probably a little upset. I told a friend, an attorney, the whole story, and he didn't believe it. He contacted my mother and he drew up the papers by which I'd be admitted to a hospital."

As it happened, there was an easy way to check Jeb's story on International Photocopy. A Chicago lawyer, Arnold I. Shure, who's won some notable victories in securities cases, had cleaned up on a big case against two Chicago firms that had underwritten International Photocopy convertible debentures. In November, 1968, Shure got a settlement of $350,000 for his client, Clifford H. Jordan, of Cedar Rapids, Iowa, who had invested in IPC. Jordan claimed that the two investment houses had misrepresented many key items in selling him the debentures. Also, the firm was really bankrupt when he was persuaded to invest in it. At the time he was battling the case, Shure recalled, he had heard that a young fellow named Wofford had invested in IPC, learned the facts, and demanded his money back. Shure tracked down Wofford in the mid-sixties, when Jeb was in a Colorado hospital, and corroborated the story.

How much did Jeb actually make in that 1962–63 trading period in New York? John Scofield of Detroit, Wofford's lawyer and family friend, says: "I had to call in accountants, Arthur Andersen & Company, to go through all the trades, all the slips to prepare Jeb's income taxes. The papers are now in storage, but as I recall them, he made no more than $50,000 at the outside. He made a lot of smart moves but also a lot of awful ones. He's probably told you about his Swiss bank operations. I think it's all fantasy. I have a list of every broker he did business with, and there was absolutely no Swiss or foreign trading at all."

Jeb called a few days later to ask me to write to "my friend in Zurich [Bluntschli]" to help him when Jeb got there to look for his trading accounts. After weighing the pros and cons, I wrote a careful letter to Bluntschli providing Jeb's background.

Early in November, 1970, Jeb flew to Zurich but had a lot of trouble with customs. He had hundreds of vitamin and health-food pills and they gave him a hard time. Later in the month he met me at the Biltmore in New York to fill me in:

"I saw your friend and he was as helpful as he could be. But I just couldn't remember what banks I had dealt with. After all, I really went to Switzerland on a hunch only. Now I doubt that there is any money of mine there. You know, I think I may have signed an authorization while I was in the hospital in Colorado enabling them to get at my bank accounts all over. Maybe they did."

A few days later Bluntschli wrote:

Your friend was here, but impressions gathered by myself and competent people higher up thought not very much of him. Not a dangerous phony, but a lot of imagination. His only *real* concern and attempt was to find out how one can trade on margin, and what the most favorable conditions would be. He was directed by my legal people to the Swiss Banking Association, and on my request got an introduction there. He never showed up.

In the fall of 1967 a book called *Beat the Market* got on the best-seller list. Besides a great title, it had the advantage of solid academic imprimatur; it had been written by two university professors, Sheen T. Kassouf, an assistant professor of econometrics at the University of California at Irvine, and Edward O. Thorp, who teaches mathematics there.

Thorp was far better known. A few years before, he had become a fleeting American legend with a book called *Beat the Dealer*. It gave a detailed program for beating the blackjack tables at Las Vegas and called for memorizing all the high and picture cards played. The casinos at Vegas got around that quickly by giving the dealer three decks, instead of one, to play with. Memorization soon became a feat strictly for Mr. Memory only. But Thorp was widely publicized and made more than $100,000 with his book.

Sheen Kassouf met me in his office at the new Irvine campus in California. He is short, bespectacled, thin, informal, and has a lively sense of humor. Born in New York—his parents are Lebanese—he went to Columbia College and got his doctorate there, too, in 1965. He went to college on the GI Bill, having served in the Army until 1952. While he was in college, he built up a technical illustration business which at its peak had twenty-five employees. He sold the firm to one of his four brothers in 1964.

"I did undergraduate work in math and got interested in the stock market. I went through in three years, even while working nights and weekends on my technical illustration business. And I got married in my junior year. By the time I was in graduate school I was earning $25,000 a year from the business. I got my PhD in three years, which they tell me is kind of fast. In the winter of 1961–62, I was tired and I took my family to

Phoenix for a rest. I just had one son then. Have two now. But I could only rest so much and I started visiting local board rooms. Up to then I'd lost the standard $1,000 that every red-blooded American is supposed to lose in the market before he's thirty. I began getting real interested in the market. But I also realized what I really wanted to do was teach economics. I was writing my thesis in 1964 when I met the dean of social studies at the new Irvine campus and he offered me a job. I finished my thesis and came out here."

He met his future co-author, Edward O. Thorp, during a faculty committee meeting. Thorp had mentioned to the dean that he was now interested in the stock market. The dean knew Kassouf was also interested.

"We got together and I told him that I had done my doctorate on evaluating stock warrants. I had worked out a hedge method that gave me 25 percent a year on my investment by going short on the securities and long, via margin accounts, on the warrants of the stock. I wasn't keeping it secret or anything. My thesis had been published and lots of people ordered it. I told many brokers about my system, but most of them ignored me because it seemed complicated. Maybe it is, a little. But I knew it worked. I had made about $100,000 in five years using it.

"But Thorp grasped it right away. He's a big, husky fellow, about thirty-seven, and when he gets enthusiastic, he almost bubbles over. He said we *had* to do a book together. After all, he'd had a best seller in *Beat the Dealer* and he was sure we could get a big advance. He sat down and wrote a one-page outline of my system and sent it on to his publisher, Random House. Naturally the title was going to be *Beat the Market*. I demurred a little, I think, but he's bigger and far more experienced in the book business and I went along. A couple of weeks later we get a check for $50,000 as advance on the book. I was bowled over. Boy!"

They spent a summer writing the book. "It was a mistake," Kassouf said. "Temperamentally we were just too far apart. I should stick to academic publications only. You're not supposed to be jumping up and down in my business."

The book's straightforward introduction set the tone:

> We present here a method by which investors can consistently make large profits. We have used this method in the market for the past five years to earn 25% a year. We have made profits during two of the sharpest stock market drops of this century. . . .
> We have used mathematics, economics and electronic computers to prove and perfect our theory. After reading dozens of books investigating advisory services and mutual funds, and trying and rejecting scores of systems, we believe that ours is the first scientifically proven method for consistent stock market profits. . . .
> This book analyzes convertible securities and their associated common stock . . . more than 300 of the 3500 securities traded on the New York and American Exchanges are convertibles. . . . We predict and analyze the price relationships which exist between convertible securities (warrants, convertible bonds, convertible preferreds, puts and calls) and their common stock. This allows us to forecast future price relationships and profits. We do not need to predict prices of individual securities in order to win. . . .

But Random House wasn't happy with the manuscript. "They said all kinds of things. Misrepresentation. It wasn't the way to beat the market they expected from the outline. They said it was too complicated. You had to be a math wizard. It wasn't for the ordinary investor and so on. Maybe they were right. As it turned out most people *didn't* understand the book. It is not easy and so not too many readers really followed it."

Random House published it, however, and it sold fifty thousand copies.

"We became overnight celebrities locally," Kassouf recalls. "Radio, TV, interviews, the works. I got about three hundred letters from readers, most of whom seemed to be engineers and scientists. All of them had been trying to develop their own formulas for beating the market. Most of the letter writers wanted me either to manage their money using the formula I had developed or to do a market letter to keep them informed on current opportunities in hedging convertibles and warrants against the common stock.

"I thought of a market letter, but it sounded like a bore to me. Too much of a discipline. Then Thorp and I had this disagreement. Temperamental differences, you might say." He preferred not to talk about it.

But he had no objection to talking about the stock market in general. "It's the last great frontier for anybody who thinks he's got it. Naturally I think I've got it. When I was younger, I wanted applause. You know, I used to go around and spend hours expounding my system free of charge to brokers and investors. Just to get a glimmer of recognition, which is what you want so badly when you're younger. Okay, now I'm older and more cynical. I'll just take the profits, thank you."

He thought there must be, right now, thousands of intelligent Americans who were spending all their spare time to figure out a formula for beating the stock market.

"They're going to waste a lot of time on technical analyses and chart reading as I did. I once tested a few chartists. I selected pages at random from a chart book, covered the name of the corporation and the last half of the chart, and asked what price change the 'pattern' indicated. Hell, they could just as well have been making random guesses. The fundamentalists are no better. It's almost impossible to estimate a stock's earnings for more than a year or two in the future. The only times I lost money in the market were when I strictly followed fundamentals."

Later it emerged that one of the reasons Kassouf was somewhat sensitive about *Beat the Market*, in addition to the fact that he had a falling-out with his co-author, Thorp, was that the book got a devasting review in the *Journal of the American Statistical Association*. Worse, the review was written by the great man himself, Professor Paul Samuelson of MIT, our first Nobel Prize winner in economics. "It was like," a faculty colleague of Kassouf's put it, "a humble parish priest being slapped down by the Pope for heresy and God knows what."

Kassouf smiled in recall. "It was one of those things you get in academic life. It passes. But Thorp went livid, I'm told, when the review appeared."

What also enabled Kassouf to take the damning review in stride was the certainty he had a winner in his system. "I was" —he laughed—"sitting like the man in that great line of Mark Twain's: 'The calm confidence of a Christian with four aces.' I had a system that worked, so naturally I started a small hedge fund to exploit it for myself, members of my family and friends. Maybe twenty-five–thirty people in it. We started January 1, 1968, with $400,000, and we now [early 1971] have $1,030,000 but then we also took in another $400,000 in new money, so it wasn't all profit. I manage the fund. It's a typical hedge fund operation and I get 20 percent of the profits. The last two and a half years weren't spectacular, frankly. In fact we only made 4 percent, but in a mutual fund they'd have lost. I think there are only five other funds that did as well or better. Yes, I know I talked in the book about making a conservative 25 percent a year on money invested in the method. Only I made some tremendous errors in judgment, so we didn't do better than 3 percent a year. In October, 1969, I figured we were due for an upside market and we didn't get it. I was wrong. Worse, I was greedy; I wanted my 25 percent, so I ended up getting almost nothing. We're still testing new strategies and trying to improve the method."

Testing? Improving? Wasn't there any *surefire* method of making money in the market? Kassouf laughed. "There is one, if you don't mind being a little crooked. I heard this story several times but could never check it out. But it has the ring of truth.

"Apparently there was this sharp bunch in Rhode Island. They brought out a newsletter unlike any ever seen before; unknown to its readers, it had two editions. One version urged buying of four hot stocks. The other edition naturally urged short selling of those same stocks. As it turned out, the short selling was great and they had a very devoted group of readers. Human nature being what it is, they didn't even lose all of the readers of the edition that advised *buying* these stocks. But now they concentrated on the ones who had gotten their solid short-sale advice. Again they broke this group up in two. One-half got short selling advice on another group of stocks; the other half were advised to buy the same stocks. The stocks went up, and now there was a group, perhaps 25 percent of the original subscribers, they started out with who believed, with good reason, that this market letter could do no wrong. Hell, they'd been right on target twice *with no equivocation.* And now the Rhode Island group prepared its final coup. They had gotten control of this nearly worthless stock, and now they pushed it in the letter; and since they had fantastically devoted readers, they got rid of the stock and made themselves maybe a million bucks. That was the end of the operation, of course. Try to check it out at the SEC, if you can."

A few people at the SEC in Washington had heard the story, too, but they thought it was one of those legendary accretions of Wall Street.

One of the most successful of the find-the-bias technique users is another academic type named Harry Markowitz. I'd been told by analysts in London and economists in New York that I must talk to him.

Markowitz is about 6 feet 2, fairly bald, with wide graying sideburns, and is developing a little pot. At forty-four he is one of the most respected, most quoted figures in the world of scholarly analysis of the stock market. His one book, *Portfolio Selection: Efficient Diversification of Investments,* published in 1959 has given him an international reputation. The bibliography on the book has long passed one thousand items, which means that many other academic types and financial analysts have spent many hours writing and talking about Harry Markowitz's book. And mostly they said nice, even warmly admiring things about it. To rate that with your first scholarly book is an extraordinary achievement, comparable to the high school runner who first time out breaks a four-minute mile—and has lots of witnesses.

Markowitz grew up in Chicago, the only child of a neighborhood grocer, and went to the University of Chicago in 1945. In high school he fell in love with a pretty sophomore of a Norwegian-English family. "She wasn't Jewish of course, but my family took it pretty well. So I got married at eighteen while I was still an undergraduate. She quit school and worked. We had two children, the first one born in 1949. He's now in college and sells life insurance on the side. Our second was born in 1951. We got divorced in 1960, and she lives out in L.A. She's remarried twice. Me, too.

"At Chicago I worked mostly in the Economics Department while I was doing my graduate work. I had a part-time job with the Cowles Commission, which was then headquartered out there, and then for the Rand Corporation from 1951 to 1958. Oh, I was doing Air Force systems analysis, input-output stuff. While I was with the Cowles group, I started getting interested in stock selection but approaching it from left field. I had been interested in matrix algebra and game theory. So I worked out a theory for finding the better among correlated risks. What combination of bets is the *best* combination—compared to their risks? What it was getting at, of course, was how the investment manager gets a portfolio of minimum risk and maximum profit possibilities."

In 1954–55, when it was time to do his doctoral thesis, Markowitz scouted around for a dissertation topic and then remembered his work for the Cowles Commission.

"I did the thesis in nine months. This whole area of 'behavior under uncertainty' was fascinating me. What's more uncertain than the stock market or an investment adviser trying to put together a package of stocks? How many does he have to put together to reduce his risk to a minimum, assuming a certain level of return on the money invested? I'll give you an analogy because the math is a little recondite.

"Let's say we're placing bets on a dart board. Every time you hit a wedge on the board you turn up ten numbers. Now you're throwing more than one dart, making more than one bet. How do you diversify your bets to minimize risk, considering the random numbers in each wedge? Well, what I finally concluded is that by investing equally among ten to twenty different risks, you've reduced your risk as far as you can. What I had worked out was a precise mathematical procedure that any portfolio manager could apply.

"Comes my thesis defense and I ran into some flack. Professor Milton Friedman said what was this? It wasn't economics or business administration or mathematics or literature. What are we giving Markowitz a doctorate *for?* Well, he was just sounding off as they do at these thesis defense sessions. When it was over, Dr. Marshak came out and said, 'Congratulations, *Dr.* Markowitz,' and that's how I became a full-fledged academic type. Even before I wrote the thesis, I had done a paper on my portfolio selection scheme for the *Journal of Finance* back in 1952, and it aroused a lot of comment. Finally, the thesis itself got printed by Wiley in 1959 and became a kind of best seller in the field. But I still wasn't thinking hard of the stock market as an occupation for an academic type. Meanwhile I had gotten interested in computer programming and theory and software. After my spell with Rand I went to GE in 1958, doing simulation work in New York. Mostly, I showed them how to use simulation on computers to help solve manufacturing problems. I was making $20,000 a year and living with my first wife up in Tarrytown."

He left GE in 1960 to go back to the Rand Corporation. There he developed a new computer language, Simscript, which has since become a standard simulating language. It makes possible much simpler communication with the computer, thus enormously reducing programming time. He left Rand in 1962 to go into his own business.

"There was another computer man, Herb Kerr. We each put in $1,000, and we created California Analysis Centers, Inc. Computer software mostly using my Simscript approach. We grew fast, and then in August, 1968, we went public. I was drawing $30,000 a year, but there were problems between Herb and myself. He and another officer in the firm had 52 percent of the stock between them and suddenly one day they fired me, the chairman and technical director of the firm. I sold most of my 300,000 shares in a public offering and I got $700,000. Good time to get out, I guess. The stock is now a buck a share, I think.

"Other big events of 1968. I got divorced again. Problems. She had two children by her previous marriage and we adopted them. Then we adopted another. Do only children like me overcompensate?"

While he was doing some consulting in Los Angeles, he was approached by John Shelton of the UCLA Finance Department to teach.

"The offer of a full professorship at the Graduate School of Business Administration was great. The teaching was enjoyable, but the committee work was getting me down. Then while I was getting a little restless, Shelton asked me if I'd be interested in joining him and a financier named Michael Goodkind who had put together the Arbitrage Management Company. I'd be the portfolio manager and get a piece of the action. While I was at it, I developed our present methods of convertible bond hedging. I also put some of my own money in the hedge fund. I quit UCLA to give the fund full time. By now I decided I wanted to get back in computer software and I was ready to move back to New York to raise money for a new venture. Then a New York Big Board firm, Mack, Bushnell & Edelman, bought the little hedge fund we had—maybe $1,000,-000 in it—and they asked me to run it for them. So I came to New York in October, 1970, with my third wife, Barbara, and her two children."

He talked a little about the mistakes he made investing his own money. "When I got the $700,000 on the stock sale, I put a lot of money in several hot no-load mutual funds, Gibraltar, Neuwirth, Ivy. But I came in at the wrong time and got clipped badly. I then moved over to fundamental research and listened to a few brokers and took their advice. In all the experience cost me $100,000. Now I have my money in the Arbitrage Management Company, some unimproved land in California, and some capital venture deals. Meanwhile, I'm starting something called Harry Markowitz and Associates. I've developed another computer language—this time for building simpler storage and retrieval systems for computers. We're raising $750,000 privately."

He returned to the hedge fund.

"It's a pretty simple operation, thanks to the computer. We buy the convertible bond of the selected corporation and short its stock. There are no great profits, but we have been averaging 2 percent a month. What we're doing is no great novelty. Others have done it and are doing it, I'm sure. Essentially we take advantage of what the pundits call a disequilibrium situation. We find something out of whack in terms of normal market price relationships and we buy the stuff. Doing that of course tends to bring the whole thing back to balance, to equilibrium. If enough people start doing the same thing, you soon have no disequilibrium, no bias, no edge. Which means that we can only go on doing this maybe two–three years. Too many people coming into the field doing the same thing. You remember the old line about how to survive on a desert island: Find a monkey your own age, eat what he eats. The trouble is if you have enough desert islanders doing that you run out of things to eat."

The slate-blue-covered booklet put out by his Arbitrage Management Company defines its purpose more formally, how the hedge works:

> . . . the basic hedge is a situation in which the investor has taken the dual position of being long one security and short the underlying related security. . . .
>
> The price of a convertible security and that of its underlying common generally move in tandem. But the price of the convertible will vary from time to time, from what we determine to be its normal price relationship to the common. When this variation produces an abnormally priced convertible a hedge is then instituted.

Harry Markowitz gave some specific examples of hedged trades. "We bought Heublein 5¾ percent convertibles of 1994 on November 16–17, 1970, for $108.64. At the same time we shorted 17.39 shares of stock per bond at an average price of

$43.34. We sold the bonds on December 8 at the average price of $122. A profit there. Then the same day we covered our shorts on the common stock at $47.47. A loss, of course. The round-trip commissions on the bonds and stocks, minus the net bond interest received during the brief period, left us with a net profit of 4 percent on the transaction for the twenty-two days. At an annual rate that's 67 percent. Our biggest profit was taken after twenty-one days in Greyhound's 6's of 1986. We made nearly 33 percent profit on that one. And we also were in Ling-Temco-Vought's $5 preferreds for only one day and made 6.2 percent on that round trip."

Markowitz spends about an hour a day on his charts at the office of Mack, Bushnell. "Fairly simple. After all, our computerized data bank has the price histories and relationships of all the convertibles available and their common stocks. And it scans the list every day, seeking out skewed relationships we can get in on. And because it's no great trick we're sure to have a lot of other characters joining us with their own hot little on-line data banks. Then when we start tripping over each other, buying the same bonds almost simultaneously, the game will be over. Two, three years at most."

Professor Paul A. Samuelson, who roasted Kassouf and Thorp's book, is listed in the Arbitrage booklet as a "Director" of the firm.

"Mike Goodkind talked him into joining the board. He has a piece of the action. But after the Nobel Prize he resigned as director but stayed on as consultant. Oh, we consult him maybe once a month. I might ask him about a certain kind of curve which we were doing by hand. How could I do it by computer, that kind of thing. I had a few lengthy conversations with him on technique. In the past he used to call in with recommendations in warrants, but he's really more interested in hypothesis than specifics."

The firm that controls Arbitrage Management—and makes the nice commissions on all its trades—is Mack, Bushnell & Edelman. They led to another seeker of the new Holy Grail— the secret way to beat the market—Bill Scheinman. Mack, Bushnell had just said in a legal complaint that Bill had, indeed, found it and it was worth at least $2,000,000 and they were suing him for just that amount because he took his great secret away. Each seemed to be linked in a Great Chain of Being: from Kassouf to Thorp to Samuelson to Markowitz to Scheinman. Academe dipping its theories and dollars into the market. And now link Bill Scheinman, who didn't even have a BA but did have the magic charts, worth at least $2,000,000, they said.

Sheen Kassouf thought that at a given moment in our here and now there were at least fifty thousand Americans seriously looking for the magic formula, the secret of getting rich in the stock market. Fortunately for our Gross National Product, for the stability of marriage, for the amenities of social intercourse, they do it only intermittently. Dabblers, really. Bill Scheinman is intense and he does not dabble. When he went looking, he spent three years, full time, twelve–fourteen hours a day. It cost him $100,000 and very nearly ruined his second marriage, but then in December, 1967, he found it. Just in time. It was Christmas and he was almost broke.

William X. Scheinman looks a little the way Tennessee Williams did a decade ago. He also talks with a side-of-the-mouth drawl and sounds vaguely Southern, which is a trick for a New York boy. He's about 5 feet 7, heavy-faced, has a broad forehead, a cowlick, rich, thick black sideburns, shiny green eyes and a beginning pot.

How come the X for a middle initial? "My middle name was Irving. When I was in the Navy, in the Pacific, I was an enlisted man. All EM laundry was identified only by initials. Trouble was, there was another WIS abroad. So someone crossed my middle initial for better identification and I became WXS and William X. Scheinman since."

His father was a doctor, but Bill also had an aging uncle, Jess Scheinman, who had a seat on the exchange for many years, and a brother, Robert L. Scheinman, who is senior vice-president and director of the Chartered New England Corporation. In 1951, when he was twenty-four, Bill was going to Columbia's

School of General Studies at night and working during the day for a distributor of hydraulic equipment.

"I got together $200 and went in business for myself. Mostly aircraft parts. Then I started manufacturing hydraulic fittings, using a small machine shop on the West Coast. We went public in 1962 with a Reg A issue of stock that yielded $300,000. But I had picked the wrong horse. Lester Avnet went into *electrical* connectors, and I picked hydraulic, which was not what aircraft were going to use. Then I took my money and went into manufacture of plastic materials for shoes. This was way before Corfam. I sold out for $1,000,000 of restricted stock in the summer of 1964. When my year was up, the stock was free but it was worth only $100,000. The firm was nearly bust by then.

"I was thirty-seven and saw forty approaching and I asked myself: Where the hell am I going and what have I done with my life? I took stock: I had $100,000, an ex-wife, a new wife and one son. And I lacked ten credits for my BA."

Then came, as it must to thousands of red-blooded Americans, the fateful whisper: the stock market. Figure it out.

"I had been a casual investor up to then. I tried everything. Fundamental analysis? Ugh! In general fundamentals, earnings, new product promise and so on only told you the obvious a little late. The market always went past the obvious. Besides, fundamental analysis couldn't tell you when to get off. Technical analysis? Just a trend-following exercise. Millions of solid hours had been put in by thousands of men studying the charts. Why weren't they all rich?

"No, there had to be a something-else factor. The human being. Crowd psychology. We're all part of the crowd. Bernie Baruch had insights into crowd psychology. So did Fred Stein, the great mutual-fund operator. The fact that he had been an ex-merchant mariner encouraged me. After all, I had been a Navy EM myself. Sure, in theory I could monitor Fred Stein twenty-four hours a day, but why should he let me? There had to be a way. I spent months on the SEC insider reports. Maybe they knew something. A dead end. They often didn't know any better. I bought myself an adding machine and a small computer, looking for the magic correlations. I had to find the statistical data available to give me the necessary insights into crowd psychology.

"One of the items that hits you early is that in the market a minority do fairly well and a majority are either habitually wrong or less right. Months passed. Nothing. I was living on $30,000 a year and had accumulated two rooms full of NYSE and SEC materials. It was harder for me because I didn't have a math background. It becomes an obsession, the way it must have been for the alchemists. My second wife, Nadine, a very lovely gal from Topeka, Kansas, gave up on me and in disgust left me for a while. My parents were unhappy with me. I had become an obsessive nut. By December, 1967, I was running out of capital and suddenly everything seemed to come together. I had it."

What he had was several sets of correlations that seemed valid when tested on 150 leading common stocks he had been assiduously following. Before a significant turning point in the market:

      One group would buy more of the stock;
        one group would sell more of the stock.

"What I had was my theory of divergence analysis. When the divergence was important enough, the smart money was invariably right."

Whose was the smart money? The large, experienced financial institutions, the stock exchange specialists, among others. The unsophisticated were, of course, the casual investor, the odd-lotter. As long as the two groups were going in the same direction, there was nothing worth doing. But when they diverged significantly, ah! Many men had been doing the opposite of what the odd-lotter had been doing but with mixed results. The odd-lotter wasn't *always* wrong. But Bill Scheinman was certain he had the key elements to predict major moves—when to buy and sell—through his divergence analysis. There were secrets here, of course. *How* he manipulated the data. How he compared statistical data. "It's not mechanical. Highly personal. I knew the methods and I wasn't going to let anyone else know exactly how. Hell, it took me three years and $100,000. I had found a way to measure significant crowd behavior in the market. Psychometrics. I really had it."

Okay, what do you do with a secret like that when you have only a few thousand dollars left?

"The easiest thing, of course, was to run a market letter. Meanwhile I also did a book. We put out 100 copies, offset, at $15. Then we ran an ad for the book and finally sold 3,800 copies. (*Why Most Investors Are Mostly Wrong Most of the Time.*)

"We ran ads for my weekly letter, 'The Scheinman Timing Forecast.' We got a lot of subs from readers of the book. Some $40,000–$50,000 came in for subscriptions. A hundred and fifty dollars a year for forty-eight issues and at the peak we had 1,000 subs.

"The trouble with a market letter is that you become a mail-order businessman worrying about lists and weekly deadlines and printers. I found myself deeper and deeper in the trap. We selected three stocks a week. I was getting unhappy, even though I was nicely solvent again. My older brother, Bob, who knew the market well, had an idea. Why didn't I go to work for a brokerage firm and let them distribute my letter to favored customers, people who had large accounts and generated nice commissions? So I made a deal with Mack, Bushnell & Edelman. I advised and did major market studies. They brought me in at $25,000 a year—this was about June, 1969—and then in August to $31,000 and then to $40,000. Some 150 institutional investors were getting my studies. Great. The only trouble was a lot of registered reps in the firm now wanted their retail customers to meet me, the house-trained seal. Things were getting hectic and I was getting unhappy again.

"Another problem, too. We had a better mousetrap. If you can't duplicate it, why, it's almost as good doing what the inventor does. They had only one floor broker on the exchange and when word got out that Scheinman's short sales were fabulous, other brokers used to follow the Mack, Bushnell floor broker around and go short on the stocks he did. It was becoming impossible to hide our moves. You go short 50,000 shares of Minnesota Mining and five other smart-ass brokers do the same, you've defeated your own position."

In October, 1970, Bill Scheinman left Mack, Bushnell—just about the time Harry Markowitz was coming to New York to run the Arbitrage Hedge Fund for them—and went to another Big Board firm, Cohn, Delaire & Kaufman. Now he was joined in a partnership with a registered rep named Alan D. Alan, so they were now the Alan & Scheinman division of the firm.

"We figured at Cohn, Delaire we could attract institutional investors only. No retail trade. And we'd get a split on the commissions we brought in as a result of my new market studies. It should be a good deal all around. Also they had several floor brokers, not just one."

But his old firm, Mack, Bushnell, now made it clear, through a lawsuit, that Bill Scheinman's services were practically indispensable. In a suit filed on October 27, 1970, Mack, Bushnell claimed that Bill had no right to take his divergence analysis material with him when he left and that he was engaged in unfair competition. They said they earned about $2,000,000 a year in gross annual commissions for the purchase and sale of stocks and bonds for customers. And of that:

> Fully 65% of the commission business can be directly attributed to the development and dissemination of divergence analysis. Consequently plaintiff regards all materials and information in relation to divergence analysis as confidential within the firm.

In effect they said Bill Scheinman and his divergence analysis were worth at least $1,500,000 *a year* to them. In all, they asked for $2,225,000 in damages plus "such punitive damages as the Court may direct."

In a sense the legal complaint was, of course, an enormous

tribute to Bill Scheinman's formula. For the first time a real dollar value was placed on it by a reputable stockbrokerage. As far as they were concerned, the three years Bill had spent evolving it were well spent.

I saw Bill shortly after the complaint was filed. He was furious.

"You know they also called in the DA and the FBI, claiming I had stolen papers from them. My divergence analysis materials. Of course the DA and FBI promptly stepped out of the picture as soon as they realized what was involved. But what gets me is here I've busted my ass for years developing divergence analysis, wrote about and publicized it, and now they come along and claim I stole *their* stuff. *They* invented divergence analysis!"

There is an arbitration clause governing disputes between members of the New York Stock Exchange, as well as with their employees. A New York Supreme Court justice ruled that the matter should go to arbitration. Since Bill Scheinman had recently become a registered rep—in order to be able to get commissions on business divergence analysis brought into Cohn, Delaire—he was covered as an employee of a member firm.

Meanwhile, Bill, studying his charts and divergences, was getting very bearish about the market in the fall of 1970. In September, 1970, he said it was "the time for aggressive selling." He thought the market wouldn't get past the 800 mark and that it was possible the market could drop to a disastrous 525 before it went up again. He thought this low could happen before the end of 1970. And the market would stay weak in early 1971. He didn't have doubts.

By the end of November, 1970, he was still very gloomy. The market was unlikely to go above the 790–800 mark, and the thing to do was a great deal of short selling. By December 4, when the market was sharply moving up, he advised his clients to cover their short sales. He said he was still pessimistic but "you just go with the market. The boat's still gonna sink but meantime the holes aren't big enough. Which means it might go up to 900 maybe. [By June, 1971, it had gone to 935.] Sure you set up standards and do your research, but once they're breached, you just go with the crowd. There's no magic formula."

(I told him I was disappointed. He made me think that he *had* one.)

His new "Timings and Transactions" studies are printed on a special vermilion paper to defy Xerox reproduction. "Boy did we have a time finding this paper." The first issue was mailed by Cohn, Delaire to more than four thousand institutions. "We're getting a good response." Eventually, of course, the reports will only go to those institutions that use Cohn, Delaire to buy or sell stocks.

Was he in the market following his own advice? "Not much. I have a real problem. I ran into debt setting up my advisory service. Now under this new setup I'll have to act first for a client before myself. Stock exchange rule."

All I could think of as I left Bill Scheinman was the classic Wall Street comment on systems to beat the market: "What's the good of a system that works except when it doesn't?"

When I checked in June, 1971, on the fate of Bill Scheinman and divergence analysis, it appeared that the Cohn, Delaire setup didn't work either. "Alan and I split up in April," Bill explained. "He's gone back to another firm as a registered rep and now I'm vice-president of Wiesenberger Financial Services. They do a lot of publications and mine will be one of them. Clients will get it only for $7,500 a year or an equivalent amount of commission in trades. I'm getting $50,000 a year base, plus a lot of other goodies, and I think this time it will work out fine. They're giving me a $250,000 budget for my department."

He was aware that divergence analysis had its weaker prophetic moments. "After all, it's not a surefire formula. It does work well at extreme points of the market, but in the interim periods it's much less clear and there's always a lot more interim than extreme points in the market."

Mack, Bushnell still hadn't pursued their claims against him via arbitration, but he was contemplating a suit against them for use of his material and harassment and several other charges.

Obviously, even when you find the magic formula, it's not an easy life. Especially if the formula doesn't work *all* the time.

12. The Schools

*I respect no study, and deem no study good, which re-
sults in moneymaking.*

—SENECA

*Most Americans probably get as far as 35 before it dawns
upon them that they are never going to get rich. Few
probably care by that time that the educational system
has failed them.*

—RUSSELL BAKER

The little ad appears fairly regularly in the New York
Times:

BEAT THE STOCK MARKET

With a unique technique that has proved out for 80 years.
Warranted to be logically indisputable. Takes only one day
of personal instruction.

The man to call for an appointment is Richard A. Garfield,
who lives on Central Park West. Garfield is sixty-one, short,
bald and has bulging eyes. "I get $1,500 for the technique," he
said. "I used to get $2,500, but maybe at a time like this I should
offer a bargain."

If he had the unique technique, logically indisputable and
so forth, why wasn't he the richest man in the world?

He nodded. "My system isn't foolproof. What throws it off?
The fallibility of the individual. My method is only 80 percent
mechanical. There's lot of room for human error in that other

20 percent. Also, I've never been able to accumulate enough money after taxes and living expenses to have a big enough stake."

Since he started teaching his system in 1947, he estimates he's had maybe two hundred students in all. Perhaps a dozen students a year.

"It takes about five hours. I generally give it at my office here or even at home. Then if they have difficulty, they have the right to call me with their problems."

He was understandably cagey about the exact mechanics of his magic system, but he went into some detail:

"I explain the different types of movement in the market: long, intermediate and short-term movements. I correlate one to the other. Then I teach them how to recognize buy and sell signals. Sure, it's based mostly on technical interpretation and Dow theory, but I add something more: what I call the Fourth Dimension. I explain what it is and how to recognize it. You can't copyright or protect a system like mine. So I have students sign a statement that they won't transmit or commercialize my system. I don't know where my former students are now or how they've done. So far my adds haven't done very well. I've run five ads in the *Times* this year [1970] and they cost me $125 each. And no students yet. Back in 1960 a man in California saw my ad in *Barron's*, phoned me, and flew here on a Friday night. He got instructed on Saturday and then flew back. Don't know what happened to him, either."

Like most system developers, Garfield is a former market loser.

"I inherited some cafeterias my father built up. Maxie's Busy Bee restaurants. I was wiped out in 1929 and then got knocked out of the box in the 1937 market crash. I spent three years studying, trying to find a recurring pattern I could latch onto. Then I found it. I took a job as a registered rep to test it, and it worked pretty well. Mostly now I make a living as a money manager. I have about a dozen clients and manage their money. The customer can use any broker he wants. I get a percentage of the amount involved. I don't do any trading for myself. That would be unethical. My last big year was 1967, when I worked for a member firm. I earned $82,000 in commissions and some $27,000 profit on trading for them. Unfortunately they got closed down by the SEC, Pickard & Company. Big troubles. Nothing to do with my trading or methods. They were a pretty cheap outfit. They had a good margin clerk who asked for a $10 raise. They just let him go and as a result acquired a real back-office mess. I think I was the only man in the outfit the SEC didn't question. So here I am with something I know works and I can't get any students or rich men to try my system for a couple of years. Only some wise guys with that old quote: Those who can do; those who can't teach. Must be something wrong. Do you think people get suspicious when you try to sell a system for making a lot of money for only $1,500? If I had the courage, I'd really charge $10,000. But I won't. You know anybody interested, send him around. Only $1,500. A special."

The biggest, most advertised and most expensive stock market school—apart from Garfield's five-hour, $1,500 run-through—is the Stock Market Institute of Park Ridge, Illinois. Its ads in the *Times* and *Barron's* and the *Wall Street Journal* proclaim it as the only school in the country "devoted exclusively to developing and improving your stock market trading skills." And it features trick headlines: "One of our students made $22,500 in the stock market last year. . . . We gave him a B-minus."

The school had been founded by Richard D. Wyckoff, a man whose writings were almost as fascinating as the legends about him. Wyckoff died in 1934 when he was sixty-one. It was also the year the SEC became operative and many of the tricks he had practiced in his lifetime were soon illegal. A few years before he died, he did a book for Harper's, *Wall Street Ventures and Adventures Through Forty Years*. It was fairly candid. Wyckoff published several market letters and routinely solicited payoffs to push a stock, which, of course, wasn't illegal then. Later he founded the *Magazine of Wall Street*.

But the most fascinating paragraphs in Wyckoff's book are on page 290. Remember now, these words were written *seriously* by a man who had grown up in the street, made money in it, and wrote about it extensively:

> For many years there have been methods of transmitting secret advices by means of code letters and words printed in certain sections of daily newspapers. Formerly these advices were brief and simple, though quite effectively used among those who were "wise." They have since been greatly elaborated. If you have some knowledge of the subject, studying these signals, advices or forecasts, you can see that they emanate from the headquarters of important interests, and that they forecast the trend of the market in general, and certain stocks.
>
> People may think this improbable; entirely too uncanny in this day of modern business procedure. But I know exactly what I am writing about.

One of Wyckoff's admirers was a contemporary stock market letter operator named Frederick N. Goldsmith, who operated the F. N. Goldsmith Financial Service, a daily letter, from 1916 on. He got anywhere from $100 to $300 a year—depending on the times, and he usually averaged two hundred subscribers. In 1916 Goldsmith latched onto the "secret newspaper code" Wyckoff alluded to, and he devoted his new market letter solely to cryptanalysis of the clues provided in, of all places, the old comic strip, "Bringing Up Father," which was about an uncouth, earthy Irish millionaire, Jiggs, and his socially ambitious wife, Maggie. "It took me an awfully long time to break the code, but once I did, it was simple to predict the market with 90 to 95 percent accuracy," he said in 1947.

He had to explain the code because in the fall of 1947 the New York State attorney general had called him in. Goldsmith had inferred in one of his ads for his market letter that he had "inside information."

Goldsmith, a short, wiry commuter from Plainfield, New Jersey—he was then eighty-three, and his rumpled seersucker suit and battered Panama hat were his Wall Street trademarks

—explained the code for the law. He showed them a Maggie and Jiggs strip for May, 1947. The first panel showed Jiggs with his right hand in his pocket. That meant, said cryptanalyst Goldsmith, "a signal to buy." Two rings of smoke were rising from Jiggs' cigar. That could only mean, "The market will go up in the second hour of trading." Then in the next frame his wife is saying: "I don't see why you can't get your name in the paper, too." The meaning? Simple: "Buy International Paper." In the last panel Jiggs' cigar is still smoking. The market would be steady at the close. In a June strip Jiggs, in a box at a Broadway show, comments to Maggie: "The intermissions are the only good things about this show." What could that mean? Goldsmith knew: "Obvious. Mission Oil was the only good buy." He put that in his market letter, and as a matter of fact, two days later Mission Oil hit a new high.

Goldsmith had letters of praise from prominent brokers and analysts: "Uncanny," said one. "There's nothing that touches it," wrote another.

One of the few men around today who admits to having used Goldsmith's market letter is fifty-two-year-old John W. Schulz, a partner in Abraham & Company and a columnist in *Forbes*. "Yeah, I gave the old man a testimonial," he told me recently. "Hell, he hit the market right surprisingly often. Sure people kidded me after the thing with the attorney general, but there was no getting around the fact Goldsmith had a helluva batting average. He missed a lot, but if you have to quit in this business when you're wrong once, who's gonna be left?"

A New York importer, Louis Mischner, testified that he made $150,000 in the market by following Goldsmith's advice. Another enthusiastic follower said Goldsmith's service was the best of all.

Goldsmith agreed to end his service in 1948 when the SEC got into the picture. There were no penalties. A year later, he died at eighty-five. George McManus, who drew Maggie and Jiggs, had been asked about the clues Goldsmith found in his comic strip. "What would I be doing with cartoons if I were so hot on the stock market?"

Seeking further clues on the Wyckoff-Goldsmith theory of secret stock market communication via daily comic strips, I visited the Stock Market Institute in Illinois. In the new 10,000-square-foot, one-story building housing the institute the boss is Lloyd I. "Bud" Andrews, a thirty-eight-year-old boyish, good-looking ex-Marine. On the far wall of Andrews' corner office—crewel drapes, off-gold rug, gold-green grass cloth wall-paper—is a full-length oil portrait of the founder, Richard DeMille Wyckoff.

I asked Andrews about the mysterious newspaper-code clue paragraphs in the founder's autobiography. Andrews, who re-membered the paragraphs, admitted that he didn't know "what in the Sam Hill" Wyckoff was talking about. "It doesn't sound like Wyckoff at all. Still, it's in the book."

He explained that back in 1931 Wyckoff had written the basic course the institute employs. "After his divorce from Cecilia, his first wife, he had a lot of financial problems. He re-married and he was anxious to get some kind of steady income. So he wrote the course and started selling it in 1933 for $500. I figure that maybe six thousand people have bought it since then. We raised the price a few years ago to $650. That is, $650 if you pay cash. More on installments."

The course is essentially based on technical interpretation of the market. As the elaborate booklet sent to mail inquirers puts it, in the words of the founder:

> The law of supply and demand controls the movement of both the market as a whole and of individual stocks. The solution of the stock market problem lay, therefore, in an understanding of this principle and in the ability to interpret supply and demand correctly.

In essence the course is designed to make you your own chartist, plotting price and volume movements in stocks, in technical analysis. (As a school for stock market technicians the institute is, of course, bitterly opposed to fundamental factors such as

profit projections, new products and the like. Andrews' prede-
cessor as president of the institute, Robert G. Evans, once said
that reading the business news in the daily papers is dangerous
for students of the technical aspects of the market. "It puts poi-
son in their mind.")

After a student signs up, Andrews explained, he is shipped
the entire course of four hundred pages. ("We've rewritten
about half of it.") The student is then asked to read it all and
learn the underlying theory.

"Then he starts sending in completed lessons and tests we
send him. We send him practice trading kits, charts and so
forth and daily statistical reports so he can plot his charts. Of
course, we answer all their questions. About 10 percent of the
students come to visit us at one time or another. And maybe
twice a year we hold seminars on the material in Boston, New
York, Chicago and San Francisco. No additional fee and we en-
courage students to bring friends along."

About 95 percent of the students are men. "Two types
mostly," Andrews went on: "Those who have the money they're
anxious to protect and those who have none and want to make
it. Everyone wants real financial independence."

Andrews explained how he became head of the institute.

"I started as a registered rep with Merrill Lynch in Chicago.
But I was pretty bad at it. I was too honest. So I left and became
a real-estate salesman. I fell on my face at that. I was married
and had a child and it was pretty rough. I went to National Cash
Register and then to the West Coast as rep for a small business
systems manufacturer, Magnedex. I rose to veepee. Then in
1966, when I was thirty-three, I decided I had to get back in
the market. I met Bob Evans who owned the Stock Market
Institute. He was looking for somebody to take over. Buy it and
run it.

"It was a very good, very generous deal. So I came on board.
I put no capital in. I'm paying off Evans out of profits. Since
I've taken over, we've increased business 170 percent. We'll
triple the enrollment this year. I think we'll get one thousand

students a year from now on. We sell the course only by mail. No salesmen getting fat rake-offs like some correspondence courses I could name. We're approved for training under the GI Bill and we're accredited by the National Home Study Council. Now we're legitimate in the eyes of the educators. We have twenty-five people on the staff. And we get 51 percent of our new students through recommends of graduates."

About one-fifth of the students are registered reps, customers' men. A few fund managers are also registered, Andrews said proudly. Mostly, though, the typical student is a businessman near retirement.

A survey in 1968 indicated that 40 percent of their students had assets of more than $100,000 and another 40 percent had at least $25,000 in net assets. Some 85 percent had attended college.

The survey also showed why graduates of the course still made unwise investment decisions. Apparently these were still possible in spite of the "scientific principles":

   37 percent said they misinterpreted data
   29 percent deviated from principles
   29 percent lacked personal discipline
   5 percent said greed or fear influenced judgment

In addition, Andrews said there were some students "destined to fail. Perhaps they find solace in losing in the market. But even if you follow all the rules of the course, you'll lose sometimes because you're dealing with the unknown, the future. Nobody knows what the market will do."

Wasn't the course designed to teach the student to interpret what the market *will* do?

"Negative. We don't assure success. We'll teach you how to speculate. That's all."

He mentioned that recently some 15–20 percent of their students were speculating in the commodity market, using the institute's methods of technical charting. I couldn't resist and filled him in on some of the wilder commodity trading incidents I had picked up from Phil and Jerry. Bud Andrews was properly shocked. "You mean things like that really still go on?" When told they did, he felt he couldn't pass that kind of information on to the students.

"No, we couldn't do that," he said soberly. "I have to feel that what I'm doing is honest *and* good."

INTERLUDE

New York, May 23, 1970

My wife and I have been invited to the wedding party of Jerry's older son, Gregory. He's marrying an attractive social worker. My wife, who has been hearing me talk about "my two rogues," is understandably curious about them and their wives.

The wedding party is held in the elaborate restaurant on the first floor of the expensive apartment building in which Jerry and Janis live on the East Side. At the luncheon I meet Jerry's father, a retired pharmacist and a widower. The only notice taken of Jerry's indictment is the fact that one of his attorneys is present. He tells me about a big churning suit he has under way for a client, a wealthy widow. She claims her broker unduly turned over her account to generate commissions for himself. Later, over a drink, Phil sounds off on the wave of churning cases being filed by disgruntled brokerage customers all over the country.

"All these cases are nonsense," Phil insists vehemently. "When the poor sucker says the account was churned fifty or eighty or one hundred times a year, what is she really *not* saying? The account could only be churned with her knowledge. After every trade she gets a confirmation notice from the broker about the transaction. If she thought there was something wrong, she should have stopped the discretionary permission she had given her registered rep. But to go to court and the SEC a *year later* is too long after the fact. There have to be two guilty parties in this kind of transaction: the broker and herself. Why should the broker alone be held accountable for her stupidity and greed? Every customer who's churned and lost money is unhappy. If she was churned and made money, there'd be no gripe.

The guilty party is not the broker; she's the guiltiest. She could have stopped the game at any time. The fact that she may have looked on the broker as a replacement figure for a son she never had doesn't enter into the court's consideration but it should."

13.

If You're So Psychic, How Come You're Not Rich?

In London an old friend interested in ESP phenomena is asked: "How come no medium ever got rich in the stock market?"

"The only rich medium we've ever had," he said, "was Eileen Garrett, and her money didn't come from the market. She was a genius at raising money for ESP foundations from rich people, particularly the late Congresswoman Frances Bolton of Ohio."

A check of the literature shows there were several reported dream cases in which the lucky sleeper "saw" a certain horse winning a race the next day but there just weren't any such cases of a winning stock.

Followers of Edgar Cayce will deny this, saying that this seer foretold in April, 1929, the great stock market crash. The only trouble was that a parcel of pessimists was also doing the same. It was all too predictable. Today there are a few astrologers who go in heavily for market predictions such as Peggy Reynolds of New York and Doris Kaye, who did a stock market horoscope book. And once the former Big Board firm of A. M. Kidder & Company had a resident astrologer, says Vartanig

Vartan, the New York *Times* financial writer who utilized the astrologer bit briefly in his interesting novel about the brokerage business, *50 Wall Street*.

How good are these astrological and other seers? No one knows. Their box scores are murky and carry too many exculpatory footnotes. The basic trouble with all these seers was spotted by Montaigne four centuries ago:

> Nobody keeps a record of their false prognostics, inasmuch as they are common and numberless; but their lucky divinations are acclaimed, being rare, incredible and prodigious. . . . For who, if he shoots at the mark all day long, will not occasionally hit it?

The British produce far more prominent public-life mystics and believers than we do. Air marshals and prominent physicists turn out to be in communication with the dead—and don't care who knows about it. Canada had a Prime Minister, Mackenzie King, who was a true believer. One of our few public figures who openly espoused belief was millionaire railroad builder Arthur E. Stilwell. He rose from a minor job in a Kansas bond and brokerage office. But he kept hearing voices that told him he must build a railroad—to link the wheatfields of Kansas with the Gulf of Mexico. He was able to raise the money and built the Kansas City Southern Railroad. Everything went well until the road was 50 miles from Galveston, where it was going to terminate. He turned to his unseen spirits for guidance. As he later wrote, they told him to forget Galveston, it was doomed; find another terminal. Galveston citizens were furious; his bankers and business associates thought he was out of his mind. But he stayed with his unseen spirits and the Kansas City Southern went to the Gulf of Mexico at a miserable spot which they called Port Arthur in honor of Arthur Stilwell. When the hurricane and tidal wave wrecked Galveston, Port Arthur's piers and rail lines were untouched. But somehow his prophetic powers didn't include his own fortunes: Two of his railroads went into bankruptcy, and he died in 1929 a comparatively poor man.

Pierre Rinfret, the corporate economist someone once called

"part Puck, part Polonius," says that he always listens to his inner psychic warnings. His widely publicized prophecies about the forthcoming state of the national economy lay him open to raucous laughs when he misses badly—as he did in 1970—but he still thinks his track record shows he's been right 80–85 percent of the time calling economic turns for the past twenty years.

"I find I can tell several days in advance when one of our clients is going to cancel our economic advisory services. I'll tell my partner, George Helmer, 'We're in trouble with this account.' He'll say, 'But we've gotten no letters from them or any anxious phone calls.' I'll say, 'You'll see. I just *know*.' And sure enough, a few days later we'll get the cancellation."

Rinfret believes that a number of people on Wall Street operate largely on their psychic hunches—even if they won't publicly admit it. "Hell, how does it *sound*?" He told me about "a very big man in the street, who has access to millions of dollars' worth of investment advice, top analysts and so on." He once bought a lot of Mary Carter Paints when it was $6. "I couldn't figure it out because it looked like nothing on fundamentals or charts or anything. He told me that he bought it because he was at a cocktail party and he heard someone say the stock would go places. *And he liked the way the person sounded when he said it.* So he bought. Mary Carter moved to 34 and he sold it in the low 30's. So much for analysts and fundamentals and the rest."

It's not just in capitalist society that the psychic hunch is denigrated. In 1915 there was a broker on the Moscow Stock Exchange named Solomon Veniaminovich Shereshevsky. He had unusual powers which neither he nor his colleagues suspected. The Revolution closed the exchange for good, as well as created a materialistic society in which psychic powers of any kind, especially the kind that leads to making money, were suspect.

Shereshevsky's story is told in a thin little volume, *The Mind of a Mnemonist,* written by Professor Aleksandr R. Luria of the Budenko Neurological Hospital in Moscow. Professor Luria, one of the great Soviet psychologists, discovered Shereshevsky in the early twenties. Shereshevsky was then a newspaper reporter who had aroused the curiosity of his editor. Shereshevsky never took notes when he went to cover a speech or event; yet his recall was full and exact. Luria tested the reporter and found that he had total recall. *Total.* Luria examined him over thirty years and found that he had an especially vivid and complex type of synesthesia. That is, every sound Shereshevsky heard produced immediately an experience of light and color, often also of taste and touch. Sixteen years after he memorized a book filled with nonsense syllables, he was able to recall them without a single error. And he could recall backward, too.

Shereshevsky drifted from job to job, and then came the Moscow Stock Exchange interlude. "At one point," he told Luria, "I studied the stock market intensely, and when I realized how important a good memory was there, I became a broker." The Revolution ended that, of course.

The good rationalist Dr. Luria absolutely refused to accept Shereshevsky's stories of what he could do with *money*—when he put his powerful imagination to work. Shereshevsky provided a typical instance:

> To me there's no great difference between the things I imagine and what exists in reality. *Often, if I imagine something is going to happen, it does.* Take the time I began arguing with a friend that the cashier in the store was sure to give me too much change. *I imagined it to myself in detail, and she actually did give me too much*—change of 20 rubles, instead of 10. . . . Deep down I think it's because *I* saw it that way. . . .

We do have a stock market type, a native son, who has attributes not as remarkable as Shereshevsky's but still worth noting. His name, right now, is Swami Amatralaya, but in a previous life he was Douglas Steen, one of the most remarkable and most successful commodity speculators of the past few decades. He was also a mathematical physicist, a statistician and one of the world's highest-ranking contract bridge players. Right now he's a meditating celibate.

Even in the new life the swami continues his commodity plotting—an hour a day—for others. The secret forces that govern his life now forbid his own active involvement in that kind of moneymaking. But there is the force of still another previous life, a life whose errors must be corrected. His father, a Los Angeles clothing salesman, got up three stakes in his life-time—and lost each one in commodity speculating.

In June, 1960, Steen was the subject of a long, admiring article in *Business Week*. It went, in part:

> Step into the Seattle office of Bache & Company and you may see a tall man peering at the commodity boards. In well-worn blue jeans and a white open-necked shirt with sleeves rolled above the elbows, he looks conspicuously out of place . . . from his desk come written slips with buy and sell orders—far and away more orders than from any other desk in the office.
>
> The man is Douglas Steen, a physicist who walked away from Northrop Corporation six years ago to devote full time to commodity speculation. Since then, he has run $6,000 into $240,000 and now holds about a $2 million position in vari-ous commodities, and has earned a reputation as one of the shrewdest of a vanishing breed of commodity traders. . . . About 40 persons are now his clients. Steen is empowered to execute, buy and sell orders for them at will. He gets a per-centage of the profits (about 8% of net, after commissions); but if there are losses the client takes the beating, but Steen doesn't get his percentage of subsequent profits until the entire loss has been made up.

Steen called Sidney Lazard, a wealthy New Orleans oil oper-ator who's also a great bridge whiz, one day suddenly in 1968 from Los Angeles. "I hadn't heard or seen him in years," Lazard told me. "He dropped out of bridge competition, you know. He said, 'I can't, but do you want to make money?' Sure, I want to make money. He suggested a $5,000 investment in commodities. I'm a gambler and I remembered he had been pretty big in commodities once. Well, in the last two months of 1968 he ran my $5,000 up into $100,000, and my broker, Shaun

Vigerie, called me: 'Hey, Sid, how long's this been going on?' So we flew to the coast and brought him back with us to New Orleans. There he told me he stopped commodity speculation on his own account because God told him to. My broker friend rolled up his eyes, but hell, Steen had made me $100,000 in two months. While he was in New Orleans, I made several hundred thousand. We gave him a percentage. He taught me his techniques, but they're just not the same without him and I blew a big bundle after he returned to Los Angeles. Now he wants no part of reality."

When reached, Steen made it clear that he was at a low point, financially. He is tall, thin, erect and white-haired. His deep-set gray-brown eyes glow, and his skin is soft and rosy as a baby's. He's forty-five. But there are what he calls "lines of suffering" around the eyes and mouth and between the eyebrows and temple. He said, "When I suffer, God suffers more."

"You must understand my background first," he said. "My father was a clothing salesman here in Los Angeles and a perpetual loser in commodity speculation. I was at UCLA seven years, after doing a two-year stint in the Navy after World War II. I get a small disability pension—$25 a month—but I am in good health. I got a MA in physics, then switched to statistics. I went to work for Northrop in 1951 and stayed there until 1954 as a mathematical physicist. I got some patents there for an accelerometer that keeps missiles on course. While at Northrop I became very interested in finance and bridge. Oh, I had a period when I was trying to beat the horses. I did fine handicapping on paper but not so good at the track. Bridge was different. In America there are 35,000,000 contract bridge players, perhaps 75,000,000 in the world. It's mighty competitive, lion eat lion. I determined to rise to the top. I became one of the four members of the U.S. team competing at Monte Carlo in 1954 for the world championship. We won. Because I had reached the top it was time to quit. It had become too mundane because there is a blocked door at the end of every mundane channel."

He got into commodities in the early fifties because a friend at

Northrop persuaded him there was a mechanical pattern, even a purely mathematical and analytical basis for trading. "I began researching the field. It's such a complex field, so many different forces at work, so many individuals involved. To me it's like a poker game to fathom the psychology of the others speculating in commodities and then to tie in the necessary mathematical patterns."

He quit Northrop in 1954 to start commodity trading.

"When I do anything, I do it fully. I became a member of seven commodity exchanges. I'd go to Winnipeg, where I was a floor member, and trade in flaxseed and potatoes. Also the New York Mercantile Exchange. Mostly I worked for Bache & Company as a registered rep. I worked there seven years and brought in a lot of business. I also had forty or fifty private clients for whom I worked on a percentage-of-the-profits deal. I think I was the first man to use computers to work out patterns for commodity trading."

He had what he calls a "potato honeymoon." He met Elsa Jo Clark-Griffin, a pretty Texas girl, at the Figueroa Ballroom in Los Angeles, and six weeks later married her.

"We got married in New York. She helped me a little charting Maine potatoes, watching prices for me. I had $15,000 which I put into Maine potato options. In four days I made $25,000 on my shorts. On the fifth day I cashed in. The market kept going up. I started selling, but it kept going up. It went up seven big jump advances in a row at approximately the limit—35-cent limit per sack—and the price of 100 pounds went from $2.60 to $5.90 in seven days at which time I had lost most of my profit. The next day when I was at the New York Mercantile Exchange, I knew if the potato rose the limit again I'd be finished. I said, oh, my God, they have me up against the wall. The market opened 40 points higher, but at the end of the day it went back to $5.40. I was back in the game. Once it fell back to $4.91, I could get out with a great profit. They got it down to $4.92, but then these guys came to block me. They knew I was trying to buy at $4.91 to cover my shorts, that I had a hell of a big block to buy. They blocked me at $4.92. At $4.96. How was I going to get out of this thing? They finally let me cover my shorts at $5.16. I did wind up making $30,000 on our honeymoon, but I aged a lot.

"After that, I had a reputation. When I came back to Los Angeles I went to the new Bache office, and Sam Smith, a partner, gave me the best desk right in front of the commodity board and they gave me parking space right next to Sam Smith's. They gave me the red-carpet treatment. I was swinging out there. We bought a $50,000 house in Sherman Oaks Hills, no children, one dog. I had an expensive study with fancy office equipment, calculators, expensive hi-fi and a pool which you went to directly from our master bedroom.

"We were members of a Moslem mosque, not Black Muslim but regular Imam Islam. We would attend mosque, and I would take turns reading the Koran to members. My wife was the religious leader in our house and she's stayed with the Moslem church, but I wandered into the Self-Realization Fellowship.

"I did an astrological chart for myself based on trans-Uranian astrology, and I found I was supposed to go to Perth, Australia, to spread the word. I had once been in Australia with my wife, but now I had to go alone. On February 6, 1963, I made the decision for celibacy and the pursuit of God. Naturally I gave up commodity trading. I lived celibate with my wife for a few months. We talked and discussed religion a lot. She saw me off at the airport. We had a very good marriage, next to no arguments.

"I haven't seen my ex-wife in two years now. I hear she went into commodities herself. She thought she had learned my techniques, but she hadn't and she lost. I helped her get a second mortgage on the house and advised her to put it in IBM. But she sold it at a loss—just before it doubled."

How does an ascetic swami feel about capitalism?

"I'm in favor of capitalism. I've always been in favor of competition, price wars, striving, initiative, enterprise. I find paradise to be exactly that way. Paradise is not a uniformity, a communism. No. You only get what you earn in paradise. Some people have real talent, others are drones. There are gradients in paradise. People that are sure and loving and determined and others that don't give a damn about anybody. It's a steep gradient of achievement; some people are going to be rewarded and others aren't."

When he returned from Australia—it wasn't the right time for his mission there—he took a small apartment in Los Angeles. "Then in 1968 my divine circuit told me that it would be all right to devote a little time to commodity trading. But of course I had no money and generally they won't let you open a margin commodity account unless you have at least $2,000. That's when I called Sidney Lazard in New Orleans. I knew him from my bridge-playing days. I handled his account on a 5-percent-of-profits basis, although I had been getting much more in my old days at Bache. But Sidney is a spiritual twin of mine, so I had to serve him on an ascetic basis. I feel very close to him. A fine gentleman, a good friend.

"I started by putting $6,200 of his money in wheat and corn, kept an average of invested capital of about $25,000–$27,000, and in twenty months had a profit of $131,500."

He described a typical day during his New Orleans stay when he was trading for Lazard at the brokerage office of Howard, Weil, Labouisse, Friedrichs & Co., where Lazard kept his account.

"Sidney Lazard would pick me up and drop me off at the broker's at 8:15 A.M. I'd study the tapes and the Commodity News Service. I kept technical charts. We did a lot of buying and selling, usually forty options at a time. Then in the afternoon I took the bus back to my apartment. There'd I'd be contemplating or chanting most of the time. I was completely celibate and vegetarian, but my inner cycle then allowed me to eat fish. I'm not vegetarian anymore, though."

He did well in New Orleans on cocoa. "We hit it beautifully, even on the swings. And then I had this experience with orange juice. The night I went to New Orleans in December, 1968, they had a freeze which hit Florida. I had this teaching, this vision. I saw seven quart plastic bottles of orange juice in the refrigerator of the Lazard home. I knew this meant that when the freeze really hit that there were going to be seven limits, seven days in which the price would hit the ceiling allowed for the day's trading in orange juice. That's what happened. On the day of the seventh limit we threw in all our options and sold at the very top. But usually I do my trading on technical factors, not dreams or visions."

The New Orleans interval had a sad finish. "In September, 1970, Sidney took over the market operations and, operating against my advice, lost $15,000. I left October 12, and by the end of November, 1970, he ran into disaster. In 41 days he lost $350,000. Now he's coming out of a difficult financial position. He had promised me $250 a month for life. I'm sure he'll get back on his feet."

Steen came back from New Orleans with $4,200, which he put into stocks that are down now. His present plan is to arrange an annuity so that he can completely abandon commodity trading. He's not trading now, but he does a weekly market letter for Howard, Weil, Labouisse, Friedrichs & Co. in New Orleans. "I do the letter which pays my rent and I phone my contact there, Shaun Vigerie, who's one of the best salesmen at Howard, Weil. I call him collect four times a week and give my opinions. For my market stuff I spend an hour a day."

Steen faces a severe moral dilemma today. He needs $10,000 to underwrite his predestined Australian mission, but he can't think of any way to make it except by selling the secrets of his commodity speculation methods to a few people. "I don't want to go back to the commodities market. I want to have a pure clear mind for God. If God tells me to go back in the commodity market, what can I do? God is telling me to do charitable works. I am not interested in charitable works, but I have some lined up in New South Wales. I have work to do in Melbourne. So I must beg, I must find a way to raise $10,000.

"I have developed a new technique, 'First Major Retrace.' My divine circuit tells me to sell it as a commodity method. The man who gets it can make more than $50,000 a year. The method is simple; it doesn't require a great intellect. Only a few minutes a day. My circuit says to sell it to a few people so as to raise at least $5,000. I'm not allowed to use the method."

The moral problem he faces in offering people a "means of making a lot of money in commodities" is that he really thinks "most people are foolish to engage in financial speculation. The same effort put in the mundane field of work could do much more for most people. Most people fail. The commission in commodities runs about 6 percent on every trade. If you broke even on sixteen transactions, you'd be practically wiped out. The average commodity speculator is going to be wiped out in six months. You get a much longer run on stocks where the commission might be only 2½ percent. Yet my divine circuit wants me to stay in the field of finance for a certain short span, which I have been doing because of the nice people I've been meeting like Shaun Vigerie. He believes in me.

"My work for Shaun, my technique, is not based on numerology, not on trading, but on definite arithmetic patterns of price fluctuations. There are certain unusual patterns of price changes that I look for. It's that simple. I study eighteen different commodities for Shaun and on several phone calls I rate each commodity. One is very bullish, two is bullish . . . eight is bearish and nine very bearish. Also I label each number with a letter: *A* means long-term, *B* is medium and so on. Long-term in commodities means at most ninety days; *C* a seven- to ten-day deal. I mail him my weekly report every Friday so he can have it in Monday's mail. I use eighteen equations for each commodity. But all this is insignificant really. My mission is to make people understand how important it is to concentrate on God. There is nothing here, nothing, only God. [His voice rises with a touch of frenzied hysteria.] This world is a projection on a screen, not reality. The real significance, the nitty-gritty of life *is to keep everything out of focus except God.* God does everything for you automatically. My ingenious four commodity techniques are not really mine, you understand . . . a blast of light, the programming of God."

Shaun Vigerie, the New Orleans broker to whom Steen was supplying weekly commodity analyses and who was now Steen's main source of income, phoned in March, 1971. He sounds like a bubbly Henry Fonda and is a partner in his brokerage firm. He's a Tulane graduate and has been a broker fifteen years with a wide and prosperous client list.

"Doug is the best market technician I ever met," he said. "I'm basically a fundamentalist, but I must say Doug has impressed me with his analyses. We used to give him a flat $600 a month, but now it varies. Mainly it's a matter of his calling me and saying, 'Boss, Divine Providence tells me to ask you for $100 to help someone.' So I send it out. He's a very sweet guy, super-emotional, which is why I don't think he could work as a broker with customers anymore. He'd just get too involved in their lives. But he *does* know the commodity markets. We don't publish his stuff or anything like that, but mostly I pass on his stuff to other brokers who are interested in, say, cocoa or silver or something, and to major customers.

"I've wondered why Doug's system doesn't seem to work without him. I've got all his systems in a desk drawer. I think his great market experience—and he's had an awful lot of it—must come into play. Without that background it doesn't work. I pay Doug out of my own pocket, by the way. You *want* to help him. You feel he's so tortured. When you have a big position in a stock, he empathizes with you, he roots for you but he's also very honest. Once I had this big position in cocoa and he'd been holding my hand. But one night he called me: 'Boss, you're going to lose on cocoa. Get out in the morning.' But I'm a fundamentalist, and from what I knew of the supply and de-mand positions on cocoa, the damn thing had to go up. He was right, though, and it collapsed and we lost heavily."

Shaun Vigerie went out to Los Angeles with his client, Sidney Lazard, to bring Doug Steen back to New Orleans in 1968. Vigerie recalls the meeting:

"He was so far out I never thought we could bring him back in and I kept wondering, What in the hell has Sidney fallen into? But then we got Doug talking on commodities and show-ing us his charts and I knew this man had something. Also, he made $130,000 for Sidney trading. Well we brought him back and then we had some strong problems in New Orleans while he was working there for us."

The first one was Alvin Pierce.

"He kept referring to this Pierce character, and at first we couldn't figure out who he was talking about when he referred to 'My boy, Alvin.' He didn't sound like a friend. Then a broker I knew called me that a strange character had opened an account with them in the name of Alvin Pierce. The way he described him I knew it was Doug. Since Doug already had an account with us, I knew this was trouble—trading under two different personal accounts. I asked, 'Who is this Alvin Pierce?'"

Pierce, Doug explained, was the operating name for the Prince of Darkness when he was on earth. For some reason he had asked Doug to open the other trading account. "We got that closed out fast, but Alvin always kept popping up in his conversation. He knew what Alvin was up to. Shortly after Doug came to New Orleans in 1968, he suddenly announced that Alvin was going after Penn Central and whatever Alvin goes after must go down. He urged us to go short. We didn't, of course. We could have cleaned up on that one."

Doug's contacts with nonearthly entities got him into trouble once with the Chicago Board of Trade, the great commodity trading center. "Doug had a client on a discretionary trading account. The client died, Doug was notified—and he continued trading for the account. Said he was getting messages from the dead man. He lost on the trades and the widow sued and there was a big mess. I think Doug was suspended for a time by the Board of Trade.

"Doug also told me that his projected mission to Australia has been postponed again by the spirits. Oh, yes, Alvin Pierce, the Prince of Darkness, has removed the curse he had on the market and everything's going to be pretty bullish for quite a while."

PART III | *The Winners*

14. *How You, Too, Can Make Three or Four Million in the Market by Following These Rules and Being a Certain Kind of Person*

Oh, how Americans have wanted heroes, wanted brave simple fine men!

—SHERWOOD ANDERSON

Next Tuesday morning, when the regular weekly meeting of the New York Stock Exchange's Public Information and Press Relations Division gets under way in George Bookman's corner office on the fourteenth floor, the subject will be heroes. More specifically, the new, needed hero of American capitalism.

It will take place because the ten people on Bookman's staff are filled with details of the disaster the exchange and American investors—all 32,000,000 of them—squeaked through in 1970. The catalog of horrors is too well known: how 35 percent of the brokerage staffers were fired (more than 16,500 men and women). How investors lost more than $113 billion in the first five months of 1970, for an average loss of $3,600 each. A paper loss for many who held onto their stocks, but still. . . . How more than 100 broker-members of the New York Stock Exchange collapsed or disappeared in the past two years. How Penn Central alone lost more than $43,000,000 in 1970.

In magazine articles, editorials, and books they continue

lacerating the still-draining wounds. *Someone* was responsible. It was the tricky, self-serving specialists on the exchange. It was the incredibly mismanaged brokerage firms. It was the fast-shuffle promoters, the Charlie Plohns, the Kleiner-Bells, the Parvin-Dohrmanns. No matter who, Guilt Must Be Paid.

The patient is feeling much better as his Dow-Jones temperature rises, but there are grim-faced doctors of economics who scorn these false starts. No recovery until the patient gets back near death's door—with a Dow-Jones of around 500, or even 300—barks Eliot Janeway. And Dr. Galbraith won't rest until his favorite and endlessly repeated prophecy comes true, and the rout is at least as bad as it was in 1929.

With all these natural pessimists, with all the bloody scab-pickers still around, George Bookman's staff of public relations experts must find hope and cheer and reasons why the American public must trust once again, should buy stocks with the optimistic brio they used to have.

George Bookman used to be a writer for *Fortune* before joining the exchange. He is a tall, double-chinned, no-nonsense fellow with short hair. His weekly staff meetings are fairly informal, and all suggestions, even the wildest, are welcome. And some great ideas have come out of those discussions, including the most successful campaign the exchange ever conducted: Own Your Share of American Business, which led to an incredible rise of shareowners. There were only 6,500,000 in 1952, compared with nearly 32,000,000 in 1971.

After this future meeting is under way a few minutes, someone at the far end of the room will begin musing out loud.

"You know what bothered me on our latest census of the 32,000,000 shareholders in America? How nameless and faceless they are. Did you know our corporations have lost track of a fourth of their stockholders; they don't know where 7,500,000 of them are?

"Out there"—he waved vaguely westward from Broad and Wall streets—"are heroes of American capitalism whose stories we should be telling and selling. Sure, a lot of wise guys think that 90 percent of the people who put money in the market must lose, but I also remember a Gallup Poll that showed half of us still believe in the traditional American dream that any man can get rich. And a lot have. Now, why can't we find those who have gotten rich in the stock market and tell their stories?"

He pulled out some notes. "There are too many fat computer figures floating around the building. We've forgotten the great allure of a simple million. If you don't do another thing for the rest of your life, a million bucks made in the market and put into tax exempts will give you $50,000 a year, tax-free, $1,000 a week, and you don't have to do a goddamned thing again or share it with IRS or your lawyer or accountant. All yours, free and clear."

Since all those present made considerably less than $50,000 a year—and what they made was heavily bitten into by the federal, state, and city income tax grabbers—several nodded in empathic agreement.

"You know what people will do for just one lousy, measly million? Back in 1967 Roper did a poll of a lot of representative Americans. He asked them: For a million dollars, would you leave your family? One percent said they would. Give up your U.S. citizenship? This time 4 percent would have made that deal. Marry someone you didn't love? Ten percent were ready to buy that package. Give up your friends permanently? Maybe it wasn't so much of a sacrifice for them anyway, but 11 percent were ready to do that. How about serving a year in jail on a framed charge? For a million bucks, 13 percent said they'd do the time. Some 14 percent said they'd take a dangerous job in which they had a one-in-ten chance of losing their life. And a big 21 percent—better than one in five of those questioned—said they'd turn beggar for a year if that would lead to a million bucks.

"What would they do for two, three, four or even five million? I'm glad Roper didn't ask. The shameless depravity, the lacerating sellouts, the humiliating copouts—I'd rather not know."

He had wandered a little, as visionaries sometimes will.

"A guy from out in left field makes a few million in the stock market. We should be celebrating it. Hosannas, cheers, hearty applause. He didn't leave his family, rat on his friends, demean himself publicly, go to jail, risk his life, or beg on the streets. A *clean* million or so. And we know it can be done. All we got to do is find these men—or women."

He had obviously done his homework.

"It won't be easy. The Swedes publish a tax calendar every year showing exactly how much each Swede pays in income taxes. For $5 a year, it's an annual best seller, for the calendar lists the names of Sweden's 100,000 families who have incomes of more than $3,000 a year—and the amounts they paid in taxes. What we need in the United States is a capital gains tax listing, say, everyone who paid more than $5,000 in capital gains for the year. That would be a great starting point, but as you know, we don't have it—and aren't likely to get it. There'd be a revolution if anyone tried *that*."

He took out another slip of paper. "The trouble with us is that we'd sooner talk about our sex lives than our money. I found this quote in Harry Golden's *For 2¢ Plain,* and it hits it right on the head":

> People never discuss their salaries publicly, or their income or their patrimony. People make a successful effort never to discuss money in front of friends or relatives, because money in our society is the ultimate reality and to discuss it is to reveal oneself.

"So what we need is a *modest* American. Our guy doesn't talk about his market winnings; in fact, his friends and neighbors don't even know he's made it. Ideally, he shouldn't be too well educated. We don't want people to feel that you can make it in the market *only* if you have a PhD or even a four-year college education. Most Americans didn't go to college.

"Of course, we want him starting out with a modest stake, say, $25,000 or even less, preferably. Everybody knows if you have a lot to start with, it isn't too hard to get a lot more. And we want him making at least a million, preferably more. Solid stuff. No day-trader character, no board-room lout touting his own stocks to get some volume out of his gullible neighbors.

"What else? I'd like him to be a man who took his own counsel. He doesn't spend a lot of money on tip sheets or hire fancy investment counselors. Don't forget, he has to do it on his own. Shrewd American know-how. And he lives modestly. No flash, no phone in the new, long Mercedes. If we're lucky, he'll be a veteran, a man who's served his country. He should have some nice hobbies. We don't want a one-track mind, some character who spends twelve hours a day on charts and knows every page of *Standard & Poor's*. And not *too* young. Fortyish would be ideal. We had too much publicity about these young whiz kids with the go-go funds, the ten-year-olds who run up a few million between classes."

Another staffer roused himself out of the trance brought on by the talk—one of the longest ever heard at these Tuesday morning meetings—and asked: "Okay. We find him. What do we do with him?"

"What do we do? We make him the new hero of American capitalism! I want to see his picture in the meeting rooms of every one of our fourteen thousand investment clubs; in each of the board rooms of every brokerage branch office. He should be on the cover of *Time*, translated into Polish and Russian for *Amerika*, the USIA magazine in Europe. He's proof that it can be done. Not one of those lucky bastards who win a sweepstakes, but a cool, calm, determined American who invested his modest savings and made a real fortune. A hero for our time."

Does such a hero exist? This new, needed hero of American capitalism?

I thought I'd try to dig up some likely candidates who fit the description, more or less. And one of them is almost ideally qualified, as you'll see.

Still, there *are* drawbacks. Making a few million bucks out of the market from a modest start takes its own peculiar toll.

Let's start with the man who is perhaps the least qualified in some ways. But he made it before the others did and in a sense showed that it *could* be done. Not only does George A.

Miller have one of those perfectly anonymous American names, but he's our only WASP. He is far and away the best-educated candidate, so it's not surprising he made the least, slightly more than a million.

"*I Don't Know How I'll Ever Pay for All This.*"

He was short, with a thinning patch of white hair. He walked with a bowlegged limp. He never had more than two suits— and both cost less than $37 each and were incredibly rumpled. He had two pairs of ancient, badly repaired shoes and a pair of mangled overshoes tied together with pieces of string and rubber bands. He seldom spent more than 35 cents for lunch and lived on $2,950 from a yearly pension.

He never went to a concert, movie, or football game. He never listened to the radio for more than fifteen minutes a day. He was a lousy cardplayer, even though he was one of the world's authorities on finite groups, a particularly abstruse field of mathematics. He was so unhandy around the house he had to move into an apartment. He had owned an Essex car for twelve years but sold it for $75 rather than spend $2 to buy a rear-view mirror required by state law. He often slept in his cluttered office by putting three folding chairs in a row and using a thick math text as a pillow. And he ran $25,000 in lifetime savings up into $1,000,000 by playing the stock market. His peak earnings had been $6,000 a year as a professor of mathematics at the University of Illinois, averaging out at 3,300 a year.

He came from a large family, a factor he had in common along with our other quiet winners. His father had been a farmer near Lynnville, Pennsylvania, who seldom had more than $100 in cash income. And like some of the others, George A. Miller got burned in the market in his early trades. He was suckered into phony gold stocks by boiler-room salesmen calling from Chicago, and he was persuaded by more reputable brokers into picking up foreign bonds designed primarily for the lush American market by Eastern underwriters and banks who knew the countries issuing the bonds almost surely couldn't pay them off when due. That was in the twenties. He got smarter in 1932, when he retired after forty-four years of teaching. He then had about $25,000 in savings, representing a lifetime of self-denial, shabby clothes and skimpy meals. He married in 1909 but had no children. He once took a trip to Chicago and another to California, both times for summer school teaching assignments. The only real vacation the Millers ever had was a one-week boat ride on the Ohio River.

His miserable ways didn't extend to others, though. When new students entered his advance course in group theory, he would give each 38 cents after advising them to buy his text. The 38 cents represented his royalty per copy. He and his wife gave $1,000 to the local Methodist church, and he was a soft touch for students who were having a hard time.

His first serious investment, after his retirement, was buying twenty-five $1,000 bonds of American Furniture Mart for half their face value, or $12,500. In 1935 the bonds were selling at a heavy discount. The Mart, a central sales and exhibit building used by leading furniture manufacturers, was going through a rough time, and there were a lot of vacancies. But Miller, who had spent a lot of time studying the firm, felt that the Mart was basically a good idea and when times improved, it would be fully rented. Also, it was located in the good downtown area and within a block of a proposed lakefront drive. He thought that on a real-estate basis alone, the building was bound to appreciate.

By 1938 the bonds were up to $800 each and Miller sold for a net profit of $7,500. He now invested the $7,500 plus another $22,000 in 1,200 shares of American Furniture Mart preferred stock. Why shift? The bonds which had appreciated to $800 each, had a topside limit of $1,000, but the preferred stock had no limit. He bought the 1,200 preferred shares in bits and pieces, paying an average price of $25. He also bought the Mart's common stock for anywhere from 40 cents to $2 a share.

The Mart did well, particularly after the end of World War II, when veterans were marrying and starting new households. In 1948 Miller sold his 1,200 shares of preferred stock

for $103.50 a share, giving him a net profit of $90,000. He held
on to his common stock, all 12,657 shares, for which he paid,
on average, about $3. When he died in 1951, they were worth
$120,000, representing a profit of $84,000. Altogether, his investments in American Furniture Mart, an over-the-counter
stock, over a period of sixteen years—bonds, preferred, and
common—realized a profit of about $212,000.

He did the same sequence with the Pickering Lumber Corporation of Kansas City. In the mid-thirties, the Pickering
$1,000 bonds fell as low as $90. But from Miller's study of the
firm, he was impressed with its sound management and, more
important, that it owned one of the few large stands of premium sugar pine—some 17,000 acres—in the United States.
He started modestly with 25 Pickering bonds in the 1935–36
period. He got them at from $90 to $150 each. Eighteen months
later the bonds had recovered nicely and Miller was able to
sell them for $380 to $400 each. His timing was perfect there.
If he had waited another two months, the price would have
fallen back to $200 per bond. The 1937 recession was on.

With his $7,000 on the bonds, Miller began acquiring Pick-
ering preferred stock at $15 to $20 each. He held these nine
years until the summer of 1946, when he sold them for $135–
$140 a share for a profit of about $48,000. Now he went into
the third stage: He began picking up Pickering common, some
5,600 shares. These he sold out in 1949. In effect, a $3,000 in-
vestment in Pickering bonds in 1935–36 was parlayed by 1949
into $110,000 worth of common stock.

He pulled his incredibly successful triple parlay again, with
Southern Union Gas, a Texas utility. In 1933–35 the bonds
were selling for anywhere from $200 to $300 each. To pay for
them, he got rid of the overseas bonds that he had been loaded
with in the twenties. For an investment of $10,000 he got
Southern Union bonds with a face value of $36,000. In 1936
the bonds began moving and continued upward. Between 1937
and 1941 Miller unloaded them at par ($1,000 each) and put
his $26,000 profit into Southern Union preferred stock. During
a four-year period, he took on some 1,200 shares of preferred

in a price range from 14 to 26. It was a risky investment; for one thing, Southern Union wasn't able to pay any dividends. In 1943 the firm was reorganized—it was a great time for reorganizing all kinds of utility companies—and Miller sold his preferred stock back to the company for $25 each, which wasn't great. But there was a nice kicker in the deal: To make up for all the unpaid dividends that had accumulated, the firm agreed to pay the preferred stockholders in common stock. Miller came out of the deal with 13,000 shares of common stock valued at $1 a share. During the war period, from 1943–46, Southern invested heavily in oil and gas fields. Then after the war, in 1946 the firm formed a subsidiary, Delhi Oil, and gave Southern Union stockholders the right to buy Delhi common at $2.36 a share. Borrowing against his common stockholdings of Southern Union, Miller bought 16,250 shares of Delhi, which he sold off in the 1948–49 period for about $16 a share, or a gain of $220,000. The original 13,000 shares of Southern stayed with him until he died, and they were worth $250,000. In effect, his original $10,000 investment in Southern's bonds in 1933 was parlayed into a lovely $500,000 profit: $30,000 in bonds; $220,000 in Delhi common; and $25,000 in Southern common.

Not all his investments were long-term. He picked up 1,000 shares of United Printers and Publishers of Joliet, Illinois, at $2–$4 a share and sold out in less than a year at $22–24 for a $20,000 profit. He had another quick one when he bought Franklin County Coal common at 22 cents–27 cents a share and sold them at $4–$5 for a net profit of $18,000. He also did nicely on Chicago and Northwestern Railway bonds and those of Consolidated Dearborn Company of Chicago.

There were some losses during the period. He once bought a preferred oil stock at $48. When it dropped to 20, he got out, taking an $8,400 loss. It never did come back. When his will was probated in 1951, it turned out he had many cats and dogs, mostly gold-mining stocks, more than 40 of them, in anywhere from 1- to 100-share lots. But it was his big ones that made the fortune.

After his wife died in 1949, he rented half his apartment to a Chinese student couple for $40 a month. He'd make himself the same breakfast after arising at 6:30; he'd have a piece of toast and a bowl of hot cereal. Once every two weeks, he'd take a bus to visit his broker, A. Burkey Gwinn, who ran the Champaign, Illinois, branch of First Securities of Chicago. He was then eighty-five and a virtual recluse. He'd walk two blocks to the student cafeteria for 35 cents' worth of lunch. Because he disliked cooking—or spending money on food—he often went supperless rather than walk back to the student cafeteria.

In January, 1951, a severe cold made him too weak to get out of bed. Gwinn urged him to go to a hospital, and in February, Miller agreed. At the hospital Miller looked at a nurse and sighed: "I don't know how I'll ever pay for all this."

When word of his death on February 9, 1951, reached his university colleagues, some of them got together a little fund of $157 to help pay for poor old Miller's funeral expenses. The money was quietly returned by Miller's attorney, J. G. Thomas, who had drawn up Miller's will in 1944. When the undertaker told Thomas that the funeral costs would be about $300 and asked if the estate could pay so much—after all, Miller was buried in one of his two frayed suits and the least expensive wooden casket—the lawyer told him not to worry.

A few days later the university learned that the poor math professor, who lived on less than $1 worth of food a day, who hadn't bought a suit in twenty years, left an estate of more than $1,000,000. Left it, moreover, to the university which had given him a munificent pension of $2,900—for forty-four years of devoted teaching. As he put it in his will: "Everything I have I received from the university, and I simply want to repay my obligation."

In all that time, Miller never talked stocks to any of his colleagues, never subscribed to a market newsletter, never read the *Wall Street Journal* or even the stock market pages of the Chicago papers.

Today, the university gets $73,000 a year from the George A. Miller endowment, which has grown to $1,700,000. Some of it goes to support the *Illinois Journal of Mathematics* and the rest for expenses of the five George A. Miller visiting professors who come to the campus for anywhere from one month to a year. The third area of support from the Miller endowment is a series of twelve–fifteen George A. Miller University Lectureships in many fields, including biology, law, literature, science, and current affairs.

But Miller is disqualified on too many grounds for possible canonization. He made his money too long ago. He made only a million. He was too well educated. You can explain long and patiently to people that his great knowledge of the more arcane areas of math had absolutely nothing to do with his splendid ability to pick market winners, but too many of them will still suspect that, somehow, there is a connection. And finally, he was a WASP, buried from a Methodist church. After all, we have many non-WASPS in the country. No, we'd better go on to the next candidate.

"The Big Bird, Kikiyon, Didn't Just Spit on Him. It Must Have Peed on Him Good."

On Saturday, February 22, 1969, some eighteen years since George A. Miller left us, Morris Ocko, a far wealthier man, is going through normal Saturday routine.

At sixty-four, Ocko is a stocky 5 feet 8, nearly bald and nearsighted. He awoke at 6 A.M. as usual. He dressed quickly in his four-room apartment at the Ravenwood, a run-down six-story apartment house at 700 West 180th Street, in the Washington Heights section of Manhattan, not far from the entrance to the George Washington Bridge. The Ravenwood was built shortly after the turn of the century, and in the thirties the old-fashioned elevator was replaced by a self-service model. Unfortunately, it is often out of order. The elevator, though, is one part of the building operation that Ocko has nothing to do with. But he is responsible for getting the filled garbage cans out of the basement into the areaway under the outside steps so that they can be picked up by the city's garbage trucks.

On the lobby directory of tenants—the Rosens, Hirschbergs,

and Kaufmans are gradually giving way to the Troias, Menendezes, Diazes and Gomezes—he is listed as M. Ocko, Basement. His is the only basement apartment in the building. To get to it, you have to go through the empty lobby—several years ago the lobby chairs were removed because of too many thefts —and across the worn, tapestried tile floor, past the long, fading mirror. Then out a side door and down a flight of worn, wooden steps to an areaway. You turn left and go through the basement door. Past the rough, dirty whitewashed walls of Manhattan schist, permeated with the sour urine stench of decades. Through an ancient wooden door to the Ocko apartment. It's dirty, dingy, and dark, with a few bare bulbs hanging from the ceiling on frayed wires. The walls and ceiling are peeling, the linoleum floors are dirt-encrusted and cracking. There is heavy rust on the bathroom tub and sink. The faucet leaks. The furniture is two levels below Salvation Army pickup standards, and most of it is covered with secondhand books, many magazines—his favorite seemed to be *True,* "the Man's Magazine"—and boxes of spare radio and TV parts, a soldering iron, and several reels of electrical wire.

After dressing—plaid shirt, ancient baggy trousers, Army field jacket—he makes himself his usual breakfast of toast, coffee, and dry cereal with milk and then checks some electrical connections near one of his windows. Among his other little jobs, Ocko was also a kind of illegal sub-supplier of electricity for some friends in the building.

When he moved into his apartment in 1941, he was thirty-five. He made a deal with the landlord. The apartment rental was $33 a month, but Ocko persuaded the landlord to let him be the assistant janitor. In return for taking out the garbage every day and other chores around the building, he'd get his apartment rent-free. Also free electricity. Gradually, over the years Ocko worked out several arrangements with some favored tenants. For one he bypassed the apartment's electric meter in the basement so that the tenant would be drawing his electricity through Ocko's free supply. For another he rigged a bypass so that the tenant got hitched onto the building's master

TV antenna without paying a monthly fee to the landlord. For most of these favors he got fees, sometimes money and sometimes food in a barter arrangement. For many of the tenants, Ocko was also the favored radio and TV repairman. His fees were arbitrary. Some he wouldn't charge at all, but most of the others paid a small fee, usually about half of what the nearby radio repair store charged.

On Saturdays he has other, outside chores. About 3 P.M., he reports to Rudy Golger, the night partner in the corner newsstand at St. Nicholas Avenue and West 181st Street, for his folder-inner job. It is not specifically covered in the fat *U.S. Dictionary of Occupational Titles*, but a folder-inner is a vital adjunct of the newspaper business in New York and other cities where the Sunday paper is a massive three- to six-pound affair. On Saturday afternoon the *Times* delivery trucks bring in huge piles of the separate sections that are printed earlier: Real Estate, Book Review, Drama, Finance, and so on. A folder-inner assembles these so that when the final news sections are delivered on Saturday night, they're merely folded around the existing packages and are then ready for sale. For his few hours of folding-in, Ocko gets $10. It's a miserable job, involving a lot of stooping and working outdoors in all kinds of weather. But Ocko doesn't mind. He did this regularly as a young man, when his parents owned a candy store in the Bronx.

Ocko has another moneymaking angle in the newspaper business. Sometimes he fishes *Daily News* and New York *Times* copies out of street corner trash cans. He has an arrangement with some newsdealers: He gets two cents per copy for the same day's paper. If they don't sell the paper, they can always return it to the distributor for a credit.

Sometimes on Saturday mornings he also helps out in a neighborhood fruit and vegetable store on West 181st Street. He gets all the fruits and vegetables he wants, and a few bucks, too.

Sundays he'd spend in his apartment, reading and listening to the radio. No TV set for him.

A man just doesn't build himself into such an iron cocoon for no reason. Morris Ocko was born on the Lower East Side of New York in 1906, two years after his parents came here from Russia. They saved, and in the early twenties were able to open a ma-and-pa candy store in the burgeoning Bronx. There were two sons and three daughters. Morris was the only one who didn't marry. His mother was naturally disappointed and kept mentioning this eligible girl or that, but apart from a few dates with a friend of his sister's he never went out.

What *did* he do? He helped out in the store, but he also tinkered with primitive model radio sets. And he pored over the stock tables in the New York *Times*. Once, when he was ten, he told his younger sister that he was going to be a millionaire. He got into Cooper Union, a free technical college founded by Peter Cooper, and studied chemical engineering. He failed a key course in calculus and had to drop out in 1927.

He got a radio repair job and saved his money. In 1929, when he was twenty-three, he made his first investment in a common stock. He bought 50 shares of Radio common on margin. It was then near its all-time high of 400, but Morris Ocko knew Radio had a great future. Late in 1929 he came to his mother for $2,000. He had his first margin call. "They'll sell me out, Ma." His mother gave it to him. It was the first of many margin calls, and he lost his stock, as did hundreds of thousands of other Americans.

In the mid-thirties his older brother, Harry, who was a math teacher at Seward Park High School, asked Morris for a good stock tip. Morris, the expert, gave him one, but it didn't work out. Morris was even more miserable than Harry: "I'll never give anyone a tip again," he promised his sister Lilian. By now the family accepted Morris as the drifter, the strange one who wouldn't marry, who had no friends, who lived at home with Mama and Papa and fixed radios and dreamed of the stock market. The family had been Orthodox, but after his bar mitzvah, Morris refused to go to the synagogue at all. He lived at home until 1941. After his mother's death, the father had remarried. Morris didn't get along with his stepmother, and in 1941, when he was thirty-five, he moved out of his parents' home for the first time—into the basement apartment on West 180th Street.

Gradually, he accumulated savings from his radio repair jobs and extra chores. Just about then, he began visiting the Sartorius brokerage office on West 181st Street, on his way to becoming the board room character, the neighborhood scrounger.

In 1953 when his sister Lilian was widowed, she wanted to go to work to support her daughter, Rosalie, who was then ten. Morris said she should stay at home until the girl was thirteen and in high school at least. From time to time he'd give her $100, sometimes $200. Occasionally, she'd visit him in his basement apartment. By then she was the only member of the family he talked to at all. He shunned invitations to family bar mitzvahs, weddings, and other festivities. Nor did he send presents.

His life was incredibly circumscribed, even for a New York apartment dweller. He had never taken a vacation or owned a car. He had never flown in a plane. In fact, he had never been out of Manhattan or the Bronx. He never went to the movies, a concert, or even a museum.

On Monday Morris Ocko finishes his janitorial chores and at noon walks over to the only club he's known for the past twenty-nine years, ever since he moved to the neighborhood from his father's house in the Bronx. Officially, the club is known as the West 181st Street office of Sartorius & Company, a member of the New York Stock Exchange. One flight up, over a lighting fixture store, the club is a long, comparatively narrow room with walls that were once painted cream and green. It faces onto a black-and-white electronic board across which runs the latest New York and American stock exchanges stock sales and prices. Most club members are in their fifties and sixties, and they come in for an hour or two, particularly at lunchtime since a lot are neighborhood merchants. They fill the worn, wooden captain chairs—held in place by floor bolts—and watch the board. The office has 3,000–4,000 accounts, but only 300–400 are really active. Morris Ocko's is one of them.

All the club members know Ocko. A few still greet him, but most know that Ocko doesn't go in for small talk. He walks over to Mrs. Sue Soyer, who's run the switchboard at Sartorius for eighteen years or more. Mrs. Soyer—she's a sister-in-law of Raphael Soyer, the artist—always has a smile for him. After all, Ocko has kept the office's public-address system in good repair these many years.

His contact with other club members is rare. Sometimes one of them brings in a radio for repairs. Ocko fixes it. Sometimes he charges; sometimes not. Depends on how the market is that day. Once a comparatively new club member, spotting Ocko, recalled with a start that he had seen him rummaging in a wastepaper basket on West 181st Street the day before. He looked at Ocko's dirty thirty-year-old felt hat, at the worn pea jacket, the fading shirt, and walked over to Charley Levine, who manages the office and is a partner in Sartorius. "Listen, Charley," he said, "I lost some weight and I have some pretty good suits. Do you think if I brought them in you could give them to Ocko so that nobody knows?" Levine thanks the man and says, "It's okay. Morris will make out."

Another time, someone sitting next to Ocko blurts out, "Listen, Morris, why the hell don't you wear another shirt! You waiting for this one to walk off your back?"

Ocko bristles—and lies: "I have six dozen shirts in my apartment."

"Okay, so why don't you wear another one?"

"I don't have to. I *have* them."

As a rule, if Ocko says hello to anyone in the board room, that's a lengthy conversation for him. If any newcomer to the club offers him a friendly tip on a stock, Ocko retorts: "Mind your own business, mister." And he moves to another seat.

Sometimes, as the office's most important customer, Ocko asserts his right to sit at Charley Levine's desk when the manager is out. Levine, who handles Ocko's trading account, is the only one who knows that Ocko, the folder-inner, the waste-basket-rummager, the assistant janitor, the crummy basement apartment dweller, is also Ocko of the Very Substantial Holdings, Ocko the Millionaire. He's the only one who knows that Ocko carries a little pillbox with nitro pills. He had a heart attack a year before. On this morning, he takes one of the pills and says casually to Levine, "I could go at any time."

Such is life for one of the richest men in Washington Heights—and such is his death. On Saturday evening, September 12, 1970, while he's filling in the final sections of the New York *Times* at the newsstand, Ocko collapses. He dies shortly after the ambulance gets him to the hospital.

The death of a millionaire is news of a sort only if you know he is a millionaire. It took seventeen days for the news to seep through via the surrogate's court, where Lilian Isaacs applied for letters of administration of her dead brother's estate. He died without a will. Mrs. Isaacs suspected her brother had been worth perhaps $50,000–$100,000. Since his entire estate was in stocks, it was easy to run up an assessment through the Sartorius office. It turned out that on the day he died, September 12, he was worth $3,900,000.

The news made a half-column in the New York *Times* on September 29. Only, by this time there was a conscious effort to cover up certain aspects of his life. For example, in the *Times* account the apartment rent he paid is given as $148. In the *Daily News,* the folder-inner job is described as "a favor for a friend." For a dead millionaire there is a tendency to lyricize his virtues. He now becomes brilliant, generous, and a kind man who couldn't do enough for his neighbors.

Pete Belea, superintendent of the building in which Ocko lived and who knew him for eighteen years, still refuses to believe that Ocko had anything like that kind of money. Belea, a bald, heavyset Yugoslav with a thick accent, is skeptical because the whole thing defies common sense. "How could a man with $4,000,000 *want* to live like this?" he says, as he takes a visitor through the Ocko apartment. "A smart pig wouldn't want to live like this. Maybe he was crazy."

A friend of Belea, the superintendent of a nearby building,

278 ROGUES TO RICHES

was furious when he heard of Ocko's wealth. "Last week he fix my TV, he charge me twenty bucks. I know he got four million, I keel him charging me so much. Must be a nut."

Once in the basement Belea saw a woman tenant give Ocko some chicken for the five cats that Ocko fed regularly. When she left, Ocko started eating the chicken. Belea said, "Hey, you not give it to the cats?" Ocko shrugged: "It's good chicken."

At the Sartorius office, Charley Levine, the manager who handled Ocko's account, explains how he accumulated $3,900,000 through the stock market.

"He started buying Natomas in 1952 when it was still owned by the American President Lines. It was low then, maybe 5–6. I asked him once why. He said he liked the name. He kept adding as it rose. Then he bought more, always on margin. It was a dividend payer and he reinvested the dividends. When he died, he held 46,000 shares of Natomas, which is a holding company with heavy interests in shipping, real estate, and mostly oil in Indonesia. In 1969, when it was near an all-time high of 130, I persuaded him to unload a lot. It wasn't easy: He said, 'What the hell will I do with the money?' But I got him to sell some just to lighten his margin. But he'd argue: 'Nobody needs my money.' Then in 1965 he started picking up a lot of Fifth Avenue Coach stock, mostly at 6–8. And it rose to $20. It was in those two stocks that he made most of his money."

Otto Stern, a registered rep in the office who knew Ocko, said almost everybody in the board room was incredulous that Morris had so much in stock. "What a waste," he said, "what a waste."

About a month after his death, his sister Lilian visited the Sartorius board room just to sit in the chair her brother favored. "They explained about the stock board to me and I tried to feel what Morris felt when he watched the numbers run across the board, but it just doesn't make any sense to me. I never owned a stock in my life. But something about it must have given Morris some joy in life."

Since he died intestate, without a will, the $3,900,000 will be divided according to a legal formula. Lilian Isaacs gets about one-fourth of the estate, and the nieces and nephews of his other brother and sisters get one-eighth or one-sixteenth. After state and federal taxes are paid on the estate, her share—one-fourth—will probably be worth more than half a million.

Mrs. Isaacs is understandably very defensive of her dead brother. "I was going down to New York in a car pool and some woman in the car said, 'Lilian, I don't care if he was your brother. He was foolish and stupid because he didn't use his money.' I got mad and I still don't talk to her. Don't make him out a miser. He wasn't. He enjoyed life in his own way. You know, he used to read a lot: history, biography, science; and he had a sense of humor. And he was gentle and kind."

One day, while visiting the Sartorius board room, one of the regulars was scornful of the publicity Ocko had gotten after death. "Crazy. Nobody gave a shit about him when he was alive, but then he really didn't care about anybody else, either. A plain nothing as a human being. He picks a couple of right stocks and now he's a somebody, a man of substance. He suddenly becomes brilliant, generous, and a kindly fellow. What crap."

Later, in a neighborhood luncheonette another board room regular, a retired dress contractor, spoke up:

"There's an old Talmudic legend about a great big bird that appears over the whole world once every seventy years. It's not like any bird man has ever seen. Very beautiful, and it's called Kikiyon. Funny name. Maybe Greek, originally. In any case, when Kikiyon comes out every seventy years for his flight around the earth, what he does is spit—once. From way up on high that saliva drifts down to earth. Now this spit is the most precious thing out of the sky. If even a tiny droplet hits you, you're the most fortunate man on earth. If you're deformed, you're miraculously cured. If you're sick, you're healed. If you're poor, you become immensely wealthy. But it can't be both. One or the other: cure or wealth. I figure the bird came around one year and somehow a droplet hit Morris up here in Washington Heights. Since the miraculous, all-

knowing droplet could sense that Morris wasn't physically deformed or sick, it gave him the blessing of wealth. It wasn't
such a smart piece of spit after all because anybody who knew
Morris could tell he was a badly deformed, sick spirit. So he
became rich. Sometimes I think that the big bird, Kikiyon,
didn't just spit on him. It must have peed on him good. Who
else would be buying Natomas at $5 and $6 a share eighteen
years ago?"

Maybe we'd better scratch Morris Ocko as a likely hero of
American capitalism. The urine-stenched basement walls stay
with you too long afterward. Just too many drawbacks. But
we do have one more possibility who fills the bill better than
any of the others.

"A Drifter Without Human Ties.
Maybe That's the Secret."

Let's turn to Edwin Lewis Clark. Even the name is splendidly American. Every schoolchild had to read about the great
Lewis and Clark expedition in the early nineteenth century,
the one that President Jefferson sent out to explore the Northwest. Edwin Lewis Clark. There he is: tall, muscular, blue
eyes, curly black hair, quite good-looking. We know he's forty-
nine, but he looks ten years younger. We observe him washing
his beautiful new Cadillac Coupé De Ville, the two-door hard-
top.

He is doing this with loving care on the narrow street in
front of his apartment house, 749 Garland Avenue, between
Seventh and Eighth streets in downtown Los Angeles, a block
away from the busy Harbor Freeway. Garland Apartments is
only three years old, a three-story white-stucco building,
trimmed with gold paint. It has forty-one furnished units.
Edwin Lewis Clark lives in 305 on the third floor. It's a one-
bedroom apartment furnished in routine modern. He pays
$130 a month rent.

The neighborhood is old but genteel. Across the street is a

new Holiday Inn motel. There are several old, turreted, wooden houses on the block, relics of another century, long since turned into boardinghouses for the elderly.

When he finishes washing and polishing his car, Ed Clark checks his oil. The stick says he needs a quart and he pours it in, out of the two-and-a-half-gallon oilcan he buys at Sears so that he saves 25 cents a quart. He wears a $2 pair of chino slacks he bought at Sears on sale and a $1.49 white T-shirt. There are weary, scuffed moccasins on his feet. Upstairs in the closet is a checked-gray suit which he bought for $38 at a sale, a tan sports jacket, and beige slacks which cost $40. There is no TV set in the apartment but two battered transistor radio sets. In a dresser drawer he has five rings with imitation stones. The whole lot is worth perhaps $20. He wears an Omega watch with his initials on the back.

There's a cheap woman's wristwatch. In another drawer is a small, black covered looseleaf notebook filled with numbers and code symbols. There are no books or magazines in the apartment, no photos of friends or family, no records, no paintings; but there is a recent issue of the *Wall Street Journal*. The refrigerator is stocked with frozen TV dinners and cans of soup and some cellophane-wrapped cookies and a few apples.

The car shiny, the oil tank filled, Edwin Lewis Clark goes up to his apartment to wash. It's Friday, near the end of the month. Time for his monthly visit to the one man in the country who knows where he is and what he's doing and how much he's worth. Not the one who *cares;* the one who *knows.* (Nobody *cares.* Clark likes it that way.) The man who knows that —and almost nothing else about Edwin Lewis Clark—is a registered rep, Edward L. Adams, at the downtown L.A. office of Merrill Lynch, Pierce, Fenner & Smith. Clark came into Adams' life three years earlier. He dropped in cold and never told Adams why he selected him of all the registered reps sitting around the big brokerage office. In many ways, Clark has been the ideal customer: He doesn't hang around bothering Adams; doesn't phone every day to see how his stocks are doing; doesn't argue; doesn't even ask for stock tips. And he never gets into monologues about himself or his stock market philosophy; never gets personal; and doesn't try to become a friend or confidant. A perfect customer.

In the bathroom, Clark starts his electric shaver. A pang. Sharp. Sudden. He draws in his breath, puts down the Remington shaver, and walks with careful steps to the living room. The pang is still with him, still sharp. No panic, man. He phones for a cab. Quickly, please. He dresses again, puts on his glasses, and slips a folding checkbook into his hip pocket.

Five minutes later he's out in front of the building. The cab's there and he takes it to a nearby hospital, Central Receiving, the Emergency Division. He's there an hour and they find out he's a veteran. Someone calls Wadsworth Veterans Hospital farther out in L.A. They send an ambulance, and by late afternoon—this is Friday, March 17, 1967—he's in the intensive care unit at Wadsworth. A coronary infarct.

Adams, his broker, isn't particularly worried. Clark doesn't come in that regularly, and besides, there's really nothing new in Clark's stocks.

A week later, Friday, March 23, Clark's dead. He's forty-nine. A clerk in the hospital's property office, sealing Clark's meager possessions, notes a folding checkbook. He goes through the stubs and Suddenly Realizes. He calls the public administrator's office and gets Peter R. Zaferis, the supervising deputy whom he knows slightly: "Pete, I think we got one. This guy has a checkbook on him and unless he's kidding himself, he's got $20,000 in a checking account downtown. We got a next of kin, a sister in Philadelphia."

Zaferis, a good-looking Greek with iron-gray hair, has been in his job eleven years. The public administrator takes charge of estates in which there is no will and no California next of kin. The office takes a small fee for its services and generally does a good job in getting the maximum return of the estate to the nearest related heirs. Zaferis turned to an assistant, Carl D. Dickinson, a jovial, freckled redhead and asked him to drop over to Clark's apartment on Garland Avenue and pick up all the papers there.

Early the next morning, Dickinson called Zaferis at home. "Hey, Pete, I found a monthly securities statement from Merrill Lynch in one of his drawers, and unless the computer burped at the wrong time, we got a rich one. He got 114,000 shares of United Artists."

Zaferis picked up the morning paper with the New York closing stock prices and found the 114,000 shares were worth, at $35.50 a share, more than $4,000,000. "Oh, my God," Zaferis said aloud to his wife. All he had was a few dozen shares of American Telephone and Seaboard Airlines worth several thousand dollars. "Four million bucks!" This called for Saturday work, and he arranged to meet Dickinson at the office in the morning.

Saturday morning, after Zaferis and Dickinson had gone over all of Clark's papers and found the 114,000 shares seemed real enough and not a computer mistake—previous statements from Merrill Lynch confirmed the shareholdings in United Artists —they decided to call Clark's listed next of kin, his sister. She was a Lenore B. Jasewicz of Philadelphia. They assumed it was her married name.

Zaferis explained who he was; that her brother was dead of a heart attack; that he had listed her as next of kin; and that there was considerable money in his estate. After she got over the shock, she asked sensibly: "What do you mean 'considerable'?" Zaferis remained a little vague because he wanted to be absolutely sure the money was really there. "I *was* pretty sure by now," he recalls, "but think what a helluva mess if I call her and tell her there's $4,000,000 and it turns out to be a bookkeeping error, a computer foul-up. If I say 'considerable' I'm safe. Everybody's 'considerable' is different."

More important, he stressed she shouldn't sign any papers for anyone, to avoid professional missing-heir hunters who might suddenly start flocking about her once the news was out. They exact a heavy percentage. Right now she was ably represented by the public administrator of the County of Los Angeles. She was in good, safe hands. And he'd be in touch with her soon.

Toward the end of their talk, he said, "Do you know if he has a wife anywhere?"

"He was married once, but he got divorced," she said. She also disclosed that she had two sisters and a brother, and she hadn't heard from her dead brother in more than eleven years. Oh, yes, she wasn't married. Her brother had changed his name to Clark while he was in the Air Force.

By Monday the Merrill Lynch office and broker Adams had confirmed that Edwin Lewis Clark was indeed the owner of 114,000 shares of United Artists stock which the brokerage was holding in its own name, since it was a margin account. But since the stock had steadily gone up since he bought the shares at 20, there had never been any need for a margin call. But Zaferis was still puzzled: How could an Air Force enlisted man have accumulated $4,000,000 worth of stock?

By Wednesday the Los Angeles *Times* had the story: AIRMAN HAD MILLIONS BUT ONLY TWO SUITS. Arrangements were made to ship the body to Philadelphia for burial after funeral services in the Oakland Cemetery of Frankford, Philadelphia.

Meanwhile, the Los Angeles *Times* Syndicate had sent the feature to subscriber papers around the country, and it hit the Miami *Herald*. There it was spotted by Judge Max Swann of the appellate court. This character with the $4,000,000 sounded just like the man to whom his sister-in-law, Helen Pinder, forty-six, had once been married. She still called herself Helen Clark. She was a legal secretary for a large Miami law firm. He called his sister-in-law: They weren't divorced, were they? Not as far as she knew. Then he put in a call to the public administrator's office in Los Angeles, and now, for the first time, Pete Zaferis could see a messy will fight looming up on what had been a nice, quiet, romantic money-out-of-the-blue scene.

Helen Clark hired a leading Los Angeles legal firm, O'Melveny & Myers. Clark's brother and sisters hired another firm.

After considerable negotiations they reached a settlement on June 13, 1968. Under its terms, Helen Clark got a little over half of Ed Clark's stock market fortune: some $1,788,488. By this time it was definitely known that he had left an estate of $4,083,750, shrunk to $3,444,366 by taxes and administrative expenses. Clark's three sisters and brothers divided about $1,466,000, or about $366,000 each, less their legal expenses, which weren't cheap.

How did Clark do it? How does a retired master sergeant who at his peak earning period, 1956, never earned more than $300 a month accumulate a stake that enabled him to go into the market and make more than $4,000,000 in a little over a decade?

In addition to his pay, most of which he saved, he received three reenlistment bonuses which averaged about $800 each, or another $2,400. And another former Air Force veteran who had known Clark slightly when he served with him in North Africa from 1950 to 1952, and again in Germany in 1955, recalled that Clark was a shrewd gambler, adept at dice and poker. "He was strictly an odds player. He knew the come-and-don't-come odds and just what chances he had of filling a four-flush. And he bluffed at the right time. I think he always came out ahead after a session."

In 1956 when Clark retired from the Air Force, it's estimated he had about $14,000. Actually, there's reason to believe that he began dabbling in the market as early as 1952 through a U.S. branch brokerage office in Germany. He bought 2,000 shares of Minute Maid on margin. The pioneering, canned orange juice concentrate company was then selling for about $6 and he had to put up only $6,000, since the margin requirement was then 50 percent. The stock low for the year had been 5⅜. He sold out in 1955 at 18 to 19, which was the high for that year in Minute Maid. On his first transaction then, he had a net profit of $25,000. In 1955 he decided on Revlon and bought 7,000 shares, on margin again, at 3 to 3½, for an investment of $23,000. Revlon began moving. There was a 100 percent stock split in 1956, which gave him 14,000 shares, and in

1958 he sold half of them at the 25–27 range for $182,000. The other 7,000 shares made another 3,500 shares, as a result of a 2-for-1 stock split. He sold these off in the mid-sixties at an average price of $65, for a total of $682,000. Meanwhile, on the first 7,000 shares of Revlon, which he sold in 1958 for $182,000, he loaded up on that old conservative bond masquerading as a common stock, American Telephone. By buying on margin, he picked up several thousand shares and again was the beneficiary of two splits: the 1959 3-for-1 split and the 1964 2-for-1. After he sold the rest of his Revlon in 1961, he put that money in Telephone, too, with a 70 percent margin. And he rode the stock until the low 70's in 1964, when he sold it all off. He was also reinvesting his dividends from Telephone in further stock purchases.

In all, then, when he first approached broker Edward Adams, in the downtown Los Angeles office in early 1964, he was worth nearly $2,000,000. It was no trick ordering about $2,000,000 worth of United Artists stock, then selling in the low 20's. At his death in 1967, the stock had just about doubled and, in fact, went even higher after his death, but before the stock was distributed to his wife, brother and sisters.

Thus, Edwin Lewis Clark, high school dropout, retired enlisted man in the Air Force, who started with a stake of $14,000, ran it up to $4,000,000 in just four stocks in a period of fifteen years.

Clearly, Ed Clark fulfills many of the qualities we want for our new hero of American capitalism: an ex-serviceman, not too well educated, keeping his own counsel, modest, not an in-and-outer. But there are some adverse factors here, too. He didn't seem to enjoy his money at all; he was unkind to his wife, miserable, in fact. But far worse, in a way, is the fact that he never made mistakes, almost always bought at the right low and almost always sold at just the right high. This is clearly unnatural, almost suspicious, in fact. It goes so much against the grain of normal investor experience that his incredible skill —luck?—is almost un-American.

His buying a new Caddy each year is a humanizing quality.

At least he used his wealth for that, but what else? No charitable donations, no gifts to family. No enjoyment of life. And
worse, no will. People who don't make wills are almost always
selfish.

Well, if none of these three is likely to make an effective
hero of American capitalism, a worthy model for our Investment Clubs, an exemplar for those thousands of youngsters
whose aunts and uncles give them copies of *Teen-agers Guide
to the Stock Market*, or who get a few shares of stock on their
birthdays or bar mitzvahs, what are we left with, except a few
deduced rules on how you, too, can do it?

1. You mustn't tell anyone you've made it, or even that
you're making it. That rules out most of us normally open
souls who'd die if we had to keep our mouths closed about our
marvelous coups in the market.

2. You can't spend a dime on yourself, or maybe just a few
dimes. After all, the gods did permit Ed Clark a new Caddy
every year.

3. The more miserably you live, the less you spend on yourself or anyone else, the better.

4. Cut all ties to family, have no friends. It seems to help
if you really don't like women at all. Just plain, old-fashioned
misogyny. For at least two of our three characters, it seemed
to be a big help.

5. You mustn't get any kind of professional help: no investment counselors, no garrulous registered reps, no market letters; you heed no rumors.

6. Join the old Rothschild animal club: buy sheep and sell
deer. Even better, you buy stocks cheap and *hold* them. No
in-and-out day trades. Not too many trades. Just a few, and
all-out on those. Clark, the wonder, did it in just four trades.

(The best case against day trading, the in-and-out operations
by the amateur, comes from an astute investor, Roger Bridwell,
who used to be on the staff of *Barron's*: "For the past 20 years
I have systematically asked my friends in the brokerage business for the names of people they knew from *firsthand observation of* their accounts who had consistently made money over

the years trading in stocks . . . profiting on the short swings in rising and declining markets. . . . *So far I haven't obtained a single name.* Therefore, I can only agree with Bernard Baruch who said that in his lifetime he had known only one successful amateur speculator.")

7. Don't make a will. Sure, old George Miller did, but he's not really one of the crew in some respects.

8. The less education, the better. You finish college, you've got yourself a mighty handicap. Graduate school? Forget it. A few years ago, the *Financial Analysts Journal* tackled the old sneer professional stock analysts often get: If you're so smart, why aren't you rich? Here are these thirteen thousand analysts, filled to their receding hairlines with P/E ratios, cash flows, and the rest of the trappings of their trade, everyone with an MBA, and years and years of special training, and they can't do what miserable Ed Clark or slobby Morris Ocko did. How come? Obviously, they were educated beyond their dreamed-of station in life.

This business of overeducation puzzled me awhile, until I came across a comment once made by Armand Erpf, a brilliant stock analyst who was a partner in Loeb, Rhoades, until his death in 1971:

> Prescience is a rare gift . . . in the stock market. It occurs only in a small minority and is not necessarily associated with tradition, intelligence or education. This also explains why so often the brutal, the uneducated, and those of obscure origins who have the gift of prescience, or of insight, and who have little to lose in following their hunches, catapult themselves to fortune and power while the nice people are swept into the dustbin of history.

And a century earlier, a wise Frenchman, Étienne Senancour, even gave the strange phenomenon a proper label. He called it *le vulgaire des sages,* the folly of the wise:

> They are too clever, they over-intellectualize the world. They are too logical; they make history a simple pattern

of cause and effect, which is not the truth. They do not allow for the unforeseen accident. More, they have no flair for imponderable things which cannot be put into a straightforward argument . . . they are lacking in instinct. . . . This is where the plain man scores. He is not intellectual. He is not too logical; but he has a curiously sound instinct, just because he is as close to real life, about what is going to happen.

As Eric Hoffer sums it up: "The well-adjusted make poor prophets."

INTERLUDE

New York, September, 1970

Phil is filled with mirth, the laughter of a cynic who's discovered a new cyn.

"I figured in a big art deal yesterday. I didn't get a dime out of it, but I learned something new. Bluntschli phoned me from Zurich. There's a woman he knows in New York, and he asked if I'd help her get around. I met her and she told me what the situation was. Let's call her the Countess.

"Now there's another fund formed in Europe that's going to deal only in art, no stocks. Supposedly the fine arts are the best hedge against inflation and so on. Paintings, sculpture, vases. Whatever. It's an offshore fund so supposedly only non-U.S. citizens can buy into it. It happens that I know the guy who is the art adviser to this fund. Which is why Bluntschli sent the Countess to me for a little introduction. She has a small collection of paintings with her. She lays them out in her apartment and the art adviser and I come up. He thought the eight paintings were absolutely magnificent. To me, well, they looked like a million other ordinary paintings. But then I'm no expert. He paid her $3,500 cash for the eight and took them down with him to his limousine. Later that day he had them sold to a dealer in Switzerland. Now this dealer is going to resell those paintings to the arts fund for something like $25,000 and rebate half the spread to the fund's art adviser, the guy in the limousine. The valuation of $25,000 is now set by the Swiss dealer and when the fund's adviser says the paintings are a good buy, why, he has a Swiss dealer's evaluation to back him up.

"Of course this isn't the first deal the arts adviser has pulled.

I figure he has made $500,000 net in the past six months with similar deals. The paintings are always bought somewhere else, sold to the dealer in Zurich, and he turns around and sells them to other dealers who sell them to the arts fund. Mostly Belgian, Luxembourg and Swiss dealers. At least 50 percent profit on each go-round which is shared with the cooperative dealer. Reminds me a little of George Herman's little stock operation with the OTC brokers around the country except in this case each art dealer knows exactly what's happening and the victims will be the people who buy into this new fund."

"I'm pretty good at thinking up schemes to make money," Phil went on, "but I got to admit that from time to time I am surpassed." He went on to tell me the story of Jack Dick.

"In my early days on the street I met this character, Jack Dick, a Brooklyn boy who had spent summers on a ranch and I think secretly modeled himself on the Marlboro man. Well, he and his father were running a factoring firm, Harper, Malone, lending money at higher than normal interest to corporations with higher than normal risks. In the 1960–62 period they became active lenders to stock plungers who wanted better margin on their stocks than their brokers could give them. So they went to this firm, Harper, Malone, which lent them up to 70 percent on their stock—at high interest. I was involved because the firm was giving me a lot of stock business, which was great. The firm had a catastrophe when the '62 market bust and Jack's father had to pick up the pieces that were left. Jack was married to a gal named Linda, who came from a wealthy family, and now he looked around for something to do. He remembered his summers on the ranch and got an idea. Cattle. Fairly brilliant, if I must say so."

Jack Dick offered to let Phil come in on the ground floor of his big idea. They had several meetings.

"I guess I didn't believe him. Maybe, it was that I just didn't like him. In any case I bowed out. Also, I just couldn't see him putting this complicated package together. But he really came through. Oh, there had been some trouble with the New York attorney general. There had been a petition filed by

the state that Dick's operation, Black Watch Farms, attempted
to mulct the New York public through fraudulent statements
and concealment of material facts in connection with their attempt to raise $5,000,000 from the public. But eventually this
problem was solved and Black Watch Farms grew splendidly.
The doctors and dentists came in with their money to buy
herds of black Angus cows."

Phil met Jack Dick again in 1964, and again he pressed
Phil to become a salesman for the herds.

"I still didn't believe," Phil recalls, "but I knew that he was
selling a helluva lot of herds and the commission was great.
He once sent his private plane down to New York to bring
me, my wife and kids up to his place, the Black Watch Farms
near Wappingers Falls, New York. I was impressed. It was
probably the most beautiful feudal estate in America. Once he
flew me up during their October sales and it was a fantastic
operation, what he called their Annual Showcase Sale. There
were cattlemen from all over the world, from Texas to Ar-
gentina.

"He'd get about eight hundred of them and their wives
and he put on a great show. There was a cocktail party, dinner
in the wall-to-wall-carpeted tents. There'd be top entertain-
ment the night before the auction. The next morning while
the cattle buyers looked over the stock, there'd be kilted bag-
pipers trooping the grounds skirling their miserable music.
Since it was a show biz operation, he naturally had a Broadway
press agent pushing black Angus. Connie Francis, the singer,
was an investor. So was Peter Revson, son of one of the founders
of Revlon."

It was essentially based on a tax gimmick, Phil explained.
There are a lot of people in our society with high current
income such as doctors, dentists, lawyers and popular enter-
tainers who need a tax shelter, who need a way of deducting
much more of their income so that they fall into a lower
bracket. The Treasury permitted farmers, even part-time farmers, depreciation deductions if they owned cattle. For example, a lawyer might buy $30,000 worth of cattle for his

farm or to be kept on somebody else's farm. The following year he could easily write off perhaps $22,000 in depreciation and other deductions on his cattle and greatly reduce his tax bracket. This was legal then. And the interest on the purchase loan for the cattle was also deductible.

"Jack first put together a syndicate deal. He got a number of high-income people together and bought this large farm upstate. There they bred black Angus cattle, which he sold to cattle breeders from around the country. Black Angus come from Scotland. When I turned down the idea of being one of the original investors, Jack suggested that I sell units for a 10-percent commission.

"These units which he figured were perfect investments for high-income people consisted of ten black Angus cows, a herd. The buyer would pay $35,000 and then $600 a year for each cow's maintenance, feeding and artificial insemination to produce offspring.

"Now, Jack is a great salesman and he described how he was going to sell these units and more. For example, he said that the highest price ever paid up to then for a black Angus breeding bull had been only $100,000. He knew he could get that price up to $1,500,000 in a few years."

The appeal of the black Angus cattle, Phil went on, was that it carried more beef for its size than any other breed and it had no horns to damage other cattle in transit. Even when crossed with commoner beasts such as Hereford, the black Angus bulls transmitted their desired qualities.

"He took me around the stalls one day and there was something bothering me. Here prize bulls were being bought and sold for $500,000, for $1,000,000 each, and I couldn't understand one thing.

"I said, 'Jack, you told me that a good bull can produce 20,000–30,000 vials of semen a year and there's a 70-percent conception rate; that is, seven out of ten cows so impregnated will conceive. Which means that one or two bulls could impregnate just about every worthwhile black Angus cow in the country. So why not use that one top bull for the job? After all he can be made to have an orgasm fifty times a day. All you need is enough test tubes. What's all this business of needing a lot of very expensive bulls when one could do the whole job?' I remember his answer:

" 'Listen, Phil, you must be out of your mind. If we used just *one* bull, the whole business would be over; we wouldn't need the other bulls and the whole business of fancy auctions for these bulls. Think of all the publicity we'd lose if the public didn't hear that one bull sold for a million bucks.'

"So they continued breeding, which meant they were making a lot of additional animals which meant that he had to find new batches of doctors to buy herds and maintain them. You constantly need more and more people coming in with money or the whole thing collapses.

"Well, Jack is no fool, and so in July, 1968, he made a deal with Bermec Corporation, a truck-leasing operation, listed on the Big Board, to buy out his interest in Black Watch in return for stock in Bermec. He got $18,000,000 in letter stock, stuff that had to be held a year or so. He turned around and sold $10,000,000 of that at a discount, for $7,000,000 cash, and promptly proceeded to buy a beautiful $1,300,000 estate in Greenwich, Connecticut, a forty-room Tudor mansion. I think it was the largest private sale in Greenwich's history. And all this without having much of his own dough into the Black Watch deal. I call that a great Class A promotion."

How smart Jack Dick was in getting out became apparent late in 1969 when the whole deal started coming unstuck. Not long ago I talked to a podiatrist named Herb Prentice who has been practicing thirty-three years and has a patient roster of top show business and business names. During an eighteen-month period Prentice sold $3,500,000 worth of herd units, mostly to patients or friends of patients. With commissions at 7½ percent and bonuses, he made about $260,000.

"I got into it," he recalled, "because I'm a big golfer and Jack Dick's sales manager, Bill Gladstone, was also one. Well, I had a built-in clientele right in my office and it wasn't hard to sell the plan to my patients. For example, just in the June–December, 1968, period I sold more than $1,000,000 worth of herds to them. Most of them would come in for at least three herds or $100,000, but a lot took six herds. I did realistic selling. I told them if they were in a high-enough bracket, the program would work out a profit to them—in addition to their annual tax deductions—*in ten years.* Ten years. That's a long time. Anything can happen. There's a guy in Great Neck, where I live, I tried to sell. Runs a string of employment agencies. I tried for weeks to sell him and couldn't. You know I have a lot of respect for his business acumen."

I got another view of the black Angus operation from Mark Drake, a crewcut, ex-Kansan who is a cattle management expert. He has a PhD in animal genetics and had been called in by Bermec Leasing after they took over the black Angus farms.

"Most investors lost on the deal. Part of it was the high prices Jack Dick set on the cattle. Cows were selling for maybe $500–$700, purebred only for breeding. He took his most daring figure—and then doubled it. So he asked for $3,500 a cow and got it.

"There were other aspects of the whole operation that almost seemed made-to-order for a con game. For example, how would you know that the cows they showed you were really yours? Well, supposedly each cow carried a tattoo on the inside of an ear, between two ribs in letters $3/8$ inch to $1/2$ inch high. But a lot of tattoos weren't put in properly. Tattoos fade. There were mistakes in numbering and as a result a lot of mistaken registration of animals. If the tattoos aren't right or readable, animals are kicked out of auctions. Then there was the trouble with the bull semen. This has to be kept in liquid nitrogen and a lot of semen just went bad in storage. In March, 1970, there was a survey of the animals at the farm to see how they rated. The U.S. Department of Agriculture has a grading system in which 17 is tops and 12 or below is commercial grade only which means the animals are fit only for slaughter, not breeding purposes. Out of some 17,500 cows being maintained at the black Angus farms for absentee owners, all but 385 were grade 12 or lower. Of some 1,400 bulls, all but 11 were grade 12 or lower. Some breeding program!"

In addition to bad management the herd owners had to face other severe problems. For one thing, the tax laws were changed in 1969 to make it much more difficult to get the great tax savings of the past. Even worse, black Angus cattle are falling out of favor. As expert Mark Drake put it: "We now have new judging standards. The new bull is taller and longer, higher off the ground, more upstanding and much more growth potential than standard black Angus, which is just a rectangular block of an animal. Packing companies are finding it doesn't cost any more to kill a 1,200-pound animal than an 800-pound animal. A lot of breeders are turning to a Swiss breed called Simmental."

The final blow for the cattle herd owners came in September, 1970, when Black Watch Farms filed a petition for bankruptcy, which meant that the Farms could no longer afford to feed and care for the cattle. As a result most of the owners either had to shift their cows to other farms or have them slaughtered. Mark Drake has found homes for many of the investors' cattle, but it still costs them about $250 a year per animal.

By early 1971 there were more than twenty-five lawsuits under way against Black Watch Farms by dissatisfied herd owners. One suit alone, a class action, was seeking $10,000,000, which is supposedly the amount investors put into cattle contracts between May, 1969, and January, 1970.

Marvin Usdin, a Long Island attorney who is representing a number of the plaintiffs, estimates that there were 540 investors in all who put up nearly $45,000,000. "A lot of them thought it was a nice clean venture with tax savings and all. But most of them will be slaughtered. So will their cattle. The Black Watch bankruptcy is a Chapter 11. Under it the company officers' salaries are being paid out of the assets that are left. The actual administration expenses are about $15,000 a week, so I don't think there's going to be much left over for the victims."

What of Jack Dick who dreamed up the original operation? He still lives in palatial splendor in Greenwich, Connecticut. I phoned him, but he felt he'd need permission of his lawyers —"y'know there's a hell of a lot of litigation swirling around" —before he could talk. They didn't think it was advisable.

Bermac Corporation, a high flier of the 1967–69 market, is now in great distress—after writing off some $13,000,000 of its investment in Black Watch Farms. In March, 1971, Bermec applied to the federal court for protection under the Bankruptcy Act.*

Phil had a final footnote on the operation. "Jack went over to London and bought a lot of paintings and silverware. He got a factor to lend him $2,000,000 on his paintings, based on official valuations and appraisals. When he didn't pay the loan, they went after him and he said, 'Just sell my collateral.' When they tried to, they found that they couldn't get much for the stuff. They're very unhappy with him. You might say that Jack Dick has himself a package of troubles. But still not nearly as big as Bermec's—or the doctors and dentists who bought the herds."

In September, 1971, Jack Dick was arrested by detectives of the New York district attorney's office on a charge of stealing $840,000 by using false information and documents to get a loan for that amount. Among other felonies, he was charged with forging eleven invoices from three well-known art galleries. The falsified bills of sale provided "astronomical values" to his recently acquired art—which he had to put up as collateral for the large loans.

* In June 1971, court-appointed trustees took over Bermec, which had a $2,900,000 loss in the last half of 1970.

15. The Sleeper

It is intelligent to ask two questions: *1) Is it possible?*
2) Can I do it? But it is unintelligent to ask these ques-
tions: 1) Is it real? 2) Has my neighbor Christopherson
done it?

—SÖREN KIERKEGAARD

Somewhere in London a man sleeps. He's been
in a cataleptic trance since 1898. He's Graham—no first name
—and he's on his way to becoming the wealthiest man in history,
ruler of half the earth's productive capacity. This will happen
in the year 2100—only 129 years from now—when he finally
awakens.

How did it start? Well, Graham had a cousin named
Warming:

> a solitary man without children, who made a big for-
> tune speculating in roads—the first Eadhamite roads—he
> bought all the patent rights and made a big company. . . .
> His roads killed the railroads in two dozen years; he bought
> up and Eadhamited all the tracks. And because he didn't
> want to break up his great property or let in shareholders,
> he left it all to the Sleeper, Graham, and put it under a
> Board of Trustees that he had picked and trained. He knew
> then that the Sleeper wouldn't wake, that he would go on
> sleeping until he died . . . then a man in the United States

who had lost two sons in a boat accident, followed that up
with another great bequest [for the Sleeper].

The Council of Trustees ruling the Sleeper's wealth is very
clever:

> They worked politics with money, and kept on adding to the
> money by working currency and tariffs. They grew—and
> grew. And for years the twelve Trustees had the growing of
> the Sleeper's estate, under hundreds of disguises and pseu-
> donyms. . . . Wielding an enormous influence and patron-
> age the Council had early assumed a political aspect. . . .
> At least the party organizations of two hemispheres were in
> its hands; it became an inner council of political control.
> . . . Steadily, steadfastly it grew. . . . In a hundred years
> Graham had become almost exclusive owner of Africa, of
> South America, of France, of London, of England . . . the
> Council bought and organized China, drilled Asia, crippled
> the Old World empires, undermined them financially, fought
> and defeated them. . . .

All this, of course, takes place in H. G. Wells' *When the
Sleeper Wakes,* one of his early prophetic novels.

Forget Graham, the Sleeper of fiction. The name to keep in
mind is Holden, the real perpetuator of fortune.

Every ten years *Fortune* magazine does a box score on our
richest Americans. Their most recent trackdown, was filled with
most of the obvious names—J. Paul Getty and Howard Hughes
leading all the rest with fortunes estimated at between $1 billion
and $1.5 billion each—but there were several surprises. Every-
one has heard of Dr. Edwin H. Land who invented the Polaroid
camera and was then credited with being worth $500,000,000 to
$1 billion, along with three members of the Pittsburgh Mellon
family, and H. L. Hunt of Dallas who underwrites far-right
causes. But whoever heard of Albert C. Buehler who was worth
$100,000,000 in Victor Comptometer stock; or William L.
McKnight whose fortune was then worth $300,000,000 to
$500,000,000 because he was the biggest single stockholder in
Minnesota Mining & Manufacturing?

There were five names in the $300,000,000–$500,000,000 list, and twenty-seven in the lesser list of $200,000,000–$300,000,000. In all, there were sixty-six men and women who each were worth at least $150,000,000. And nowhere on the list was anybody named Holden.

Everybody knows money begets money, and the odds are that the Rockefellers and Mellons and Du Ponts and Gettys will leave very wealthy descendants. But clans die out; willful heirs make mistakes, lose interest in moneymaking; the gods frown. Shirt sleeves to shirt sleeves in three generations, and so on. But the Holdens have something else going for them, besides the measly $5,000,000–$6,000,000 with which they are making their ascent to the most rarified heights of wealth. They have the tax laws and five hundred years.

True, they are opposed by the lawyers of the Internal Revenue Service who have been battling the peculiar ideas of the Holdens since old Jonathan Holden put the crazy package together in 1945. Every year or so, the government gathers its legal forces in the second-floor hearing room of the U.S. Tax Court in downtown Federal Plaza in New York to battle the Holdens and their dangerous ideas of perpetual accumulation. The federal government says the Holden idea is dangerous because, if unchecked, the Holden descendants would be controlling $10 *quadrillion.* That's the one that comes after mere trillions which, of course, is the step up after billions.

So far, the Holdens have more than held their own in the legal battles. Often, the government's legal forces can wear down an opponent and force him into a miserable compromise, but in this case, the Holdens have a little edge: They take their legal expenses right off the top of their five little trusts which are growing very nicely, just as Jonathan Holden planned.

Many enormously wealthy men on the *Fortune* list prefer to live with a comparative lack of ostentation. One car. One house. Public school for the children, and so on. But Randal Holden outdoes them. His office and headquarters for the Holden trusts that may someday rule the world is an abandoned candy store on East Third Street in New York's East Village.

The store, in a tenement which Randal Holden owns, has blacked-out windows. An orange juice can holds pencils. Until recently, he had no secretary but used his neighbor, P. Yeung, a Chinese laundryman, to take his phone calls. But that was getting a little awkward and Randal Holden has since taken on two women secretaries, part time. The desk is thirdhand, the ledger dog-eared, and only a fairly new IBM typewriter indicates that this might be something other than the headquarters of a teen-age gang.

There's a beat-up Firestone bike in the store which Holden uses to visit his various properties in the East Village and also to get to his car, which he parks on East Fourteenth Street, after driving down from his home in Larchmont.

Holden is fifty-five and 6 feet 1. He has blue eyes, darkening blond hair and a permanently creased forehead, as befits the man who has to worry about the fledgling steps of what might just barely turn out to be the greatest accumulation of money in the history of the earth.

It didn't start with Randal Holden. It was his father, Jonathan, a lawyer with several fascinating ideological addictions, which he loved to talk and write about. All of them contributed to the founding of The Trusts which, if the world is still around in a couple of hundred years and capitalism has still survived and there are Holdens about—well, if these conditions are met, there's a chance The Trusts *will* be world capitalism, writ large.

Jonathan Holden married when he was thirty and had seven daughters and three sons. (Two of the children were adopted.) When he died in 1967, he left, in addition, twenty-eight grandchildren and four great-grandchildren. He loved the role of family patriarch.

He set forth most of his ideas on wealth, posterity, compound interest and the proper uses of money accumulation in the book he put together in 1932 and had privately printed. He ran off one hundred copies, one of which is in the New York Public Library. In many ways, the book is a good summary of his odd views and laid the groundwork for The Trusts.

The volume is grandly titled:

THE HOLDENS OF HARTWICK: THE FUTURE LIFE
Life for Many or for Few
Nationalized Thrift and Other Papers
BY
Stephen and Jonathan Holden
AND
Holdens of The Hartwick Clan

Arranged by Jonathan Holden

By page 54 he gets into his real meat:

> Do you rarely take thought of your future life? Are you
> sure there may not stretch before you and me, an immense
> span of future existence to which we unwisely give little
> heed. . . ?
> Let us imagine a group of believers in and cultivators of
> the "Future Life." Suppose they asserted that their present
> greatest duty was to assist the probable plan of creation
> . . . by promoting the progress of humanity toward its poten-
> tial optimum of quality and quantity. . . . Suppose a group
> even of a single family which might be of more than average
> size [*his* large family, for example] and they believe that the
> members of the group would live again in the lives of the
> posterity of the group.

He saw members of this family employing "propaganda of almost hypnotic intensity directed toward the young of the group"
designed to win them over to the "Future Life" concept. For
several centuries, the group adheres to this propagation "so that
the same faith and practice was handed down from generation
to generation. . . ." As a result:

> a single family could within twenty or perhaps even
> ten generations by its expansion displace the organization of
> human society . . . without resorting to force or proselyti-
> zing . . . by underliving the multitude of unbelievers thru a
> less costly standard of living in material things, so that thus
> the requirements of the believers in the way of food, cloth-
> ing and housing would be easily satisfied . . . by saving. . . .

All this was preliminary to the basic concept: the powers of compound interest. He collected all sorts of interest tables and knew that $1 invested for a century at 4 percent became $50, or in 235 years $10,000. That if a single cent should be kept invested at a mere 4 percent interest for 1,000 years, it would become $1,000 trillion. He wrote this in 1912 when he calculated that all the real and personal property in the world was worth less than a trillion dollars. And, of course, he had the old one about how Peter Minuit, when buying Manhattan Island from the Indians in 1626, would have done better to put out $24 cash at 7 percent interest. By 1912 it would have become more than $5 billion. (In 1970, the buildings and land of Manhattan had an estimated worth of $40 billion. But if Minuit had simply invested the $24 at 6½ percent interest for the 344 years from 1626 to 1970—he'd have a hell of a time finding a bank that would endure that long—the money would have grown to nearly $62 billion and his descendants would have been spared the headaches of erecting those structures.)

He worked out compound interest tables showing what would happen to $10,000 invested in 1912 under a trust providing that the income accumulate and be added, with only a tiny expenditure each year. In 100 years, 2012, at a mere 3 percent interest, there would be $187,000 in the fund; in 200 years $3,420,000; more than $2 billion in 500 years; and $3 trillion in 1,000 years.

Or forget a mere $10,000. Start with a million. At compound interest of 4 percent in 100 years it becomes $50,505,000. At 5 percent, $131,000,000 and at 6 percent—the current prevailing rate—$339,000,000.

Inevitably, he asked in his book:

> Why has not some family invested a dollar so that its descendants might obtain billions? . . . No individual or family has yet put the cumulative power of compound interest to the test for more than about two centuries. It is fortunate for the general welfare of humanity that such is the case, as otherwise too great wealth would be acquired by a few. [That was just for the record.]

Naturally, his patron saint was Benjamin Franklin, our great apostle of compound interest. In 1790, when Franklin died, he set up two trust funds with about $5,000 in each, one to be administered by the city of Philadelphia, the other by Boston. It provided that these funds should be lent out to "young married artificers" under twenty-five who had served their apprenticeships in those cities. The loans would enable them to set up their own businesses. They were to pay 5 percent on the loans. The trusts were to run two hundred years and then the funds were to be divided between city and state according to a formula.

As the years passed, there were fewer and fewer "qualified artificers" and the courts put the age up to thirty-five. Still not enough: From 1885 to 1917 the trustees of the Philadelphia trust couldn't find any qualified applicants, and by 1908 the fund had grown to $175,000. In 1890, after the first hundred years had passed, $133,000 was given the Franklin Institute of Philadelphia for its building fund. Eventually, in 1990, the remainder will be divided between Philadelphia and the state of Pennsylvania.

A contemporary of Ben Franklin's named Peter Thellusson was born in Paris in 1737 and settled in England, where he made a great deal of money in trade. He died in 1797, leaving £100,000 to his wife and children—in today's terms, something like $2,200,000—and the rest of his estate, then about £700,000 [about $15,000,000 in today's purchasing values], he left to trustees. The money was to accumulate for the lives of his sons and their sons—Peter's grandsons—even those who weren't born at the time Peter died. Reasonable estimates were that the trust would last at least seventy-five years and would accumulate incredible amounts—anywhere from £27,000,000 up to £140,000,000, or roughly $650,000,000 to $3.6 billion in today's dollar values. There was a great outcry. Somehow the idea of letting such enormous fortunes—and their potential power—accumulate had menacing overtones. As the great legal pundit James Kent put it in his *Commentaries on American Law*: "Such an iron-hearted scheme of settlement, by withdrawing property for so long a period, from all the uses and purposes of social life, was intolerable."

As it happened, three of Thellusson's sons were members of Parliament. Since they had been, in effect, partially disinherited in favor of *their* sons, they weren't happy with their father's will. The litigation was long, bitter, and expensive, but the strange will *was* upheld. As it happened, the trust lasted only fifty-nine years, and because it had been badly managed and the litigation costs took a deep bite, the grandchildren inherited only a few million instead of billions.

The case led to legislation providing that a will can provide for trust accumulations only for the lives of beneficiaries alive at the time of probate; or for twenty-one years from the death of the willmaker; or until twenty-one years of the life of the youngest, even though he was still in his mother's womb at the time of probate.

The twenty-one-year rule has since been copied in more than a dozen U.S. states, and as a result, "The Rule Against Perpetuities" is a knotty subject in every law school curriculum in the United States.

But all this applies only to bequests for the benefit of living persons. When it comes to charitable donation, there is no time limit for accumulation. A trust for charity can last forever. And since charitable accumulations are exempt from taxation, there are all sorts of fascinating possibilities. As one of our leading legal commentators on the subject, Professor Lewis M. Simes, put it: "By this device, the vanity of the dead capitalist may shape the use of property forever."

This was the device Jonathan Holden had in mind. He clothed it in the most altruistic of rhetoric:

Suppose some citizen were to give $10,000 in trust toward the support and improvement of public schools or some other educational, philanthropic purposes, and that the . . . income should accumulate for 2,000 years. If the interest averaged 3% for the first two centuries and then progressively declined to 1%, the income accumulated would reach 180 trillion dollars.

He knew that this wasn't a popular position:

> The "practical" man will say: Our concern is with the present. Let the future take care of itself. What good will it do us that in the future all mankind shall be richly endowed . . . there is scarcely anyone who has not some altruism. . . . How many of us if asked for a dime and assured that it would be the means of providing a delightful banquet or entertainment for a million persons would refuse to spare the coin even if the giver could not be present or ever know any of the guests and even if the banquet were to be postponed several centuries. . . . We owe a debt to past humanity which we can only discharge by payment to the future. What we can accomplish for our contemporaries is slight compared with what the same effort will do for posterity.

(Holden wrote this in the golden age of 1912 when there were no serious questions about mankind having a posterity.)

Having brooded on the possibilities for more than forty years, Jonathan Holden was finally ready to do something in 1945. He set up six trusts that year with a total of $180,000 in them. Two were for 500 years and four for 1,000 years, and all were "for the benefit of humanity." More specifically, the trusts provide small annual incomes for the various charitable groups, such as the Unitarian Foundation of Boston—Randal had once been a Unitarian, but he was basically an agnostic who believed religion was all right for others but not for him. Another trust, which the Holden family calls the Indian Trust, is for pregnant mothers in India. The eventual beneficiaries are Hartwick College in Oneonta, New York—which his daughter, Janet, attended; West Virginia Wesleyan College; and Talladega, a black college in Alabama. Ultimately—in the year 2444—all the trusts will revert to Pennsylvania, partly because it was the home of Ben Franklin and, more important, because that state looks with benign favor on long-term charitable trusts.

By 1958 the original trusts with $180,000 in them had grown to more than $3,000,000, largely because Holden kept adding to them. That year, the litigation—which may yet exceed the longevity of Dickens' great classic of endless estate litigation, *Jarndyce v. Jarndyce*—began when Holden asked the government for a refund of $112,000 paid in taxes on the income of the trusts, which he felt they shouldn't have had to pay.

It wasn't just the $112,000, the IRS attorneys said. The trusts themselves were "against public policy." In effect, Holden really was out to destroy the tax base of the nation. *His beneficiaries might well end up with all the money in the country.* One of the government witnesses testified that the trusts might end up owning nearly *$10 quadrillion,* which was then ninety thousand times more than all U.S. savings on deposit in all our banks.

In July, 1961, Holden won his greatest court victory when the U.S. Court of Appeals ruled that at least two of his 500-year trusts were tax exempt. The government hasn't given up yet. There are some ninety-two related tax court cases pending involving the tax liabilities of the various Holden trusts. In their most recent court skirmish, the Holdens won. Eventually, there will be some kind of settlement on how much tax the trusts owe the United States, but the trusts themselves are likely to go on and on, accumulating, waxing fatter and fatter.

The importance of great trusts is not really who gets the money when the trust terminates, or even who is drawing small amounts out of it during the life of the trusts—the Unitarian Foundation in Boston, for example, does get a few thousand every year—but who *controls* the trusts. And in this case the control is vested in Randal Holden and his sister, Janet Adams, of Main Street, Pine Plains, New York. She's married to a prosperous Ford dealer. She's slender, brown-haired and two years older than Randal.

"The way it works is this," Randal Holden explained recently. "There is right now maybe $8,000,000 in all the trusts.

About two-thirds of the money is in the long-term charitable trusts. About one-third in family trusts which benefit us and our children. These trusts will end when the beneficiaries die and the remainder will go into the charitable trusts. My sister and I are the trustees in most of the trusts. Janet does most of the paperwork up at her home in Pine Plains, and she draws $3,000 a year or a little more for her administrative duties on the trusts. Janet and I are supposed to make the decisions on what stocks to buy for the trusts, but I guess most of the decisions are really mine. So far, the decisions have been pretty good. I do a whole lot better, somehow, on my stock investments for the trusts than I do for myself.

"Sure, Janet's children and mine—she has five, I have three —think the trusts are terrible. They'd love to get hold of the money for spending here and now. So would my wife, who thinks my father was just a terrible, sarcastic skinflint. But then, my wife is a Democrat and you know how Democrats are about spending money." He's a Nixon Republican.

"We hardly talk about the trusts and their future implications. My father made the money, and if that's what he wanted to do with his money, that was up to him. Hell, he could have given it all away for indigent Shetland sheepdogs or widows in Uganda. I suppose Janet and I were brainwashed sufficiently by him so that the fact that quite a lot of money is accumulating, money we won't be able to get our hands on, really doesn't bother us too much. Some. I'm fifty-five now, and if I have another twenty years, it's going to be pretty sizable, given the investment luck I've had to date.

"The next generation of trustees? We really don't know. They'll be Holdens, we assume—God knows there are enough grandchildren, nieces and nephews around to pick from—and I hope they can take on the same attitude toward the mounting pile of dough."

Told the story of H. G. Wells' *When the Sleeper Wakes,* he nodded. "Look how wrong Wells was in his projections just for seventy-five years. I just avoid thinking of what the world will be like one hundred years from now—or how large the Holden trust accumulations will be. Idle thinking. Just think of the fantastic changes that have taken place in the world only since my grandfather got out of Yale in 1857."

One day in New York I talked to a former government tax attorney who had been involved in the Holden litigation. "Things are more complicated now since the 1969 tax law changes. There are different provisions on accumulations and we have to see how it will affect the Holden trusts. But I suppose basically the damn things could go on nearly forever. Charity is a sacred cow under tax law. But I'd bet anything that these trusts are going to be annuities for generations of lawyers. Sure, the old man saw his trusts marching, bigger and stronger every decade, to the biggest pile ever accumulated. It was just his way of building his own beautiful Taj Mahal of money. He could talk all he wanted to about showing people the usefulness of thrift, the joys of compound interest, and the rest of that crap, but let's face it—what this old crank really did was to try to build himself the most fantastic memorial in history—if it lasts."

Why shouldn't it?

"Human nature. What makes you think the third and fourth generation of Holdens are going to accept the old man's dictate? These trusts can be busted wide open. Under state law, the beneficiaries could come forward and declare the trusts illegal and distribute what's in them. Probably be even easier to do now, with the 1969 tax laws. Sooner or later one of the Holdens is going to do just that, just as the Thellusson sons tried to bust the old man's will in London."

But what if they didn't; what if the trusts were allowed to run as long as Jonathan Holden said they should?

"The odds are way against," he said. "First place, all this presumes the survival of capitalism as we know it. There is a worldwide trend toward some kind of Socialism, state or otherwise. Then what kind of odds would you give on us surviving, period, in the face of worldwide pollution, H-bombs and overpopulation? Still, *if* we did manage to come through, by the skin of our teeth, and the trusts survived, they would have a helluva lot of money. And power, too."

This interested me particularly, since I had wondered if the trustees of the Holden trusts would have the power, say, that Wells envisioned for the trustees of the Sleeper.

"When you are trustee for several billions—let's not even think of the trillions and quadrillions that are ultimately what the trusts are supposed to amount to—when you *command* that much money, the fact that you don't *own* it doesn't make much difference. You live on it. You get fees. You appoint the law firms and the accountants and the stockbrokers who buy the stocks for the trusts. You appoint and control the investment counselors, the public relations people, the computer experts. You decide where and how the Trusts spend the moneys accumulating; where and how it should be invested; what companies should be favored; what real estate should be bought. You swing five, ten billion dollars' worth of power around like that, and the fact that you personally aren't a billionaire or even a centi-millionaire doesn't matter. You have the *power* of one and that's what counts. I wouldn't bet much on it, but there's always the off chance that some Holden, one hundred years from now, could be one of the most powerful men on earth. That is, if some of his ancestors didn't decide that pie now was better than power later."

16. What It Really Takes to Make Money in Wall Street

Lessons are not given, they are taken.

—CESARE PAVESE

Are there only fifty thousand Americans seriously looking for the magic formula, the golden wand, *the* secret of getting rich in the stock market? That was Professor Sheen Kassouf's estimate. Surely there must be hundreds of thousands. They spend hundreds of millions on financial how-to books, charts, market letters and financial advisers. They haunt the reference rooms of our public libraries going through New York Stock Exchange tables.

You can't blame them. Anyone who finds the formula will have a great life. As one of the stock market schools paints it, this is the way a successful stock market operator lives:

Trading in stocks is an ideal business when you know how to operate scientifically. Hours 10 to 3. Stay away when you like. Take long week-ends. And frequent vacations. Travel abroad for months. Surely those frequent trips to Zurich would be tax-deductible. Go and come when you please. No overhead. No partners. No employees. *No boss.* You are in business for yourself. Bank account increases steadily after you know how.

And in their determined, frantic search for the magic formula some men would even sup with the devil. Even a poet seeking wealth. His name was Joaquin Miller, a third-rater who had a nice run of popularity at the end of the nineteenth century when many Americans thought the devil was on earth in the shape of Jay Gould, financier. One of the kinder things friends said about Gould was that he would cheat his father out of a dollar to make an honest penny.

Joaquin Miller hit the jackpot with a Broadway play. His royalties gave him a sudden $90,000. He would now make a real fortune on Wall Street, just as lots of others seemed to be doing. First he decided to consult his good friend, Jay Gould, who said he never, never handed out tips. But in deference to Joaquin Miller's poetic genius he would break his ironclad rule.

Gould's tips were to buy Vandalia railroad stock and to sell Western Union short. Gould said he was personally putting every dollar into these situations. He made Miller promise total secrecy. Miller invested his $90,000 as advised and sat back.

Gould, the devil, had of course done just the opposite; he sold Vandalia short and bought Western Union. Vandalia soon went into receivership and Western Union didn't stop climbing that year. Miller never got over his terrible betrayal; he did a terrible, unreadable novel about the iniquities of Wall Street. Gould died very, very rich.

After I talked to my two rogues on and off for a year, Phil and Jerry didn't sound very devilish to me. Only very shrewd, cynical and clever. I asked them for some specific approaches for making money in the market—without running afoul of the SEC or the dictates of a middle-class conscience. And what did it take besides hard work, first-rate thinking, money, guts and luck?

Well, you have to enjoy hard thinking, Phil said. Most people don't like it. But let us assume you have all those marvelous virtues, and you want to know how to make a great deal of money in the market in the shortest possible time. "Now you're a bright, intelligent guy who's learned a few of life's lessons. You have sense enough not to want to run a factory and worry about inventory or unions. Let's get even more specific. Let's suppose I was a stock promoter, which of course I'm not. I'm out to make a lot of dough, quick. First, I try to find a listed company because the best ad for promoting any stock is the ticker tape. The over-the-counter market doesn't show volume, which is a disadvantage for our purpose. But you want a stock that is fairly thin, not too many shares out. Ideally, it should be a stock on the American Stock Exchange. Say, one with a million shares or less outstanding. And it should be selling for $5–$10 a share. A good price range. Under $5 is difficult to sell, and over $10 gets a little sticky. Okay, you got the stock. Now you want a story for the stock. Without the story you got nothing. The best kind of story is science-oriented, which almost no one will really understand, and that's all to the good. Okay, now you got the stock and its stock distribution is, say, 775,000 shares outstanding. Say about 480,000 shares with the public and the rest held by management. Now you're ready to move.

"You get together a group of brokers. Talk to them individually and give them the basic picture so that they can come in at relatively low levels, between $5 and $10. Bring them in early and they'll want to bring in their best clients soon, too. So with this push you start the ball rolling. The stock goes to $8, $9. Why are the brokers doing this, in addition to being fascinated by your charm and your story about the stock? Well, the easiest method is to give the broker a cash payment or an option. *I* won't do this because this leads to indictments if the SEC gets nosy. So if *I* were to do it, I'd do it only on the basis of the value of the stock."

He mentioned the case of a promoter who, the SEC says, wasn't as scrupulous about broker payoffs as Phil said *he* would be.

"He's a very bright promoter with a simple philosophy. He'd find a good stock, one that deserved to go up. Never junk. He'd then buy positions in the open market. He got interested in something called Alloys Unlimited, which was selling around $7 then. They were making silicone wafers and stuff. He had bought himself 50,000 shares at 4½–7. Then he'd go around from broker to broker; he'd go to bars where brokers and registered reps hang out and tout the stock to everyone who could hear him. Or he'd go to a broker with a powerful following and recommend the stock to him. Sometimes the broker would need further persuasion and this promoter would provide it.

"Very simple. Alloys was then selling for 7. This promoter would offer the broker an option on 1,000 shares at 10 or 11 or 12. That is, if the stock rose to any of those levels, the co-operative broker would get a profit of three, four or five thousand dollars—just for pushing it onto his big customers. And he wouldn't have to invest a dime himself.

"He approached Jerry and me, but I wasn't interested in getting involved in option deals. Even though I knew his judgment was very good. Well, this promoter did the right things with the right people, and when Alloys went to the 22–23 level, he unloaded. And that shows how little even an expert who has studied the stock closely really knows. The damn stock went to the 130–140 level. So he missed the really big profits. It's not uncommon, by the way. Usually the man who knows most about the company will make the least. Juan Trippe, the ex-president of Pan American, sold a big block of the stock at 19—just before it shot up to 100.

"The only trouble with the promoter on Alloys, though, was not only did he underestimate the stock's ability to push up, but he got the SEC nosy about the rise. So now he's under indictment for pushing the stock with his option route. Yet everybody he got into the stock made a fortune. Lots of funds have the stock now; it split three-for-one and was taken over by an English firm, Plessey.

"There, basically, is the formula to use. But you've got to do it without payoffs, which is a little harder. Yet most Amex stocks that made big moves had this kind of setup. It's very rare that a stock goes up by itself. It's better to buy the wrong stock at the right time than the right stock at the wrong time. And the wrong time is if nobody is pushing it. Okay, end of Method One."

Method Two, Phil went on, calls for more patience, but then you don't have to make any payoffs to anyone and it's strictly legit.

"Let's say you're thirty years old and you have $25,000. I deliberately chose a young man because most of them lack patience. And patience is what you need for Method Two. What you do is call five or six different firms and ask which industry is most out of favor right now, which stocks in those industries are least likely to move. Let's say four out of five say airlines, which they probably would have right now. [This was June, 1970.] So buy airlines. They look horrible. The straw-hats-in-winter principle. The companies are selling at all-time lows. The registered reps will look at you with horror: 'Airlines? You must be kidding. There's no statistical reason to buy airlines' and so on. Or they'd give you the same reason not to buy steels. So you buy them. You wait a year and at the very least you'll probably make 50–60 percent on your investment."

Method Three calls for some intelligence work, and Phil admitted that it might be beyond the average investor. Still, he thought it worth trying because it was the surest method of all.

"Find a deal where a stock promoter is stuck with a big block of stock. Say a promoter with 300,000 shares for which he paid $3 and it's now selling for 2½. The only assurance you need is that the company isn't bankrupt or about to go there. Apart from that, the risk is minimal. If the promoter can't make the stock rise, he's going to find someone—another promoter—who can. *Someone* is going to make that stock go to 10. And for God's sake, don't ask your Merrill Lynch or Bache broker if it's a stock worth going into. They'll say you're crazy. But when the stock goes to 10, they'll suddenly find it interesting."

Phil was eloquent on the subject of stock market analysts.

"Why aren't most any good?" he asked. "How many *good*

lawyers, how many *good* doctors are there? Not many. But you got to remember there's less professionalism on Wall Street than anyplace else. Schooling alone won't make you a good analyst. One reason: It also takes an intuitive sense and you can't learn that from a book or a professor."

Jerry said: "Any other job takes a hell of a lot more doing; it took ten times more work for me to make $10,000 a year as a publicity man on Broadway than it takes me now to make a whole lot more a year."

Phil: "Consider the average businessman. Against considerable odds he's put together a business because he's smart. He has to worry effectively about merchandising, inventory, unions, operating a good sales force. If he has to spend $10,000 for a new drilling machine, he shops around carefully, talks to a lot of people first, and then does a lot of figuring to see if he can stretch the old machines a little further. But take the same businessman in the market with $10,000. He goes to an idiot who makes a tenth of what he does and he asks his advice. Does that make sense?"

So I asked if they knew of any good analysts.

Sure, said Phil. "Me."

"He's right," said Jerry.

And then they added up the proofs. What it came to was a long and fascinating case history of their latest adventure with a stock called Chief Consolidated Mines.

As I lived through the ups and downs and quirks of the stock with them, it became a kind of postgraduate course on what it really takes to make money in Wall Street. During its unfolding I wondered how many of us outsiders could be— would be—willing to run the great risks, the endless uncertainties, the murderous wear and tear on psyche and body to make a real pile of dough. Which you might, when it was all over, still *not* make for a variety of miserable reasons that had nothing to do with brilliant financial thinking, splendid market insights, enormous interpretive gifts and lots of courage.

Why did Chief Consolidated sound vaguely familiar to me?

"Yeah," said Jerry, "it's the same stock we picked up a few years ago at 3 and it went to 9¾ and most of our people got out at 7–8. But it had all sorts of problems, flooding and so on."

What had brought them back to the stock?

Phil explained: "We've always kept an eye on it, and in August, 1969, we noticed some activity and we soon heard that three insiders were buying heavily. And we tried to talk to them, but nobody would talk to us. Ninety-nine times out of a hundred when a president of the firm refuses to talk, he's sitting on something great. When they become expansive and want to buy you lunch, you can be sure he's ready to unload some stock."

I was a little puzzled. Here they had filled me with tales of how *un*knowing insiders often were and so on.

"If it was just what insiders were doing, we wouldn't be enthusiastic," Phil said. "It's what you find out *after* that separates the good men from the two-bit operators who call themselves analysts."

Chief Consolidated Mines, listed on the Pacific Coast Exchange and the tiny National Stock Exchange in New York, was then selling for 3½. There were 2,600,000 shares outstanding. Chief didn't operate its own mines in Utah but leased them out to Kennecott Mining.

The first thing Phil did in checking on Chief was to go to a Kennecott interim report. He quoted from it:

In the lead-zinc business Kennecott is a relative newcomer. Our Tintic-Utah operation [Tintic means Chief Consolidated Mines, Phil interposed] which commenced in 1963 has reached its planned daily production rate of 500 tons of ore last summer. This was shipped to custom mills and smelters . . . a 500-ton a day concentrator is being constructed . . . a significant part of the output of this operation will continue to be direct smelting work . . . if development work in adjacent areas comes up to expectation the production of Tintic will be expanded to 1800 tons of ore a day. . . .

This should result in production of around 45,000 tons of lead, 25,000 tons of zinc and two million ounces of silver per year. . . .

"Take any average analyst with a mediocre firm and you saw all this in the Kennecott report," said Phil. "And unless you were very stupid you would know that when Kennecott talked about Tintic, it was talking about the mines it was operating on lease from Chief. Now our little analyst knows that and he knows something about mining. So he starts adding up figures on prices that are *likely* to be current in the next year or two. Forty-five thousand tons of lead is worth roughly a $13,500,000 gross. Some 25,000 tons of zinc is worth roughly $8,500,000 gross, so that's roughly $22,000,000, right? Now 2,000,000 ounces of silver at, say, $1.50 an ounce, another $3,000,000. In all, a $25,000,000 gross. Based on average costs in the industry, after deducting mining, concentrating and smelting costs, I figure a net profit of at least $10,000,000 to Kennecott. This could give Chief—based on its lease agreement —a profit of about $2,500,000. Now Chief has 2,600,000 shares out. Let's deduct $100,000 for inconsequential operating costs. So what we come down to is Chief earning something in the neighborhood of 90 cents a share and the damn stock is now 3½. Let's assume the worst: Cut the figures in half, even though Kennecott is usually very conservative in its estimates—but cut it in half and you're still talking of a share earning maybe 50 cents a share. Now any stock earning 50 cents a year has to sell for more than 3½. At least 7 or 8 in a mining stock."

Phil and Jerry advised foreign banks to pick up substantial positions in Chief. They were also working with another group that had 300,000 shares.

"Now if I make money in Chief and the bank makes money, they're going to say: Phil Stoller is a genius. But I'm not. All I do is spend some time reading."

Would he have stumbled on the Chief situation if he hadn't already known something about the outfit?

Phil: "Oh, I'd have stumbled on something else. But that's

not the point. These big outfits have analysts who are supposed to be specialists. Dozens of men making anywhere from $12,000–$40,000 a year scanning every mining stock, outside the Toronto penny crap, to find things like Chief. But most of the analysts are incompetent or lazy. Sure there are imponderables. The mines could flood or collapse; there could be a prolonged strike. God knows what. But analyzing what I see on paper, I see 1,800 tons a day of very profitable production."

He continued: "There's a rich man I work with. I had lunch with him the other day to tell him the Chief story. I showed him reports and maps and drilling reports. He said, 'Phil, I don't want to hear about that. I don't know anything about mining.' I said, 'Jay, please, let me explain why you're going to make money with Chief.' He said, 'Phil, I don't care. Is it going up or isn't it? If up, I'll buy a lot. So tell me. . . .' "

Phil hesitated. "And right there you have the typical attitude that leads to the basic fault of the securities business. They won't listen. But maybe it's my fault."

Did he mean he wanted a measure of recognition for being so smart in finding Chief?

Phil: You're being too simplistic. I want to get the credit if I'm right, but I don't want the total blame if I'm wrong. I want to *share* it.

M.T.B.: You want a footnote cushion.

Phil: All right, but he *should* know about the imponderables.

M.T.B.: But he's typical. To ask the proper question, to appreciate the full answers, he'd have to study mining procedures. And the typical investor isn't going to.

Phil: The nub of it is not that the public doesn't have the time, but they don't have the inclination to *think*. I want them to understand all the risks so that they can't point a finger at me.

M.T.B.: You want your position to be 100 percent safe. You point out the possibilities but want them to be aware of the possible pitfalls.

Phil: Right. And if the whole securities business operated

this way, the public wouldn't be raped so often. Maybe it's not even rape; just masturbation.

M.T.B.: What it comes down to, Phil, is that you want insurance for your recommendations.

Phil: If you went out and bought 1,000 shares of Chief, you're a schmuck for buying it just because we said buy it. If, however, you *understand* our reasons and you buy 5,000 shares and lose money, I don't feel as bad as if you lost money on 1,000 shares and didn't understand what was involved.

[I bought 1,000 shares.]

M.T.B.: I think my reaction is typical. At the time I knew nothing about Chief. I knew you had checked it out. You guys were living by finding such situations. If a Swiss bank thought you could and was paying Jerry $5,000 a month to do so, I assumed you had a good track record. They don't throw $60,000 a year around loosely.

Phil: Let's get back to basics. I once sold piece goods. I'd bring up the samples. We'd go through maybe one hundred samples. We'd lay them out on a cutting table. We figured out how the plackets should be made; how the sleeves should be laid out and so on. We worked together because what I sold him had to be resold to the public. And that's no different from stocks. Because like stocks, it has to be resold at a higher price to the public in order to make a profit. We had to make an intelligent advance picture of an eventual product. So out of one hundred samples we took ten, maybe a dozen shirts. We worked together. Sure he knows his milieu, it's his business. He's *survived*. And survival in business or stocks is a question of doing your best and *knowing* your best. Why should it be any different in the securities business?

M.T.B.: You're saying that the man who hasn't studied a stock and doesn't know it as well as his own business shouldn't be buying the stock? But let's assume your shirt manufacturer just can't give the stock market the same equal study he does his own business. So he says: "Okay, I have a shortcut. There's a very smart guy named Phil Stoller. I know Phil has made money for others and I trust his judgment. Admittedly I'm not going to be an expert on mines. I don't have the time. Yet the proposition attracts me and I trust his judgment, so I'll go along with it. He'll spend thirty minutes telling me about the possible things that could go wrong, but really I'll be going into Chief because I trust his judgment." What do you say then?

Phil: I'd say he should go to Puerto Rico or Vegas. I've told people for years: "If you have $100,000 that you're not using in your business, put $80,000 in what I would call relatively safe bonds and speculate like crazy with the other $20,000. In a bad year the market could go off 20 percent. So you're going to lose 20 percent anyway."

M.T.B.: You really want a whole new set of relationships between broker and customer. *Full* information and *full* disclosure. A broker says to a client, "Look, I want you to buy this stock which is now 18. Frankly the firm bought a big block of stock at 10."

Phil: Or we bought options for a penny a share.

M.T.B.: What else should he be telling the client?

Phil: Everything he knows about the company, the projections. Still, if the broker turns out to be wrong, the client will still blame him, but the broker will have performed an honorable service. But today nobody is trying that hard.

M.T.B.: Most brokers on their house tipster sheets say they're doing this, to a certain extent. They may not disclose that the firm bought a large position at a much lower price, but still they do give a fair rundown on the stock's prospects.

Phil: Ha! If I had to tell a client that I'm urging him to buy a stock at 18 and *I'm* selling at 18, how many orders would I get?

M.T.B.: That would be *real* disclosure. Should brokers be required to be that honest?

Phil: You're kidding. If they had to tell it just that way, the volume of trading might drop 50 percent—but the integrity quotient would increase 1,000 percent.

The Chief position was reinforced by other curious purchases. Phil explained: "You remember the Texas Gulf run-up.

You know who made the *real* money? Not the guys who bought Texas Gulf, although some of them made a real bundle. There was this geologist who was fined $43,000 for utilizing insider information. Hell, less than 5 percent of his profits came from buying Texas Gulf. He bought a lot of cheap mine stock bordering on the Texas Gulf properties. These were 10-cent and 20-cent stocks that jumped to $2 and $3. So with Chief; there are some cheap mine stocks right around its property. Crown Point and East Crown Point. Chief owns 12 percent of one and 62 percent of another. These are 30-cent stocks. So we bought a batch of this crap. Once the good word on Chief gets out, we figure the peripheral properties will move up to $2.50–$3."

They kept accumulating Chief, but the stock wouldn't move much. Then at the end of March, 1970, it jumped to 4⅞ on a turnover of 10,000 shares. But it fell back, and by the end of 1970 it was down to 2–2¼.

The boys were depressed. They were using a friend's office in November, and when the phone rang, Phil would open: "If it's bad news, don't tell me."

Kennecott had a profit in November. "Nobody cares. It's that kind of market," Phil said.

But by late 1970 they had another more pressing worry: They were speculating in silver contracts on the commodity exchange.

In November, 1970, we meet in their temporary office and they're more depressed than I've ever seen them. "Chief doesn't get off its ass and silver falls to $1.65 an ounce. I'm out $55,000, so far," Phil moans. "I have fifty-five contracts for a half-million ounces of silver."

Phil calls his commodity broker, Nat. "How's January [silver to be delivered that month]?" He's told it's 164.90. Phil: "I'm gonna cry. But I've got lots of company. Anyone who bought silver in the past three months is broke."

He explained. "Just about everyone buys silver, or any other commodity on margin. That 10 percent margin goes fast when silver drops. I just can't believe it; I'm about to go broke on silver. And I had it all figured out. So far I think we've lost $500,000 on silver. Yes, I know: Playing with commodities is absolute masochism. But I also know smoking is bad and I smoke; overeating is bad and I overeat. Chief won't move until the price of silver rises. Everyone figured that when the United States stopped selling its stock of silver, the price had to jump. So everyone was wrong. Us, too."

Jerry: "Nothing goes up when there's a big public interest."

To show that he still retained a sense of humor in spite of the month's calamities, Phil pulled out a clip which he had heavily marked. It was a recent New York *Times* obituary on Dr. Theodor Reik, one of the early psychoanalysts. The sections Phil had circled included some of Reik's well-known quotations: "No one is as stubborn and successful in having bad luck as the masochist." "The masochist is basically a pleasure-seeking person. Masochism is a revelation of universal need; and the masochist degrades and humiliates himself and often ingratiates himself for only one aim: to be loved."

"I show it to you," said Phil, "only to show you how wrong the shrinks can be. I may be a masochist for going into commodities and this miserable silver, but no one can say of me that I ever tried to *ingratiate* myself with anybody. Not that."

In all, November, 1970, was a disastrous month for Phil and Jerry.

Item. Phil and his wife, Mickey, went to Aruba for a vacation. The boys stayed home, got in an argument, and the older one slammed the door on his brother, who lost the tip of a finger. After the Stollers were back home, the first night the younger boy awoke in a sweat and came running to his parents' bedroom: "I want my finger back, I want my finger back."

Item. Jerry must decide this month how he's going to plead on his indictment on the Pentron stock manipulation. The case is shortly coming up for trial. Should he plead guilty and hope for the best? Very mixed feelings. His lawyers—to whom he's paid $38,000 so far—want him to cop a plea. "I'm fighting it. Hell, I could have copped a plea two years ago."

Why didn't he? Jerry: "I was broke then. I needed the time

to make some money. If I copped a plea, then I'd have gotten probation, been forced out of the securities business, and been broke. This way at least I was able to make a bundle. The thing that bothers me is that after the Pentron thing there's the Terminal-Hudson stock case. If I plead guilty on Pentron and get probation, what happens when I come up for sentencing on Terminal-Hudson as a 'hardened offender'? Sure, the lawyers want me to cop a plea. It's easier for them. No trial, nothing. They make more money sitting around the office than the courtroom.

"In this district," he went on, "the government wins 80 percent of its securities cases. In Texas I'd walk off scot-free."

After a week of fierce inner wrestling Jerry decides to take his chances and plead guilty. It's a bad waiting time for Jerry. A diet he started has been abandoned. In his mind's eye he's previewed several gruesome scenarios of the day of sentence. He seems more harried, paler than I've ever seen him.

Item. Dinner at the Palm Restaurant. Bad news from Switzerland. Their friend and associate, Bluntschli, is out of commission for two months with a badly shattered leg. Auto accident —his new Maserati. A new boss comes in to run the bank. First decision: All clients of the bank must now put up cash for all their transactions. He's getting even for Penn Central. Why the hell isn't Chief moving up? Why is silver falling? What's the matter with his New York experts?

Phil: "We should have known. Silver was a sure thing and sure things with a big public interest never work out. There was that sure thing back in '58. Remember?" he asks Jerry. "The Treasury bonds?" Jerry nods.

Phil goes on: "The Treasury was bringing out $2\frac{5}{8}$ percent bonds in 1958, maturing in 1965. You could buy the bonds for only 5 percent margin. Everyone—and I mean just about everyone—knew it was a sure thing. So they bought the bonds on margin. It had to go up as Treasury bonds usually did after they came out, because they figured interest rates would fall lower and these bonds would rise as a result. So the bonds were way oversubscribed because everyone and his cousin was

uying them on margin. All the smart money was out for this
ure thing, this big, free ride. So they guessed wrong. Interest
ates rose and the bonds fell. The damn bonds fell to $952 on
$1,000 bond and millions were lost by the smart moneymen.
Vell, silver was the same. It had to go up, and when something
1as to go up' in Wall Street, it generally doesn't. Everyone
gured silver had to move when the U.S. Treasury stopped
elling silver on November 10. So everyone was wrong."

Phil bets me, dinner for three, that silver won't go any
ower between now and January, 1971. It does. So does Chief.
The boys are miserable and glum. Phil is drinking more than
sual. Jerry thinks wildly of countries they can run to. Phil
urses the day they started buying silver futures. "We must
ave been out of our goddamned minds." Jerry nods. Still,
ays Phil, there are great possibilities with silver because silver
s one of the unregulated commodities like cocoa and sugar.
There shouldn't be any unregulated commodities, but there
re. (Corn, wheat, potatoes, bacon are regulated commodities.)

"You must know a little about me by now," Phil goes on.
And maybe you realize that for me the great joy is thinking
p a moneymaking gimmick. After I've figured it out—and
now it will work—it becomes uninteresting to me. Well,
he silver commodity deal I worked out was one of my proudest
noments.

"It goes like this: You're a legitimate member of the Com-
nodity Exchange without any larceny in your heart; and you
nustn't be a gambler. Either one will ruin you. You are pure
f heart and you're going to make a lovely perennial living
loing nothing. You start in with ten of your customers. You
ersuade them to go short on silver; borrow silver now for
uture delivery in the hope that the price will go down. Now
ach of these persuaded customers of yours has to put up $1,500
silver contract of 10,000 ounces. You get another ten cus-
omers to go long, buy in the hope that silver will go up. They
lso give you $1,500 a contract. In all both sets of customers
vill have given you $30,000. What do you have to do with that
noney? Not a thing. The Comex, the clearinghouse for com-

modity deals in silver, doesn't ask you, the broker, for a penny
as long as you stay in balance: ten contracts long, ten contracts
short. You lend out the $30,000 at 7 percent or 8 percent or
whatever you can get.

"Okay, you got the hang of it. Now let's forget a lousy ten
or twenty contracts. Let's say you work up to a fat, faithful set
of one hundred clients who have invested, say, $1,000,000 in
balanced long and short positions. You have that million, and
you put it out at Certificates of Deposit. What could you get?
In 1970, 7 percent and 8 percent. So for just six months you
have at least $35,000–$40,000 free and clear for doing nothing.
If the price of silver rises, you have to notify your short clients
to ante up more margin; the same if it falls. As long as you
keep them balanced, you're playing the game.

"Sure there are steps to watch. It's important to get your
clients in their positions the same month. If in different months
you would have to give the clearinghouse 20 percent of the
amount, but you'd still have most of the money to lend out.

"Brilliant, no? And I figured it out all by myself. The only
thing wrong with it was when I really got to know the silver
and cocoa markets, I realized that smart brokers *had been
doing this all along;* that my brilliant gimmick was a tarnished
antique. Now there's absolutely nothing illegal about it. As I
say, the only time you get in trouble is if you decide to gamble
on the future of silver.

"In a way you could even pull this stunt on regulated commodities, which are regulated by the CEA, the Commodity
Exchange Authority. But it would be harder. They're looking
over your shoulder and they'd probably get nosy if you were
encouraging your customers in nearly duplicate shorts and
longs. If the regulated commodity price didn't move much, you
could get away doing it quite awhile."

The use of customers' money, especially in commodity trading, often makes the brokering business the banking business,
Phil continued. "And as everybody knows, that's much more
profitable. Sophisticated investors know their broker is borrowing money at 6½ percent from the bank and lending it to

hem at 8 percent or even 8½ percent for their margin ac-
ounts. But the big commodity brokerage firms with large
ommodity departments such as Merrill Lynch or Bache don't
ave to go to banks for the margin money. They get the money
rom their own commodity customers. After all, these firms
re likely to have lots of customers who are long or short on a
iven commodity such as silver, and nearly all the money those
ustomers put up can be lent out at 8½ percent. As long as
he long and short positions are in balance, there's a lot of
noney available to lend out, since the firms don't have to turn
t over to the commodity clearinghouse. It's called the straddle
noney and it's very sweet."

There was even a commoner variation of the gimmick worked
very day, Phil said. "I know this registered rep at a major
irm. He doesn't have too much faith in the recommendations
f his firm's analysts, but he does believe in arithmetic. He also
nows that every broker, every customer's man is going to
ose a lot of his clients for passing on advice that doesn't work
ut too well. He'd concentrate on five or six high-flying stocks
nd divide his active customers in two. One-half he'd advise
hort selling, the other half buying. He had to be right, very
ight, with at least one group. And they stay with him.

"His firm, like a lot of others, usually publishes an annual
ist of stocks they think will do very well that coming year.
Ie'd pick the top ten and give a different one to a different
roup of his customers. If three or four in those groups worked
ut, why, he'd have a helluva loyal bunch of customers who'd
tay with him no matter what. Naturally, they'd recommend
heir friends to him. After all, he's a broker who brought them
nly winners. Pathetically simple, no? The guy is still doing it.
Ie figures that with simple arithmetic he can't lose."

December, 1970, was a better month for the boys. Phil had
een working for several weeks figuring out a way to beat the
lackjack game at Vegas. Anything to take his mind off miser-
ble silver, dormant Chief. After thousands of hands he had
oe Arden play according to what Phil calls his Progressive
'ress Method. The system seemed to work. Joe was sent to

Vegas with $2,000. This time he took one of those gamblers' junket flights, which cost him almost nothing. He played eighteen hours straight and made a net profit of $300. He played only one hand at $1 a hand and never really had to dip into capital.

"Next time," Phil said, "he goes out and tries it at $5 a hand. We figure he could make $400–$500 a day. Me, I don't have the *Sitzfleisch* for that kind of sitting. Joe does. The only thing that could knock out my system is for you to lose to the dealer ten times in a row. This happens, on average, once in twenty-five times. All other times you average at least two wins out of ten, which keeps you in the running. The croupier told Joe he had never seen a cleverer gambling system." Phil was visibly pleased with himself.

Just after Christmas came their first major nibble on Chief Consolidated. Phil and Jerry were cautious. There had been other interested groups anxious to take over their big positions but too many of them were just greedy con men, according to Phil. "They'd come to us with propositions which they thought were very clever because they were two steps ahead of us. Options, calls, God knows what combinations they dreamed up for us to turn over our positions. They took us for *putzes* and we don't even look like *putzes*. Hell, we were five steps ahead of them. But this time I think maybe it's the real thing."

It was a group of sophisticated investors interested in mining properties. They had a clever analyst who had also stumbled on the marvelous possibilities in Chief. The group was exploring the possibility of taking over the stock of Phil and Jerry's clients and that of the other group and then winning control of the corporation.

"If it works out," Phil predicted, "the stock will move to at least 10. Let's see what happens."

January 15, 1971. Jerry phones. He got sentenced today. "I got a suspended sentence in the Pentron case and placed on probation for two years. Also a fine of $3,500 on each of the three counts I pleaded guilty to, or a total of $10,500. I paid it. I got the highest fine. In fact I was the only one to get a sizable fine. Probably the probation reports showed I was the only one of the bunch who was currently flush. A couple of others got $1,000 fines and all of them suspended sentences."

February 2, 1971. A lot of buying in Chief Consolidated today. Some 12,100 shares are suddenly traded in the stock on the Pacific Coast Exchange after it had been running along at 300–400 shares a day. The stock, which had fallen as low as $1\frac{3}{4}$, is now up to $2\frac{7}{8}$. By mid-February the steady buying gets it up to $3\frac{1}{2}$.

The same week Bluntschli comes over on one of his regular visits to New York. Things have improved at the bank, not as black as Jerry thought they'd be. The boys have their playpen back again with only minor restrictions.

March 10, 1971. Silver moves up again to $1.69. Phil has made money on potato contracts. "You can't lose if you buy potatoes at less than 3 cents a pound. I bought a lot. In a week it moved up to $3\frac{1}{2}$ cents."

But the miserable Chief deal isn't off the ground. The mining stocks group has acquired 60,000 shares without seriously affecting the price because the market is very sticky. Now they've decided that the best thing is a proxy fight to get control of the company. If they combine their shares with the stock Phil and Jerry control for various clients, plus some other big blocks, there would be a starting group of perhaps 600,000 shares out of the 2,600,000 shares outstanding. But Phil and Jerry are against a proxy fight. "Takes too damn long," says Phil. "We've made enough business for lawyers."

Besides, Phil thinks they now have the ammunition they need to get Chief out of the 2–3 rut it's been in. He's gotten a copy of the Kennecott report on its mining operations in the Chief mines which it leases. The report covering 1970 was dated February 24, 1971. It reveals that Kennecott has substantially enlarged the reserves in one of the Chief mines, the Burgin; that they have found a silver-bearing fissure zone of "significant grade" at the Trixie mine; that sample ore at another of the mines, the Ballpark, shows a high rate of recovery; that they have had their first recovery of 2,000 ounces of gold in sample shipments out of one of the mines.

Phil taps the report. "Absolutely wild. Kennecott shipped $6,500,000 worth of ore, net, out of the Chief mines and managed to show a loss of $500,000 on the operations."

He'd long since given up trying to understand why Chief's management hadn't trumpeted the great news with a press conference.

Now this week the boys see another way out. Jerry in Florida has been having talks with a pair of investors, a Canadian and a high-flying American millionaire plunger. They are enthusiastic about the Chief's possibilities and are considering buying 300,000 shares.

Phil sends Joe Arden down to Miami with copies of the Kennecott report as the final persuader for the two men. I ask Phil why he and Jerry, veteran promoters, hadn't been able to pull off the Chief thing by themselves.

"Ah, we're burned-out promoters by now. I'm out of touch with the right people. I've been fooling around with commodities too long, but these two guys are just the right combination. Between them they have the right synergism, the right combinations to move the stock. I think we've got it this time." He admits that he's said that several times before about Chief.

He was wrong again. The investors decided it wasn't for them. Another false hope. "That's the trouble with the righteous path. You got to break your balls on a strictly honest deal." Jerry is depressed and traveling around. For the hundredth time Phil plagues himself with why they had to get into silver futures. "We had to be crazy."

At the end of May, 1971, Phil was again ebullient about Chief, even though the stock had fallen to 2½. What drove the stock down, Phil explains, was the gloomy Chief annual report that the stockholders received early in May.

"It was so down, so goddamned gloomy you'd almost think Chief management wanted them to sell their stock. All they had to do is quote verbatim some of the sections of Kennecott's own

eports to them on the significant new silver strikes they've made
on Chief's properties, the 2,000 ounces of gold they shipped
recently. Just a few quotes like those and the stock would
have jumped to 6."

Now for the first time, though, Phil's group has two of the
four members of Chief's executive committee. One of them
is Phil's lawyer, an expert in SEC law.

At the Chief annual meeting in Salt Lake City on May 18,
Phil's group discovered that their 850,000 shares represented
real control of the company. Later in the executive committee
meeting it was agreed that the Chief stockholders would receive in early June a full report on the Kennecott discoveries
in the Chief properties.

Meanwhile, Phil has bought more Chief stock for clients.
For the first time I notice how much grayer his hair has become
in the year I've known him. He mentions in passing that he
takes at least one tranquilizer a day but that during a recent
nine-day Florida stay he was off them completely.

"That did it. I think I've persuaded my wife that we move
down there permanently. If you do your business on a phone
as I do, what the hell difference does it make where you're
operating from?"

In August, 1971, Jerry gets the news: The government has
dropped the indictment on him in the Terminal-Hudson case.
For the first time in three years he's free of the threat of criminal
trial. He goes down to Panama for a vacation.

The same week Bluntschli, the Swiss banker, is in New York
on his way to Mexico City. He throws out footnote addenda as
we walk to his plane: "I found out there are at least 4,000 of
those secret Liechtenstein corporations with unknown owners
—the bull market must be on us. Now in those inside deals I'm
getting, nearly six out of seven seem to be working out . . .
they never did find out what happened to all of Frank Kaftel's
money, but I discovered he used to provide a little extra service for some of his European market letter subscribers. For
$500 extra a year he'd phone the day before the issue was going

to be mailed and tell you the name of the stock he was going to push. So his smart customers could buy the crappy stocks before the mooches pushed it up."

September, 1971: Phil is on his way to the Bahamas for some vacation and a little gambling-theory checking. Chief is still at the $3 level. Phil still thinks it's going to be a great stock, but he doesn't know why it's taken so long to work out. "If everything works out right on Chief, it's gonna be a whole new kind of life," he says. "Safe, comfortable, *respectable*—don't laugh, it's not such a dirty word—and boy, am I looking forward to a life without headaches, strain, ulcers or a new generation of Eddie Jaegermans. The new, lovely quiet life. That's for me."